FEDERAL RESUME GUIDEBOOK

SEVENTH EDITION

First-Ever Book on Federal Resume Writing Featuring the Outline Format Federal Resume

KATHRYN TROUTMAN

The Resume Place, Inc.

P.O. Box 21275, Catonsville, MD 21228
Phone: 888-480-8265
www.resume-place.com

Printed in the United States of America
Federal Resume Guidebook 7th Edition
ISBN-13: 978-1-7334076-0-1
ISBN-10: 1-7334076-0-X

Copyright © 2020 by Kathryn Troutman

The Resume Place® and Ten Steps to a Federal Job®
are trademarks of The Resume Place, Inc.

We have been careful to provide accurate Federal job search information in this book, but it is possible that errors and omissions may have been introduced. The word Federal is initial capped throughout this book based on the GPO Style Manual.

Sample Resumes: Sample resumes are real but fictionalized. All Federal applicants have given permission for their resumes to be used as samples for this publication. Privacy policy is strictly enforced.

Publication Team
Cover Designer: Brian Moore
Interior Page Design/Layout: Brian Moore and Paulina Chen
Contributors: John Gagnon, PhD; Emily Troutman, MPP
Copyediting/Proofreading: Heather Donofrio, PhD, CFJST/CFCC; Robin Quinn
Federal to Private Sector Chapter: Carla Waskiewicz, CPRW, CFJST / CFCC
Information Technology Federal Resume Writing Chapter, Rita Chambers, PMP

Sample Federal Resumes and Accomplishments were written by RP Certified Federal Resume Writers: Pam Sikora; John Gagnon, PhD; Rita Chambers, PMP; Carla Waskiewicz; Heather Donofrio, Ph.D; Emily Troutman, MPP; and Debbie Hahn.

Table of **Contents**

17 FEDERAL RESUME SAMPLES
20 KEYWORD SETS
20+ ACCOMPLISHMENT STORIES

PART 1: STRATEGIES FOR WRITING A SUCCESSFUL FEDERAL RESUME

Strategy 1. Write Your Federal Resume in the Outline Format 9

A Federal Resume is NOT a 11

	Series	Grade	Page
Administrative Specialist, Sneak Preview Outline Format 301 GS 7 301		GS 7	13
Jenny - Overseas Military Spouse 341		GS 11	16-18
Before & After - Seeking Promotion in Administrative Job Series in Naples Italy			
Milton - Private Sector Insurance Claims 1101		IC13	19-21
Before & After - Seeking FEMA Insurance Specialist			
James – County Law Enforcement 1811		GS 12	22-24
Before & After - Seeking Federal Law Enforcement Specialist (Instructor)			
Deborah - Private Sector IT Specialist 2210		GS 11	25-27
Before & After - Seeking IT Specialist (Cloud)			

Strategy 2. EXERCISE: How Many Hats Do You Wear at Work? 31

	Series	Grade	Page
Maintenance Mechanic 1419		GS 09	32
Human Resources Specialist 201		GS 07	33
Family Program Specialist 301		GS 12	33
Transition Manager 301		GS 12	33
Occupational Safety & Health Specialist 18		GS 07	33

Strategy 3. Use Keywords to Match The Vacancy Announcement...... 35

	Series	Grade	Page
Emergency Management Specialist	89	GS 12	38-42
Law Enforcement Specialist	1800	GS 11	43
Program Analyst (Mobilization)	343	GS 12	43
Program Analyst (Workforce)	343	GS 11	43
Administrative Assistant	301	GS 7	44
Administrative Officer	341	GS 9	44
Technical Writer / Editor	1082	GS 9	44
Marine Transportation Specialist	2150	GS 12	44

Strategy 4. Tell Your Accomplishment Stories 45

EXERCISE: Start Writing Your Acccomplishment Stories			48
Using the CCAR Format			49
Executive Assistant	301	GS 12	50
Public Affairs Specialist	1035	GS 13	50
Nurse	0610	GS 14	51
Emergency Management Specialist	89	GS 12	51
PILOT targeting Aviation Safety Inspector	1825	FG 12-13	51
Financial Management Analyst	501	GS 11	52
Aircraft Engine Mechanic	8602	GS 9	52
Construction Control Technician	809	GS 12	52
New Graduate, BSEE Mechanical Engineer	0083	GS 9	53
Licensed Vocational Nurse	620	GS 9	53
Clerical (OA)	303	GS 5	53

Strategy 5. Add Your Core Competencies 55

OPM Core Competencies			58-59
USAJOBS Announcement Core Competencies			60-61
FBI Special Agent Core Competencies			62-64
Career Change - Entrepreneur to FBI Special Agent	1811	GS 10	65-68

Strategy 6. Write Your Work Experience 69

USAJOBS: What should I include in my Federal resume?			70-71
How long should your Federal resume be?			72-75
Who is going to read your resume?			76
OPM Classification Standards			77
Factor Evaluation System / FES Criteria			78-81
Before-and-After Contract Specialist	1102	GS 12	82-84

Strategy 7. Edit Carefully 85

EXERCISE: Words to Avoid 87
Editing Suggestions 87
Use Powerful Words. 88
Use Active Voice. 89
Beware of Acronyms. 90
Be Consistent with Verb Tenses 90
Use "I" Intelligently. 91

Strategy 8. Pay Attention to Document Design and Formatting 93

	Series	Grade	Page
Good Example - Supply Specialist - Federal Employee.	2001	GS 11	96-97
Good Example - Office Automation Assistant	0326	GS 5	98-99
Bad Example - USAJOBS Builder	2001	GS 11	100
Bad Example - One Page Private Sector	2201	GS 9	101

SUMMARY- Does your resume cover the Federal Resume Puzzle Pieces? 102-103

Strategy 9. Submit Your Resume and Questionnaire on USAJOBS 105

Questionnaire Case Studies: What NOT To Do 107
Self-Assessment Questionnaire Samples. 108-110
QUIZ: What are the Correct Answers to this Tricky Questionnaire? 110

PART 2: TEN STEPS TO GETTING PROMOTED 111

The 10 Steps to Getting Promoted. 112
**Strategies for Federal Employees Seeking
Promotion and Career Change**. 113-114

1. Make a Decision: It's Time to Get a Promotion 115
    Danielle - Federal Employee
    BEFORE: DHS, Supervisory Law Enforcement Specialist 1811   GS 13   115
2. Find and Update Your Resume 116-117
3. Find and Review Performance Evaluations 118-119
4. Write Your Top Ten List of Accomplishments. 120-121
5. Research Promotion Job Announcements 122-123
6. Make a List of Keywords from the Announcements 124-125
7. Study Executive Core Qualifications to Understand Leadership Competencies. 126-127
8. Write and Target Your Federal Resume for a Promotion. 128-129
    AFTER - Target GS-14 Federal Resume - Ready to Submit! 1811   GS 14   128-129
9. Practice and Prepare: Telling Your Best Accomplishments for Interview. 130
10. Interview and Get the Promotion 131

PART 3: FEDERAL CAREER CHANGE - FOUR CASE STUDIES 133

How do you get started with a career change? 134-138
Four Federal Career Change Stories 139-167

	Series	Grade	Page
Career Change: Private to Federal			
Eric - Veteran / Driver seeks Material Handler 6907		WG 8	139
Before "Bad" Resume - Too Short			140-141
After "Good" Resume target Material Handler 6907		WG 8	142-145
Recent Graduate Seeking Federal Job or Pathways			
Phillip - MS, Engineering, BS Aerospace 0830		GS 9	146
Before "Bad" Resume - Too Short			148
After "Good" Resume - Outline Format 0830		GS 9	149-151
Career Change: Federal to Federal: Extreme Career Change Inside Government			
Meet Margaret – Federal Career Changer to Park Ranger			153-154
Margaret Before – Current Embedded Social Worker 0185		12	155-156
Margaret After – Target Park Ranger 0025		9	157-159
Career Change: Federal to Private Industry			
What's Important to Know for a Two-Page Resume			160-162
Ann Government Contractor – Two-Page Resume			163-164
Ann Government Contractor – Cover Letter			165
Walter USAF – Two-Page Resume			166-167

PART 4: SPECIAL INSIGHTS FOR INFORMATION TECHNOLOGY SPECIALISTS, GS-2210 169

	Series	Grade	Page
Government IT Jobs in the 21st Century			170-172
Selecting the Right Job Announcement for You			174-175
Developing Your IT Resume			176-179
Good Resume - Recent Graduate, IT Specialist (Cyber) 2210		GS 9	180-182
Good Resume - Mid-Career IT Specialist (Network Security) 2210		GS 12	183-185

RESOURCES 186

Top 30 Jobs in Government 187
Best Agencies in Government 188
Top Hiring Agencies in Government 189
Federal Resume Writing Resources - Resume Place, Inc. 190
RP Federal Career Training and Ten Steps to a Federal Job Certification. 191
Kathryn Troutman, Author and Publisher. 192

INTRODUCTION BY KATHRYN TROUTMAN

7th Ed. - NEW BOOK EDITION INCLUDES BOTH FEDERAL RESUME WRITING AND FEDERAL CAREER CHANGE STRATEGIES AND FORMATS.

I wrote the first-ever book on Federal resume writing, the *Federal Resume Guidebook*, in 1996 after the government eliminated the SF-171, a monster of a form that sometimes exceeded 30 pages in length and needed its own table of contents to navigate. Since publishing the first book, I have been teaching Federal job applicants how to write the best Federal resume format, starting with the paper format (sometimes 10 to 14 pages), which evolved to the Resumix format, and is now the USAJOBS format.

The seventh edition of the Federal Resume Guidebook continues the tradition of delivering the most up-to-date information on Federal resume writing. The new edition includes 17 entirely new sample Federal resumes from real Federal jobseekers—including 11 dramatic BEFORE and AFTER Federal resumes.

The new edition partitions the book into four parts, helping you look at the Federal resume from any angle! I am so excited to share all of this new content with you. Go ahead, take a look:

1. Federal Resume Writing Lessons – 9 Strategies - Including 3 New Strategies!
2. Ten Steps to Getting a Promotion in Government – All New Content!
3. Special Insights for Federal Career Change – All New Content!
   - Career Change for Federal Employees (changing occupational series)
   - Private Sector Seeking Federal Careers (Wage-Grade/Veteran; and Recent Graduate)
   - Federal Employee Leaving Government – Two Page Private Sector Resumes and cover letter
4. Writing the IT Specialist Federal Resume – Updated for latest format!

My team uses this book all around the world as the primary and authoritative text for delivering training to Federal government agencies on Federal resume writing. This book is, without question, a must-read if you want a Federal career, are already a Federal employee but want a promotion, or are thinking about a career change. This is—as it has been since the first edition in 1996—the ultimate guidebook for Federal resume writing. Read it, follow the instructions, and leverage its proven insights to create the foundation for the Federal career that you want.

Good luck with your Federal job search and Federal resume. I hope you get Best Qualified, Referred, Interviewed, and HIRED!

KATHRYN TROUTMAN

Author and Publisher, Federal Resume Guidebook, 7th Ed.

Strategy 1

USE THE OUTLINE FORMAT

The Federal resume is the most important document you can write to support your entrance into Federal service or obtain a promotion to a new position.

If you're like most people, the application process for a Federal job can feel both mystifying and overwhelming. Part of the problem is that there are so many different ideas about what constitutes a "good" Federal resume. If you ask five different people, you're more than likely to get five different answers. So, what really makes a resume competitive for Federal job applications?

The key to the answer is to remember that Federal resumes are read by Human Resources Specialists; the resumes are <u>not</u> evaluated by automated systems. Therefore, put yourself in the shoes of the Human Resources Specialist who reviews upwards of hundreds of applications for a single job announcement, rates each resume based on whether it meets specific criteria spelled out in the job announcement, and determines which resumes get ranked "best qualified" and "referred."

Obviously, a winning resume would be as easy to review as possible. By making the Human Resources Specialist's job easier (i.e., making the resume as easy to rate as possible by making key information readily identifiable), you have a better chance of receiving a favorable review.

Furthermore, think of the Federal resume as an argument—your job is to make the best possible argument as to why you're the best possible candidate for the position you're applying to. All too often, Federal jobseekers view the resume as an information dump, putting as much of their professional history into the document (which leads to extraordinarily long resumes). Here's the thing: if the resume is an argument, all the content in the resume should be strategic and directly relevant to the position for which the jobseeker is aiming.

> Our format, the Outline Format, is based on years of feedback from Federal Human Resources experts and accounts for changes to the Federal jobs application process since Hiring Reform in 2010.

The Outline Format is specifically designed to accomplish both of these goals: it is easy to read and makes a clear, targeted argument. The key features of the Outline Format are that (1) it uses short paragraphs, rather than bullets; (2) it emphasizes keywords and key phrases from the announcement in left-justified ALL CAPS headliners that lead each paragraph; and (3) it highlights accomplishment stories as separate from duty descriptions. The Outline Format combines strategically selected keywords and key phrases with supporting paragraphs; each keyword or key phrase is backed by evidence in the supporting paragraph.

For Human Resources Specialists, the ALL CAPS keywords and key phrases render resume review simple: all they must do is scan down the left-hand side of the resume to see what qualifications you're claiming and whether they match the announcement. By highlighting accomplishments, you also make it easier to identify that value-added you bring to the table.

Now, let's take a closer look…

A Federal Resume **Is NOT a...**

... Private Industry Resume

WHY: Too short. Not enough info.

... Bulleted Resume

WHY: This format is usually just another version of the Private Industry resume. Even with bullets, it is still too short and does not have enough detail.

... Big Block Resume

WHY: Have you tried to actually read one of these lately? It's nearly impossible!

... Functional Resume

WHY: You must list your most recent employment first, not last.

If you ever receive a message like the one below in response to an application, it is time to fix your Federal resume format!

"Your resume did not document either the number of hours worked per week for all jobs listed, a detailed description of your duties performed, or the month/year to month/year worked for all jobs listed, as required by the vacancy announcement. Please be sure to read each announcement for complete qualification requirements and instructions on 'How to Apply.'"

A Competitive **Federal Resume...**

Is 3 to 5 Pages in Length

WHY: The Federal resume must include certain information in order for you to be rated as Best Qualified for a position. Each generalized and specialized skill that you have developed in your career has to be written into the document.

Matches the Job Announcement

WHY: To be successful, the Federal resume must match the job announcement by making sure KEYWORDS are very easy to find and showing how you have the Knowledge, Skills, and Abilities for the job, including those listed in the Questionnaire, which is Part 2 of the Federal job application.

Includes Accomplishments

WHY: In order to be rated Best Qualified, you must include accomplishments that will prove the Knowledge, Skills, and Abilities or Specialized Experience in the announcement. This information will prove your Past Performance and help you get REFERRED to a supervisor.

Lists Employment in Reverse Chronological Order

WHY: This order is used by the resume builder in USAJOBS.gov. Refer to the USAJOBS builder to make sure your Federal resume includes the required information.

Includes Information Required in Your Federal Resume

The Federal resume **must match** the USAJOBS Resume Builder fields. We recomend that you use the USAJOBS Resume Builder to create your resume for the first time.

- Month and year of each job you held for at least the last ten years
- Supervisor names and phone numbers (if they are available)
- Street addresses, city, state, and zip code of employers for at least ten years
- Education with hours completed
- Majors and colleges with city, state, and zip code
- Training with titles, sponsoring organizations, and classroom hours

> And last but not least...
> ## Uses the Outline Format!

The Outline Format resume **was developed by Kathryn Troutman in 1996 for the first edition of the** *Federal Resume Guidebook.* This format is still preferred by Federal Human Resources specialists because it is easy to read and rate. The following example provides an introduction into how a single job block written in the Outline Format should look. Keep in mind that this is just one job block from a resume. This approach outlines your knowledge, skills, and abilities in an easy-to-read and easy-to-rate format that makes it simple for the Human Resources Specialist to identify what you bring to the table.

Paragraphs, not bullets

GENERAL CLERK III
Coastal Development Services
3704 Pacific Ave • Virginia Beach, VA 23541

11/2015 – Present
40 Hours per Week
Salary: $45,000 per Year

Coastal Development Services is a major human resources organization and defense contractor that specializes in personnel management, data oversight, and pay administration. The company has approximately $1B in annual revenue and is the largest regional private sector employer.

PAY ADMINISTRATION: Proactively administer and maintain accuracy for military pay accounts across 3,800 officers and enlisted personnel. Devise, develop, and disseminate information and advice on military customers on pay, electronic service record entries, dependency data guidelines, and benefits/entitlements.

PROBLEM SOLVING: Investigate issues and resolve problems relating to military pay using in-depth knowledge of the Military Personnel Manual, Command Pass Coordinator Manual, and other Department of Defense instructions and policies. Analyze military records for discrepancies and deficiencies; deliver recommendations for resolution.

ALL CAPS headlines for each paragraph using KEYWORDS from the announcement

EDUCATION & TRAINING ADMINISTRATION: Deliver one-on-one and group training on a variety of education and professional development opportunities. Offer mentorship and guidance on advancement opportunities to more than 300 personnel annually, while also overseeing the review and approval of 100 tuition assistance requests for personnel pursuing degrees.

Add your accomplishments at the end of each job block

KEY ACCOMPLISHMENTS: During a routine audit of transaction data, I identified troubling gaps in the data-sets that appeared to indicate a problem with system-to-system communication. Recognizing the seriousness of this issue, I immediately informed my superior and launched an investigation alongside my counterpart at Department of Defense. Working in concert, we discovered a database glitch that could be fixed via system update. My efforts quickly resolved the issue, closed gaps in the data, and ensured accurate pay for 3,800 personnel. I received a commendation for my quick action and problem solving.

What to Include in **Your Federal Resume**

There are some pieces of information that must be included in your Federal resume, and others that are merely optional. In the lists provided here, you have a quick breakdown of the information your Federal resume should present.

Personal Information

> ❯ Full name, mailing address (with zip code), day and evening phone numbers (with area codes), and email address (one that you can access outside work if necessary)

Work Experience

Give the following information for your paid and nonpaid work experience related to the job you are applying for (do not copy and paste your job description into the resume):

> ❯ Job title (include series and grade if it was a Federal job)
> ❯ Duties and accomplishments
> ❯ Employer's name and specific address, city, state, and zip code
> ❯ Supervisor's name and phone number (if you have this information)
> ❯ Starting and ending dates (month and year)
> ❯ Hours per week
> ❯ Salary (optional, not required)
> ❯ Permission (if you choose) to contact your current supervisor (Saying "no" is acceptable and will not affect your chances of being considered for the position.)

Education

> ❯ Colleges or universities
> ❯ Name, city, and state (zip code)
> ❯ Majors
> ❯ Type and year of any degrees received (If no degree was received, show total credits earned and indicate whether semester or quarter hours.)
> ❯ Courses that will be relevant for the position and descriptions of your major papers, course projects, or capstone projects

Other Qualifications

> ❯ Job-related training courses (title and year/classroom hours and certificate if applicable)
> ❯ Job-related skills (for example, other languages, computer software/hardware, tools, machinery, and typing speed)
> ❯ Job-related certificates and licenses (current only)
> ❯ Job-related honors, awards, and special accomplishments (for example, publications, memberships in professional or honor societies, leadership activities, public speaking, and performance awards. Give dates, but do not send documents unless requested.

This information is listed in the OPM OF-510, *Applying for a Federal Job*
www.gpo.gov/pdfs/careers/apply/of0510.pdf

Before & After **Sample Federal Resumes**

In the following pages, we'll show you four examples of before and after Federal resumes. Each "before" example will demonstrate the pitfalls of the following popular resume formats:

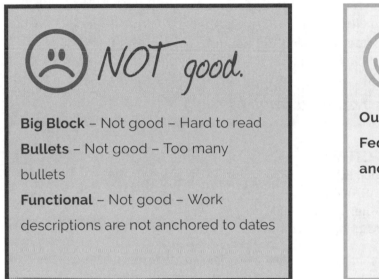

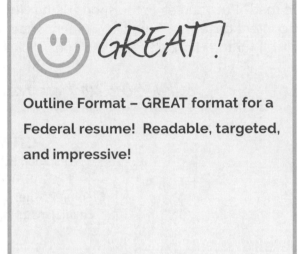

Big Block – Not good – Hard to read

Bullets – Not good – Too many bullets

Functional – Not good – Work descriptions are not anchored to dates

Outline Format – GREAT format for a Federal resume! Readable, targeted, and impressive!

Each "after" example will demonstrate the resume as revised using the Outline Format, which IS the example you should follow. The examples look at few different jobseeker scenarios:

Sample 1 – FEDERAL TO FEDERAL

Jenny is a current Federal employee, GS-0301-9. She is seeking a GS-0301-11 position in the same agency she was working for in the Housing Department in Naples, Italy. She was promoted with this Federal resume!

Sample 2 – PRIVATE SECTOR TO FEDERAL

Milton has been in auto insurance claims and emergency management claims for 15 years. He wanted to get hired by FEMA in emergency claims work. He was HIRED with this resume. You will see accomplishments and special claims examples featured!

Sample 3 – COUNTY EMPLOYEE TO FEDERAL

James has been in county law enforcement for 15 or more years. He wanted to move into government and the 1811 job series. He succeeded with this resume!

Sample 4 – PRIVATE SECTOR TO FEDERAL

Deborah wanted an Information Technology Specialist (Cloud), GS 2210-11 position in government. There are MANY positions in this field in government.

Before: Big Block Resume

Overseas Military Spouse Seeking Promotion | Target: GS-11 Program Analyst

☹ *This example shows what NOT to do.*

In the Big Block resume format, all the job blocks exist as single giant paragraphs. This approach stems from the days of Resumix, when resumes were scanned by an automated system. But Resumix was eliminated in 2010. Now it is time to write in a more readable format. Do you see how this format is hard to read? Put yourself in the shoes of the Human Resources Specialist who has to review and rate this content based on a specific job announcement. The Big Block format makes this process more difficult for the Human Resources Specialist, which is not the outcome you're aiming for!

See how the big block resume is hard to read!

Jenny

PSC 000 BOX 000
FPO, AE 09618 US
Evening Phone: 000-000-0000
Email: jan111@gmail.com

Work Experience:
NSA Naples Housing Office
PSC 808 Box 7
FPO, AE   09618 United States
07/2015 - Present
Salary: 44,250.00 USD Per Year
Hours per week: 40
Series: 0301 **Pay Plan:** GS **Grade:** 9
PRINCIPAL ADVISOR/ASSISTANT TO HOUSING DIRECTOR in preparing, developing and presenting housing program information for the Naples area. ACTING ADMINISTRATIVE OFFICER; provided administrative housing support within the command. Ensured quality of life for service members and/or family members through provision of adequate, affordable housing by the housing program. Confirmed that all transactions conformed to regulatory housing requirements. ADMINISTRATION: Advised command on training, program, regulatory requirements and procedures; administrative and secretarial duties requiring extensive knowledge of Navy Housing management and mission. Consultant to management on personnel staffing matters; resolved controversial, complex and difficult issues. Reviewed proposed directives for consistency with established directives and proper distribution. Served as the central point of information, resolving questions and problems. Established/maintained administrative business files about policies and procedures, plus logs to track the status of actions and correspondence. Received incoming correspondence, screened material prior to distribution for suspense dates, established controls and followed up for the Housing Director. Ensured daily reports were compiled and verified. Arranged travel, schedules of visits and reservations, notifying organizations and officials to be visited and submitting travel vouchers and reports. Coordinated counseling/mediation meetings with Housing Director, military members and their chain of command to discuss violations of Housing regulations in government quarters. Coordinated administrative hearings when occupants appealed eviction from military family housing. Served as recorder for hearings. MARKETING: Planned/coordinated special studies, satisfaction and market surveys, facility assessments and housing program reviews.

Before: **Bulleted Resume**

Overseas Military Spouse Seeking Promotion | Target: GS-11 Program Analyst

☹ *This example shows what NOT to do.*

In the Bulleted Resume format, all the job blocks exist as long lists of bullet points. Many people prefer to write their resumes this way. However, because the Human Resources specialist is looking specifically to identify knowledge, skills, and abilities, the list-based approach takes too long to review. Do you see how this resume is hard to read? Now, put yourself in the shoes of the Human Resources Specialist who has to review and rate this content based on a specific job announcement. It is simply too difficult to identify the relevant skills and accomplishments in this format.

It's too hard to find the relevant skills in this format.

Jenny
PSC 000 BOX 000 FPO, AE 09618 US
Evening Phone: 000-000-0000   Email: jan111@gmail.com

Work Experience:

NSA Naples Housing Office
PSC 808 Box 7
FPO, AE 09618 United States
07/2015 - Present

Salary: 44,250.00 USD Per Year
Hours per week: 40
Series: 0301 Pay Plan: GS Grade: 9
Administrative Support Specialist (This is a Federal job.)

- ADMINISTRATIVE OFFICER: deals directly with operation level managers regarding all aspects of administrative management.

- Provides guidance on personnel management, security, administrative internal control, department marketing program, training program and briefings/presentations.

- Directs Family and Bachelor housing staff to develop enhanced processes and procedures.

- Conducts briefings to managers on study findings and recommendations to improve the effectiveness of the housing program.

- Researches, interprets, initiates, and communicates administrative policies, regulations, procedures, and processes to all levels of the command.

- Resolves complex problems affecting the housing program and organizational requirements to improve the efficiency of operations.

- Develops, plans, schedules, and prepares data for project/planning and progress review.

- Identifies and conducts special studies and gathers data from subordinate organizations to resolve variances and to solve complex problems. Conducts housing management surveys, reviews and inspections to assess the effectiveness of program operations.

- Implements changes to organizational, resource controls and benchmark studies to evaluate significant complexity.

After: Outline Format Federal Resume—HIRED!

Overseas Military Spouse Seeking Promotion | Target: GS-11 Program Analyst

 *This example shows a format that works!*

Human Resources Specialists in the Federal government have the following to say about the Outline Format:
"I wish all resumes looked like this. It would make my job so much easier to find the best qualified candidates and decide who should be referred to the Selecting Official." The Outline Format makes keywords and accomplishments stand out, making it easier for the Human Resources Specialist to identify what knowledge, skills, and abilities you bring to the table.

Jenny

Work Experience:
PSC 808 Box 7
FPO, AE   09618 United States
NSA Naples Housing Office
07/2015 - Present
Salary: 44,250.00 USD Per Year

Hours per week: 40
Series: 0301 **Pay Plan:** GS **Grade:** 9
Administrative Support Specialist (This is a Federal job.)

The Housing Department, Fleet and Family Readiness Programs at Commander, Navy Installations Command, Navy Region Europe, Africa, Southwest Asia (EURAFSWA), Capodichino, Italy, is responsible for policy development, resourcing and oversight of quality of life programs for Sailors and their families.

ENSURE QUALITY OF LIFE for service members/families by providing adequate and affordable housing options at NSA Naples, serving 5000+ residents. As Administrative Officer, deal directly with operation-level managers regarding administrative management.

HOUSING PROGRAM EXPERTISE: Understand mission requirements, program goals and objectives, regulations/laws/policies/precedents, methods and procedures that govern operations. Analyze, coordinate and review tasks, projects and organizational goals.

- Conduct complex housing-related studies to evaluate the impact of changes in regulatory and legislative requirements. Study structure of the housing operation to improve processes and maximize mission accomplishment. Prepare Business Case Analysis and Business Process Reviews regarding courses of action for cost effective renovations for more than 1,000 family units in two years.

PERSONNEL/WORKFORCE MANAGEMENT: Create Requests for Personnel Actions (RPAs), civilian reports and other documents in Defense Civilian Personnel Data System (DCPDS) and Total Workforce Management System (TWMS). Prepare/process all personnel actions for department, ensuring requests are processed promptly and appropriately.

- Position Creation – We needed 2 new positions, 1 in Showing and 1 in Referral. I created the positions, obtained approval for them, advertised them, and interviewed and selected candidates. This complex process took about 1 year, but it filled a need and improved morale among staff.

MARKETING: Design, develop and implement the Housing Marketing Program for proactive internal/ external information distribution. Develop and produce materials, pamphlets and other promotional materials for distribution to customers. Liaise with Public Affairs office; advise management/staff and recommend policy regarding public affairs matters related to housing and command operations.

- Edited and improved the content of Housing's Facebook page, which receives 700 views per day, and answered an average of 3 messages per day. The Facebook page promoted the housing programs, quality of life for families and events for open houses.

Before: **Big Block Resume**

Private Sector Seeking FEMA Position | Target: FEMA, Insurance Specialist, IC-13

☹ *See how the big block resume is hard to read!*

Milton

Professional Experience

GEICO
Auto Damage Field Claims Supervisor   02/2016 to present

Providing support to my adjusters in the field to provide excellent claims service. Delivering to customers the most accurate estimates and completing shop supplements while maintaining our cost severity within competitive margins. Managing the entire repair process for customers to reduce cycle time by communicating with both the rental car companies and body shops of choice. Commercial Claim Experience: I recently had a commercial apartment complex claimant that suffered damage to their property from a motor vehicle accident. I visited the site, took photos of the damage, and wrote a preliminary estimate after taking a statement from the property manager. I then recommended a vendor for repair from a vendor list I have on file.

Travelers Insurance
Account Manager Underwriter   02/2015 to 02/2016

Assisted agent and insureds with products, pricing and availability for Assigned Risk Workers Compensation. Collaborated extensively with auditors during preliminary and year-end audit processes. Coached and mentored staff members with constructive feedback on obtaining additional premium. Manages relationships with Account Executives, agents, Managing General Agents (MGAs), as well as peers and business partners. Negotiates and resolves conflicting priorities. Partners with Account Executives/Underwriters to establish support needs for new and renewal policies (i.e., identify/gather relevant account information to quote and/or bind the policy; create exhibits, etc.). Prepares documents and participate in pre-renewal meetings. Prepares underwriting/pricing exhibits (i.e., exposures, experience rating, profit and loss analysis, expense models, updated account information, etc.). Manages account documentation (i.e., proposals, agreement letters, reinsurance contracts, collateral agreements, pricing doc, policy change, endorsements, cancellations, etc.). Ensures accurate and timely servicing and billing of accounts. Communicates with brokers/agencies, MGAs, and internal departments. (i.e., researches and resolves issues, responds to inquiries and questions). Quotes accounts by reviewing exposures and experience rating, updating account information, rates and adjusts the price, as requested.

Before: **Bulleted Resume**

Private Sector Seeking FEMA Position | Target: FEMA, Insurance Specialist, IC-13

It's too hard to find the relevant skills in this format.

Milton

Professional Experience

GEICO

Auto Damage Field Claims Supervisor   02/2016 to present

- Providing support to my adjusters in the field to provide excellent claims service
- Delivering to customers the most accurate estimates and completing shop supplements while maintaining our cost severity within competitive margins
- Managing the entire repair process for customers to reduce cycle time by communicating with both the rental car companies and body shops of choice
- Commercial Claim Experience:
  I recently had a commercial apartment complex claimant that suffered damage to their property from a motor vehicle accident. I visited the site, took photos of the damage, and wrote a preliminary estimate after taking a statement from the property manager. I then recommended a vendor for repair from a vendor list I have on file.

Travelers Insurance

Account Manager Underwriter   02/2015 to 02/2016

- Assisted agent and insureds with products, pricing and availability for Assigned Risk Workers Compensation
- Collaborated extensively with auditors during preliminary and year-end audit processes
- Coached and mentored staff members with constructive feedback on obtaining additional premium
  - Manages relationships with Account Executives, agents, Managing General Agents (MGAs), as well as peers and business partners
  - Negotiates and resolves conflicting priorities
  - Partners with Account Executives/Underwriters to establish support needs for new and renewal policies (i.e., identify/gather relevant account information to quote and/or bind the policy; create exhibits, etc.)
  - Prepares documents and participate in pre-renewal meetings
  - Prepares underwriting/pricing exhibits (i.e., exposures, experience rating, profit and loss analysis, expense models, updated account information, etc.)
  - Manages account documentation (i.e., proposals, agreement letters, reinsurance contracts, collateral agreements, pricing doc, policy change, endorsements, cancellations, etc.)
  - Ensures accurate and timely servicing and billing of accounts

---

 *This is an example of what to do!*

Milton

PROFILE

Dedicated insurance agent with 18 years of experience in insurance sales, underwriting and claims management. Consistently achieved high customer satisfaction ratings. Strong understanding of insurance to effectively manage a team to meet customer expectations.

PROFESSIONAL EXPERIENCE

AUTO DAMAGE FIELD CLAIMS SUPERVISER
GEICO
3535 W Pipken Rd, Lakeland, FL 33811
Supervisor: John Smith (202) 222-2222 Please do not contact.

02/2016 to Present
40 hours per week
$64,900 per year

GEICO is the second largest auto insurer in the United States and provides coverage for more than 24 million motor vehicles owned by more than 15 million policy holders. In my role as an Insurance Claims Supervisor, I oversee a 10-member team of field adjusters and office-based insurance agents, focusing on auto damage claims while also providing products insuring personal and commercial property.

FRONT-END SUPERVISION & TRAINING: Deliver training and support to adjusters in the field to provide excellent claims service. Ensure agents in the office professionally and courteously serve customers coming into the office looking for insurance products.

COMMERCIAL CLAIMS PROCESSING: Process claims for commercial customers, including property management companies. Conduct claims process in accordance with commercial-specific guidelines, such as requiring claimants to obtain repair estimates from multiple vendors, who are then vetted for sufficient coverage, insurance and bonds to ensure estimate integrity and guard against overcharging. Issue payment via two-party check to avoid fraud. Communicate with customer and vendors throughout process.

FLOOD INSURANCE / NATIONAL FLOOD INSURANCE PROGRAM (NFIP): Maintain current knowledge of NFIP. Routinely interact with the local county flood department for any changes in the flood zone for individual risks. Obtain elevation certificates for customers that require flood coverage per the mortgage carrier and help customers understand both the requirement and all of its protections. Handle auto and property claims including damage from flooding due to storms and other circumstances.

KEY ACCOMPLISHMENTS:
· Developed, implemented, and managed an emergency claims drive program in response to widespread damage from Hurricane Irma in September 2017. My team set up locations to provide immediate payment to repair salvageable vehicle or full value payment for vehicles that were total losses; we also immediately placed customers in rental vehicles. This expedited response helped affected customers return to their jobs and provided transportation when it was badly needed.

· As an adjuster in 2017, I paid out over $1.2M in claims settlements for insured and claimants. One of the claims received was for a claimant who sustained damage from one of our insureds because they drove off the road, hit a brick mailbox, and ran the vehicle into their home. We replaced the brick mailbox, received estimates for stucco and concrete block repair to the home and paid out over $18K in damages to the claimant.

Before: Big Block Resume

County Law Enforcement Officer Seeking Federal | Target: Law Enforcement Specialist GS-1811

See how the big block resume is hard to read!

JAMES

PROFESSIONAL EXPERIENCE

DETECTIVE, SPECIAL INVESTIGATIVE DIVISION　　　　　　**7/2016 – Present**
Howard County Police Department　　　　　　　　　　　　　　40 Hours per Week
Street address, Columbia, MD　　　　　　　Reference: Lt. John Smith (000) 000-0000

Responsible for coordinating high-value investigations and conducting joint operations with similar units in other jurisdictions to respond to violations of Federal law, state law, and violations of regulations, policies, and procedures. Liaise with Federal government law enforcement agency representatives, including those from the U.S. Marshals Task Force, to plan strategic and tactical investigations and operations to identify and apprehend fugitives. In April 2017, I deployed to Baltimore, Maryland for the Baltimore City Riots. In this role, I coordinated with Federal, state, and local law enforcement to conduct critical security operations in an exigent and fluid set of circumstances. I was instrumental in overseeing the deployment of less lethal munitions that resulted in the protection and preservation of numerous lives and property. Responsible for conducting, coordinating, planning and evaluating tactical operations pertaining to the Fugitive Unit, such as: small team tactics, dynamic entries, takedowns and vehicle assaults. Engage in room clearing, close quarters combat, marksmanship, legal considerations, deadly force and less lethal encounters, vehicle take down operations, barricaded suspects, hostage rescue, high risk warrant service, officer rescue and active shooter response.

I possess a vast knowledge of special weapons and tactics. As a result, served as an instructor in a Basic SWAT School for 4 consecutive years. Developed curricula and taught classes in both classroom and "real world" environments. Evaluated training and student performance relating to vehicle assaults, entry tactics, active shooter response, less lethal munitions, and physical fitness. Member of the Fugitive Unit, a plain-clothes undercover unit comprised of the most seasoned, capable and successful detectives in the agency. Responsible for locating and apprehending the most violent fugitives whose crimes originated in Prince George's County, MD. Routinely conduct investigations utilizing traditional and electronic surveillance, general investigative skills, and interviews and interrogations, resulting in the apprehension of over 185 fugitives annually. Well-versed in constitutional law, state statutes, Federal and state case law, search and seizure, arrests and detentions, and officer safety. Proactively coordinated and liaised with Federal law enforcement agencies to assess national security threats, ensure continuity of operations, and provide personal protection for senior officials. Provided protective services for governmental officials, including President G.W. Bush, President Obama, and other dignitaries. Routinely served as a member of Quick Reaction Force Teams prepared to respond to emergency incidents at major events in the DC metropolitan area. Led and implemented department-wide programs on special weapons and tactics, as well as strategic operations planning. Ensured that all members of the Special Operations Division were well-versed in constitutional law, state statutes, Federal and state case law, search and seizure, arrests and detentions, and officer safety techniques. As a member of the Emergency Services Team (SWAT), I was responsible for handling high risk situations such as those involving hostages or barricaded subjects. Participated in the execution of over 600 high risk search and seizure warrants, several barricades and a hostage rescue. Planned, conducted, and reported on high-level threats by dangerous groups and persons.

☹ *It's too hard to find the relevant skills in this format.*

JAMES

Professional Summary

Seasoned professional with over 18 years of experience in the Public Safety Field and in serving the community. Skilled at conducting and managing complex investigations, surveillance operations, undercover operations and testifying in said investigations. Proven ability to work effectively in a team environment or independently.

Work History

DETECTIVE – SPECIAL INVESTIGATIVE DIVISION (FUGITIVE UNIT)   7/2015 to present
HOWARD COUNTY POLICE DEPARTMENT – STREET ADDRESS, COLUMBIA, MD

- Responsible for locating and apprehending violent felons within Prince George's County and other jurisdictions
- Responsible for training members of the Fugitive Unit involving situational awareness, small team tactics and dynamic entries

POLICE CORPORAL– SPECIAL OPERATIONS DIVISION (EMERGENCY SERVICES TEAM/SWAT) 4/2011 to 7/2015

PRINCE GEORGE'S COUNTY POLICE DEPARTMENT – 6700 RIVERDALE ROAD, RIVERDALE, MARYLAND

- Handles high risk situations such as those involving hostages or barricaded subjects
- Executes search and seizure warrants and vehicle assaults
- Provides protective services for governmental officials and other dignitaries
- Conducts training programs on special weapons and tactics

DETECTIVE – NARCOTIC ENFORCEMENT DIVISION   7/2001 to 4/2011
PRINCE GEORGE'S COUNTY POLICE DEPARTMENT – 7600 BARLOWE ROAD, LANDOVER, MARYLAND

- Worked as an undercover narcotics detective
- Investigated narcotic traffickers, arrested narcotic traffickers and testified in those cases in court

After: Outline Format Federal Resume

County Law Enforcement Officer Seeking Federal |
Target: Law Enforcement Specialist GS-1811

This is an example of what to do!

JAMES

PROFILE

Seasoned law enforcement professional with 18+ years of experience in conducting and managing complex investigations, surveillance operations, undercover operations, and testifying in court cases. Skilled Investigator in all aspects of law enforcement operations, with substantial experience in protracted strategic investigations, urgent tactical investigations, and managing mission critical threats and risk mitigation.

PROFESSIONAL EXPERIENCE

DETECTIVE, SPECIAL INVESTIGATIVE DIVISION	**7/2016 – Present**
Howard County Police Department	40 Hours per Week
Street address, Columbia, MD ZIP	Reference: Lt. John Smith
(000) 000-0000	(000) 000-0000

The Special Investigative Division handles the most serious criminal cases, such as violent crimes and robberies. Investigations often involve surveillance operations, covert details and search and seizure warrants, as well as interviews of victims, witnesses and suspects. Detectives also investigate arson, auto theft and fraud cases.

INVESTIGATIVE COORDINATION WITH FEDERAL STAKEHOLDERS: Coordinate high-value investigations and conducting joint operations with similar units in other jurisdictions to respond to violations of federal law, state law, and violations of regulations, policies, and procedures. Liaise with federal government law enforcement agency representatives, including those from the U.S. Marshals Task Force, to plan strategic and tactical investigations and operations to identify and apprehend fugitives.

— In April 2017, I deployed to Baltimore, Maryland for the Baltimore City Riots. In this role, I coordinated with federal, state, and local law enforcement to conduct critical security operations in an exigent and fluid set of circumstances. I was instrumental in overseeing the deployment of less lethal munitions that resulted in the protection and preservation of numerous lives and property.

LAW ENFORCEMENT OPERATIONS: Conduct, coordinate, plan and evaluate tactical operations pertaining to the Fugitive Unit, such as: small team tactics, dynamic entries, takedowns and vehicle assaults. Engage in room clearing, close quarters combat, marksmanship, legal considerations, deadly force and less lethal encounters, vehicle take down operations, barricaded suspects, hostage rescue, high risk warrant service, officer rescue and active shooter response.

— I possess a vast knowledge of special weapons and tactics. As a result, instructed the Basic SWAT School for 4 consecutive years. Developed curricula and taught classes in both classroom and "real world" environments. Evaluated training and student performance relating to vehicle assaults, entry tactics, active shooter response, less lethal munitions, and physical fitness.

SPECIAL INVESTIGATIONS – FUGITIVE UNIT: Member of the Fugitive Unit, a plain-clothes undercover unit compromised of the most seasoned, capable and successful detectives in the agency. Located and apprehended the most violent fugitives whose crimes originated in Prince George's County, MD. Routinely conduct investigations utilizing traditional and electronic surveillance, general investigative skills, and interviews and interrogations, resulting in the apprehension of over 185 fugitives annually. Well-versed in constitutional law, state statutes, federal and state case law, search and seizure, arrests and detentions, and officer safety.

Private Sector to Federal | Target: Information Technology Specialist (Cloud), GS 2210-11

 *The duties and responsibilities must be anchored to the dates.*

Deborah

CERTIFICATIONS
Certified CloudHealth Platform Associate, CloudHealth, 2018
AWS Certified Cloud Practitioner, Amazon, 2018

SUMMARY OF INFORMATION TECHNOLOGY SKILLS

CLOUD TEAM MEMBER: Dedicated Cloud Management Systems Specialist in the 9-person GriffinNet Cloud Team. Provide pre-sales technical assistance to account managers and cloud architects in the design of cloud solutions tailored to the specific business needs of each customer.

CLOUDHEALTH ADMINISTRATION: As the corporate Subject Matter Expert (SME) on the CloudHealth platform, demonstrate CloudHealth capabilities to prospective clients. Compatible with Amazon Web Services (AWS), Microsoft Azure, and Google Cloud Platform (GCP), the CloudHeath Software as a Service (SaaS) platform collects and analyzes data from the client's cloud computing services to inform their business decisions through enhanced visualization, optimization, cost management, governance, and security.

IT PROJECT MANAGEMENT: Project Manager for 200+ concurrent, short and long-term projects for customers across the Northern CompuNet territory, which includes Eastern Idaho, Spokane, WA, and Billings and Missoula, MT. Use ConnectWise to manage the full project management life cycle, from project concept through execution, control, and closure.

COMMUNICATIONS: Communicate sensitive issues orally and in writing to a diverse group of technical and non-technical professionals. Participate in biweekly team meetings to track the progress of each customer project, ongoing risks and issues, and the tracking of employee training and certifications.

WRITING DOCUMENTATION: Develop a broad range of written products, including project plans, proposals, SOWs, Change Orders, and Processes & Procedures. Update customer site and project documentation to keep current with configuration changes. Routinely brief customers and corporate management, keeping them up-to-date on project status and projected system upgrade schedules.

CLIENT BILLINGS: Led a project to automate the manual corporate process to generate CloudHealth customer bills. Met with the Finance Department to map out the "as-is" billing process and recommend alternatives to introduce automation and streamlining. Developed the technical specifications for a billing model using features of the ConnectWise application. Served as the liaison between the ConnectWise vendor and the corporate software development team throughout the successful design of dropdown keys that streamlined the client bill processing process.

EMPLOYMENT HISTORY:
Cloud Management Systems Specialist (01/2017 – Present)
Griffin Networks, Cloud Team

Systems Analyst / Client Services, Eastern Region (01/2015 – 2/2017)
System Source is an Amazon Partner, 338 Clubhouse Rd Hunt Valley MD 21031

After: Outline Format Federal Resume

Private Sector to Federal | Target: Information Technology Specialist (Cloud), GS 2210-11

 *This example shows what to do!*

Deborah

CERTIFICATIONS

Certified CloudHealth Platform Associate, CloudHealth, 2018
AWS Certified Cloud Practitioner, Amazon, 2018

TECHNICAL SKILLS

Platforms: Microsoft Windows Desktop (7/8/10), Red Hat Linux, VMWare
Cloud Platforms: Amazon Web Services (AWS), Microsoft Azure, Google Cloud Platform (GCP), CloudHealth
Project Management: ConnectWise, MicroSoft Planner
Enterprise Applications: SharePoint, Direct Messaging, Rhapsody
Electronic Health Records (EHR): Orion, Epic, OAS/Gold
Electronic Medical Records (EMR): Meditech, Cerner, Allscripts, Centricity, McKesson
Video Teleconferencing (VTC): VTEL, Cisco Webex
Helpdesk: Remedy, Salesforce, LiveAgent
Office Products: Microsoft Office

RELATED PROFESSIONAL EXPERIENCE

Cloud Management Systems Specialist (01/2017 – Present)
Griffin Networks
Cloud Team
4509 Metropolitan CT, Frederick, MD 21704
Full-Time: 40+ hours/week; Base Salary: $45,000
Supervisor: Travis Davis, (xxx) xxx-xxxx; Please do not contact.

Cloud Management System Specialist for the GriffinNet Cloud Team. GriffinNet partners with market leaders in the cloud technologies sector, including Microsoft, Google, Amazon, and VMware, to provide comprehensive IT solutions for small to large businesses, from Managed Services and Enterprise Networks to Collaboration, Data Center, and Cloud Services.

SYSTEMS ANALYSIS: Dedicated Cloud Management Systems Specialist in the 9-person GriffinNet Cloud Team. Guide development of feasibility studies. Oversee fact-finding measures designed to ascertain the requirements of the system's end-users. Gauge how end-users would operate the system in terms of general experience in using computer hardware or software.

SYSTEMS ADMINISTRATION: As the corporate Subject Matter Expert (SME) on the CloudHealth platform, demonstrate CloudHealth capabilities to prospective clients. Compatible with Amazon Web Services (AWS), Microsoft Azure, and Google Cloud Platform (GCP), the CloudHeath Software as a Service (SaaS) platform collects and analyzes data from the client's cloud computing services to inform their business decisions through enhanced visualization, optimization, cost management, governance, and security.

IT PROJECT MANAGEMENT: Project Manager for 200+ concurrent, short and long-term projects for customers across the Northern CompuNet territory, which includes Eastern Idaho, Spokane, WA, and Billings and Missoula, MT. Use ConnectWise to manage the full project management life cycle, from project concept through execution, control, and closure.

EFFECTIVE COMMUNICATION: Communicate sensitive issues in oral and written formats to a diverse group of technical and non-technical professionals. Participate in biweekly team meetings to track the progress of each customer project, ongoing risks and issues, and the tracking of employee training and certifications. Develop a broad range of written products, including project plans, proposals, SOWs, Change Orders, and Processes & Procedures. Update customer site and project documentation to keep current with configuration changes. Routinely brief customers and corporate management, keeping them up to date on project status and projected system upgrade schedules.

KEY ACCOMPLISHMENT

CloudHealth Billing Enhancements: Led a project to automate the manual corporate process to generate CloudHealth customer bills. Met with the Finance Department to map out the "as-is" billing process and recommend alternatives to introduce automation and streamlining. Developed technical specifications for a billing model using features of the ConnectWise application. Served as the liaison between the ConnectWise vendor and the corporate software development team throughout the successful design of dropdown keys that streamlined the client bill processing process.

We started this chapter by observing that the Federal resume is the primary document upon which Human Resources Specialists determine your eligibility, qualifications, and applicant ranking for a Federal position. After looking at both good and bad examples of Federal resumes, it is clear why Human Resources Specialists prefer the Outline Format. As you work on your new Federal resume, we hope that you'll take strategy #1 to heart: use the Outline Format. Why? The answer is simple: because it works!

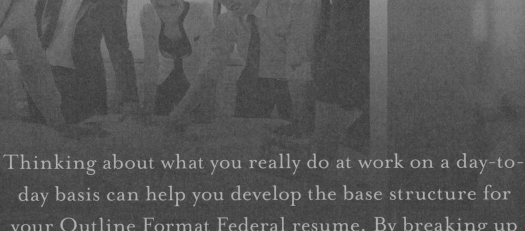

★ ★ ★

Strategy 2

HOW MANY HATS DO YOU WEAR AT WORK?

Thinking about what you really do at work on a day-to-day basis can help you develop the base structure for your Outline Format Federal resume. By breaking up what you do—the "hats" you wear—you can gain a better sense of what skills can be highlighted in the small paragraphs required by the Outline Format.

If you're like most people, you probably haven't updated your resume in quite some time. Maybe you don't even have a resume! Whatever your situation, figuring out where to start can be one of the most challenging aspects of writing your new Federal resume. We find it helpful to begin with what you know best—your current work experience. That's where Strategy 2 comes into play.

It is easy to show up, do your job, and go home at the end of the day without giving serious thought about the variety of things you do in a professional setting. When asked, people will say, for example, "Oh, I'm an analyst. I analyze things" and leave it at that. But what all goes into that job? What hats does the analyst wear? In reality, that person is probably collecting documents, looking at databases, interviewing people, synthesizing information, writing memoranda and reports, preparing presentations, conducting trainings, briefing senior managers, and so on.

A job title doesn't really convey the entirety of what you do. So, if you're struggling with where to start and need to build your resume from the ground up, begin here: how many hats do you wear at work? And what, exactly, are those hats?

Spend some time thinking about this and come up with a list of the top 5 to 7 core functions or work activities you engage in daily. Don't overthink. Just come up with a list. The list you create represents your hats. Then, for each hat, think of specific evidence-based examples that demonstrate your claim. Let's go back to the analyst example. If one of the analyst's hats is "research" then we might build out that hat with evidence-based examples like this:

> RESEARCH: Conduct research into human-rights related legislation and legal advocacy campaigns using primary and secondary sources. Routinely search databases—such as Lexis-Nexis, Westlaw, and JSTOR—to identify and locate source material. Manage a complex research program, including oversight of research assistants to develop, draft, and publish research findings. Apply research acumen to evaluate policies, governmental procedures and operations, and legislative impacts. Leverage research findings to develop strategic goals in memoranda and briefing materials.

If you take the hats-based approach, it simplifies the writing process into list-making and then building content based on the list you've created. The benefits of this are multiple:

1. it allows you to claim credit for the work you really do (not just what is in your position description)
2. it creates a framework for the Outline Format resume for your current job block
3. it opens the space for you to think about the evidence that you can use from your own experience to demonstrate each "hat" or skill.

Exercise: How Many Hats Do You Wear at Work?

When we teach Federal resume writing for government agencies, we ask each attendee to write out a list of the "hats" they wear at work every day. Then, we ask them to compare that list of hats to their resume. Attendees are often surprised to find that some of the hats in their new list do not appear in their resume at all. Doing the hats exercise allows an individual to identify core knowledge, skills, and abilities that they haven't considered putting into the resume.

What are the 5 to 7 hats that you wear in your job?

No matter where you're at in the process of developing your Federal resume, identifying the hats you wear at work is an important exercise. It will help you develop content for your resume. It will lessen the reliance on duty descriptions and help you put your experience into your own words. And, importantly, it is a good exercise to help you take credit for the work that you do day in and day out! The hats exercise can also be an excellent way of reacquainting yourself with your work as a form of interview preparation for your next job.

Begin writing your Federal resume with the "HATS" and "KEYWORDS" in ALL CAPS. Each paragraph will have a headline that will represent the most important skills needed for your target position. Use the Outline Format with the ALL CAP KEYWORDS to build your Federal resume! You will stand a FAR BETTER chance of getting Best Qualified for the position.

Sample Hats

In the following pages, we provide samples of the "hats" employees wear in a variety of different positions. These samples are based on real-life exercises that we conducted across the country. From a mechanic to an ecologist to a quality assurance specialist, you'll see that each role is tied to some pretty specific hats. You can use a short list of hats to help develop content for your Federal resume! For example, in our first sample—the Maintenance Mechanic—you can see that each of the identified hats can be used to build the outline of the resume, and each hat then becomes the headliner for a full paragraph with evidence-based examples.

Sample 1:

Shenandoah National Park, Maintenance Mechanic

- Maintenance Mechanic
- Preventative Maintenance
- Communications / Team Work
- Safety and Sanitation Knowledge
- Equipment Skills
- Small Tools
- Problem Solving

> For example, in our first sample—**the Maintenance Mechanic**—you can see that each of the identified hats can be used to build the outline of the resume, and each hat then becomes the headliner for a full paragraph with evidence-based examples.

Maintenance Mechanic   05/2018 - Present
National Park Service

MAINTENANCE MECHANIC - Repair facilities, buildings, and historic structures. Experienced in carpentry, painting, and roofing to maintain park buildings and facilities. Performed wood repair and painting for the Hoover Building, Interior and Exterior. Every room in the property. Exterior, Front Porch and Deck. Ensured paint colors and types of paint to meet Historic Preservation Requirements.

PREVENTATIVE MAINTENANCE: Preventive and construction maintenance on structures that require a knowledge of woodworking tools and equipment and historic preservation methods.

COMMUNICATIONS / TEAM WORK: Communicate with staff concerning repairs, schedule and maintenance requirements.

COLLABORATE WITH SAFETY AND SANITATION. Coordinate with sanitation group cleaning comfort stations and buildings throughout the park as needed.

EQUIPMENT SKILLS: Operate 4x4 pickups, small trailers, etc. to complete work projects.
Perform normal carpentry, painting, and roofing repairs and maintenance such as replacing door frames, constructing stairways and decks, repair/replace roofs and rafters.

SMALL TOOLS: Experience includes using common tools such as: hand saw, table saw, sander, framing square, chisel, etc.

PROBLEM SOLVING: Skilled in solving problems with carpentry, maintenance projects.

Sample 2: Human Resources Specialist, GS-0201-7

- Employee Relations
- Senior Advisor
- Knowledge Of Employment Law
- Case Management
- Representation
- Negotiator

Keywords from the announcement:
Employee relations
Senior management and supervisory advisor
Knowledge of complex case law
Maintain documents and files for case management
Represent management before third parties
Experienced negotiator

Sample 3: Family Program Specialist, GS-0301-12

- Family Program Manager
- Operations Manager
- Supervisor
- Studies / Analysis / Improvements
- Administrative Processes
- Communications / Customer Relations
- Computer Skills

Keywords from the announcement:
Develop and recommend policy
Organize military and family programs
Evaluate and recommend changes in methods for operations
Supervise staff
Manage studies, analysis, and evaluations leading to improvements
Study administrative practices and policies
Communicate in writing and orally
Computer skills / database skills

Sample 4: Transition Manager, GS 0301-12

- Transition Service Manager
- Resources Coordinator
- Marketing Director
- Instructor
- Customer Services
- Computer Skills

Keywords from the announcement:
Plan, direct, and implement transition services
Coordinate resources with service providers
Devise and manage a marketing program
Interpersonal skills / instructor
Customer services
Computer skills

Sample 5: Occupational Safety & Health Specialist, GS-0018-07

- Safety Manager
- Inspector
- Compliance Reviewer / Advisor
- Analyze Processes
- Case Management / Investigations

Keywords from the announcement:
Occupational and safety health laws and regulations knowledge
Inspect or survey workplaces
Review for compliance of established safety and occupational health policies
Analyze and evaluate new and existing processes
Determine existence of severity and outcome of hazards

Strategy 3

USE KEYWORDS TO MATCH THE VACANCY ANNOUNCEMENT

Your Outline Format Federal Resume must include the keywords from the vacancy announcement. Every single USAJOBS announcement contains the important keywords, skills, and keyword phrases that you can copy into your resume for a great match to the announcement.

All too often, highly qualified jobseekers apply to Federal job after Federal job and don't get results. Their applications come back with a dreaded notification: "Not Qualified." This is usually less due to their actual qualifications and more due to the fact that they haven't shown how they meet the qualifications listed in the USAJOBS announcement.

If you're new to searching for and applying to Federal jobs, you need to understand that there is a key that will unlock the door of opportunity. You can choose to use the key or not; but, if you don't, you won't land that Federal job.

So, what's the key?

The key to successfully applying for Federal jobs is to read the USAJOBS announcement carefully and critically, taking note of the keywords and key phrases. Then you turn the key by incorporating those keywords and phrases into your resume before submitting the application. Essentially, this is all about targeting—the resume must match the announcement.

Every USAJOBS announcement has its own set of important words and phrases, but you have to know where to look to find them. Too often, Federal jobseekers will read the duty description in the announcement and then quickly apply. To be successful, you have to know how the Human Resources Specialist is going to look at your resume. The wonderful thing about announcements on USAJOBS is that they convey exactly what is being looked for and evaluated in your application.

> **There are three primary areas where you can locate keywords and key phrases:**
> 1. Qualifications section, which articulates the required "specialized experience" for the position
> 2. How You Will Be Evaluated section, which lists additional knowledge, skills, and abilities (KSAs)
> 3. Self-Assessment Questionnaire

1. *Specialized Experience.* The Specialized Experience section is crucial as it outlines the types and scope of work experiences that will render you minimally qualified for the position. While reviewing your resume, the Human Resources Specialist looks specifically at whether you possess the required specialized experience. If it isn't clearly demonstrated, guess what? You're deemed "Not Qualified." The trick here is to read through the section, identify the essential words and phrases, and come up with a list of keywords based on your analysis. Those become ALL CAPS headliners for your Outline Format resume. For each one, you'll want to build out a paragraph of content with evidence-based examples.

2. *How You Will Be Evaluated.* The How You Will Be Evaluated section usually provides a list of additional KSAs and competencies. These can vary wildly, from highly technical knowledge to soft skills like "effective communication." You need to pay attention to the words listed in this section because they, too, need to show up in your resume. Remember, this section of the announcement is explicitly telling you how you will be evaluated! Ignore it at your peril.

3. ***Self-Assessment Questionnaire.*** The questionnaire isn't in the announcement itself; rather, it is usually located in the Application Manager that the announcement directs you to after you apply. However, most USAJOBS announcements allow you to preview the questionnaire with a link, usually located near the bottom of the announcement. This is another important place to look for keywords and phrases because for each question for which you claim expertise or proficiency, your answer must be supported in the resume itself.

You simply cannot ignore this strategy if you want a Federal job. Remember: the resume must be matched to the language of the announcement. Anything less will result in a failed application. Identifying keywords and key phrases can seem like a lot of work because, well, it is. It can also be tricky. If you're looking at a long paragraph of content in the Specialized Experience section, you might feel overwhelmed by the attempt to essentialize it down into a list of 5 to 7 words or phrases. Even so, remember those who succeed at applying for Federal jobs are those who emphasize quality over quantity—this isn't a numbers game. Really, it is simply about doing a quality job of reviewing the announcement and reflecting the announcement back in the resume.

With practice, you can master this process. This chapter is designed to help you learn the process and to guide you through the careful analysis of each section in a USAJOBS announcement.

Analyzing a job announcement to identify keywords is both an art and a science. It is an art in the sense that it requires a bit of a subjective feeling about which words are important and which are not. It is also an art in the sense that the more you do it, the more naturally it will come to you. Analyzing the job announcement is a science because it can be broken down into distinct steps and applies an analytical approach that requires you to identify core competencies from each section of the announcement. Most people struggle with this process. So if you don't get it quite right on the first try, that's okay!

So, let's turn the key and get started...

⊗ Every USAJOBS announcement has a set of different keywords / phrases.

⊗ Find keywords in the announcement: Duties, KSAs, Specialized Experience, and the Questionnaire.

⊗ Keywords will become the ALL CAP HEADLINES.

⊗ Use at least five to seven keyword phrases for your Outline Format resume.

Keyword Search Examples

Here are a few tips to help you identify what makes a keyword a keyword:

1. First, a keyword is critically important to the job. That is to say, the job could not be done without the action or function described by the word.
2. Second, a keyword summarizes specific job actions or identifies the scope of responsibility.
3. Third, keywords can be readily identified by asking yourself: what are the competencies being looked for in this position?
4. Finally, think about keywords in the context of knowledge, skills, and abilities. Which words denote a specific knowledge, skill, or ability required to do the job?

Let's take a look at a specific example. In this example we'll look through each component of a job announcement—duties, qualifications, and how you will be evaluated—to identify keywords.

How does your analysis of each section of the announcement match up?

Keywords are underlined.

Use these keywords as HEADLINES in your outline format Federal Resume.

SAMPLE VACANCY ANNOUNCEMENT

JOB TITLE: Emergency Management Specialist, GS-0089-12
DEPARTMENT: Department of the Army
AGENCY U.S. Army Corps of Engineers

DUTIES:
Serves as senior level <u>Emergency Management</u> Specialist for the South Pacific Division (SPD), <u>Readiness and Contingency Operations</u> Division. Provides <u>technical staff advice</u>, assistance, and planning, coordination, acquisition and maintenance for the Regional Emergency Operations Center (EOC), Emergency Relocation Site, and emergency alternate assemble points. <u>Manages the operational readiness</u> of the Regional Deployable Tactical Operations Center (DTOC), a HQUSACE asset assigned to Sacramento and Los Angeles Districts, and oversees SPD's Planning and Response Team. Ensures operational readiness of the SPD <u>communication systems</u>, <u>emergency information reporting</u> systems and emergency relocation of command and control facilities.

KEYWORDS

- ❯ EMERGENCY MANAGEMENT
- ❯ READINESS AND CONTINGENCY OPERATIONS
- ❯ TECHNICAL STAFF ADVICE
- ❯ COMMUNICATIONS SYSTEMS AND EMERGENCY INFORMATION REPORTING

QUALIFICATIONS SECTION (Keywords underlined)

QUALIFICATIONS REQUIRED:
In order to qualify, you must meet the education and/or experience requirements described below. Your resume must clearly describe your relevant experience; if qualifying based on education, your transcripts will be required as part of your application.

Experience required:
To qualify based on your experience, your resume must describe at least one year of experience which prepared you to do the work in this job. Specialized experience is defined as: Experience <u>engaging Federal, State, local and non-governmental partners</u> which support the <u>development of evacuation plans</u>, <u>strategies</u>, policies and procedures in times of disaster; preparing <u>analysis of data</u>, budgets and contracts; <u>interprets complex policy</u> and prepares reports that outlines complex guidance for the purpose of <u>creating instructions</u>; prepares recommendations, guidance, written and oral summaries for senior level briefings.

KEYWORDS

❯ FEDERAL, STATE, LOCAL AND NON-GOVERNMENTAL PARTNERS

❯ EVACUATION PLANS, STRATEGIES

❯ ANALYSIS OF DATA

❯ INTERPRETATION OF COMPLEX POLICY

❯ CREATE INSTRUCTIONS FOR EVACUATIONS

KNOWLEDGE, SKILLS, AND ABILITIES (KSAs) SECTION (Keywords underlined)

You will be evaluated on the basis of your level of competency (knowledge, skills, abilities) in the following areas:
- Knowledge of <u>Emergency Management Operations</u>
- Ability to <u>Develop Emergency Operations Plans</u>
- Ability to <u>Communicate</u>
- Ability to <u>Operate in an Emergency Operations Center</u>

KEYWORDS

❯ EMERGENCY MANAGEMENT OPERATIONS

❯ DEVELOP EMERGENCY OPERATION PLANS

❯ COMMUNICATIONS

❯ EMERGENCY OPERATIONS CENTER LOGISTICS & OPERATIONS

USAJOBS SELF-ASSESSMENT QUESTIONNAIRE

Thank you for your interest in an Emergency Management Specialist position with the Department of the Army. **Your resume and the responses you provide to this assessment questionnaire will be used to determine if you are among the best qualified for this position**. Your responses are subject to verification. Please review your responses for accuracy before you submit your application.

> Your application will be given a score to determine if you are in the Best Qualified category to be referred to the hiring supervisor for selection.

1. Select the one statement below that best describes the experience that you possess that demonstrates your ability to perform the work of an Emergency Management Specialist at the GS-12 grade level or equivalent pay band in the Federal service.

A. I possess at least one year of specialized experience equivalent to the GS-11 level in the Federal Service which includes experience <u>engaging Federal, State, local and non-governmental partners which support the development of evacuation plans, strategies, policies and procedures in times of disaster; preparing analysis of data, budgets and contracts; interprets complex policy and prepares reports that outlines complex guidance for the purpose of creating instructions; prepares recommendations, guidance, written and oral summaries for senior level briefings associated with emergency situations.</u>
B. I do not possess the experience as described above.

For each task in the following group, choose the statement from the list below that best describes your experience and/or training.
A- I have not had education, training or experience in performing this task.
B- I have had education or training in performing the task, but have not yet performed it on the job.
C- I have performed this task on the job. My work on this task was monitored closely by a supervisor or senior employee to ensure compliance with proper procedures.
D- I have performed this task as a regular part of a job. I have performed it independently and normally without review by a supervisor or senior employee.
E- I am considered an expert in performing this task. I have supervised performance of this task or am normally the person who is consulted by other workers to assist them in doing this task because of my expertise.

> **Give yourself all the credit you can.** You will need to answer E for at least 85-90% of the questions in order to achieve Best Qualified. If you cannot, then you need not apply.

6. Apply statutory and regulatory requirements (Public Law 84-99, Public Law 93-288 and ER/EP 500-1-1) and mission responsibilities under the Emergency Support Functions to support the <u>National Response Framework and National Disaster Recovery Framework</u>.

7. Perform evaluations, maintenance, revisions and corrective actions of emergency management program plans. Such as <u>preparedness exercises, training, and/or actual emergencies</u> and associated After Action Reviews (AARs) in support of the organizations accreditation.

> Your Federal resume needs to demonstrate these skills.

8. Develop planning documents and procedures pertinent to <u>Deployment and Emergency Operations Center (EOC) operations</u>, Division Continuity of Operations, Catastrophic Disaster and all Hazards.

9. Apply Department of Defense (DoD), US Army Corps of Engineers (USACE), or Federal Emergency Management Agency (FEMA), <u>rules and regulations related to natural disaster and national preparedness</u>, response and recovery to ensure the readiness of the organization.

10. Develop annual <u>budget requirements for emergency management programs and funding sources</u> to stay within budget.

11. Manage regional operations of <u>overseas contingency deployments</u> and Planning and Response team, cadre readiness and deployments.

12. Manage <u>employee data, equipment readiness</u>, disaster event updates, and equipment loan tracking using USACE ENGLink program.

For each response of "E" above, please indicate what position(s) on your resume supports this response (such as title, organization & date). If you fail to include this information, your application will be considered incomplete and you will be removed from consideration for this position.

A. Yes, I verify that all of my responses to this questionnaire are true and accurate. **I accept that if my supporting documentation and/or later steps in the selection process do not support one or more of my responses to the questionnaire that my application may be rated lower and/or I may be removed from further consideration.**

> This is a test! Give yourself all the credit that you can!

Keyword Search **Examples Continued**

When you have identified the keywords from a job announcement, the trick is to label which ones are "primary keywords" and which are "secondary keywords." The primary keywords become ALL CAPS headers for each paragraph, while the secondary keywords are to be described in the paragraph of text. Think of this as identifying individual buckets (the big, primary ideas) and then filling the buckets with secondary, supporting ideas. In reality, what you're doing is building the skeleton of your targeted Federal resume. Let's look at an example of how we might break down primary and secondary keywords to build the resume's framework.

Work Experience:

Baltimore County Fire Department
1000 Frederick Road
Baltimore, MD   21228 United States

01/2014 - Present
Hours per week: 40
Supervisory Firefighter

Duties, Accomplishments and Related Skills:

Primary keywords =
ALL CAPS headings

EMERGENCY MANAGEMENT OPERATIONS
Emergency Operations Center Logistics and Operations

DEVELOP EMERGENCY OPERATION PLANS
Evacuation plans and strategies

Secondary keywords =
Paragraph content

Readiness and contingency operations
Create instructions for evaluations

COMMUNICATIONS
Federal, state, local and non-governmental partners
Technical staff advice
Communications systems and emergency information reporting

ANALYSIS OF DATA
Interpretation of complex data
Quantitative and qualitative analysis

ACCOMPLISHMENTS
Write a couple of accomplishments that demonstrate the KSAs to stand out and get Best Qualified and Referred.

More Keyword Examples **from Actual Announcements**

MATCH YOUR RESUME TO THE ANNOUNCEMENT WITH KEYWORDS!

The following pages provide samples of the keywords that routinely appear for a variety of different positions. From a law enforcement specialist to an administrative specialist to a marine transportation specialist, you'll see that each role is tied to some pretty specific keywords. Although these keywords are pretty common for these types of positions, remember that you'll always want to look at, review, and match your keywords to the specific announcement of the job you're applying to. We're sharing these here to give you a sense of the depth, breadth, and variety of keywords that you'll find across the Federal jobs landscape.

LAW ENFORCEMENT SPECIALIST
GS-1800-11

- Technical Operations Specialist
- Plan And Execute Electronic Surveillance
- Expert In Use, Installation And Operation Of Electronic Surveillance Devices
- Investigate Potential Hazards And Implement Electronic Countermeasures
- Conduct Complex Technical Investigations
- Gather Intelligence And Evidence
- Oral And Written Communication
- Perform Lead Technical Security Advances

PROGRAM ANALYST (MOBILIZATION)
GS-0343-12

- (Acting) Mobilization Program Specialist
- Program Management
- Personnel Management
- Contract Oversight
- Mobilization Procedures
- Operations Management
- Administrative Planning

PROGRAM ANALYST (WORKFORCE)
GS-0343-11

- Director
- Organizational And Workforce Issues Leadership
- Interviews, Surveys, And Focus Groups
- Management, Program, And Data Analysis
- Strategic And Performance Planning/Workforce Development
- Training And Development
- Process Improvement
- Oral And Written Communication
- Data Mining/Trend Analysis
- Workforce Retention Strategy Creation

More Keyword Examples **Continued**

ADMINISTRATIVE ASSISTANT
GS-0301-7

- ❯ Administrative Assistant
- ❯ Medical Administrator/Manager
- ❯ Demonstrate Knowledge Of Medical Terminology
- ❯ Gather Data To Prepare Reports
- ❯ Communicate Orally And In Writing

ADMINISTRATIVE OFFICER
GS-0341-9

- ❯ Senior Military Advisor/Training
- ❯ Training And Program Management
- ❯ Management Advisor
- ❯ Logistics/Supply Management

TECHNICAL WRITER / EDITOR
GS-1082-9

- ❯ Technical Writer/Editor
- ❯ Research
- ❯ Communication .
- ❯ Automation
- ❯ Workload Management
- ❯ Project Research

MARINE TRANSPORTATION SPECIALIST
GS-2150-12

- ❯ Marine Transportation Specialist
- ❯ Business And Logistics Support
- ❯ Project Management
- ❯ Analysis
- ❯ Quality Assurance
- ❯ Emergency Logistics
- ❯ Contract Management
- ❯ Training
- ❯ Knowledge Of Federal, State, And Local Regulations
- ❯ Communications And Customer Service

As we noted at the beginning of this chapter, the key to successfully applying for Federal jobs is to read the USAJOBS announcement carefully and critically, taking note of the keywords and key phrases. Then you turn the key by incorporating those keywords and phrases into your resume before submitting the application. Essentially, this is all about targeting—the resume must match the announcement. Your analytical ability becomes a key player in this process, as does your attention to detail. Many Federal jobseekers find this to be quite tedious. But with effort, practice, and time, it should become second nature to you. Are you ready to turn the key?

Strategy 4

TELL YOUR ACCOMPLISHMENT STORIES

Supervisors appreciate employees who work hard to meet a mission. Demonstrating your value through accomplishment stories is a crucial part of the Federal resume. Highlighting accomplishments is the best way to show how you stand out above the crowd.

The Federal resume isn't just about demonstrating specialized experience and KSAs through keywords and phrases. Those are centrally important aspects of constructing a competitive Federal resume, but to be successful the resume should ultimately be accomplishment-focused. As we noted in Strategy 1, by highlighting accomplishments you also make it easier to identify the added value you bring to the table.

> **It is common for resumes to leave out accomplishments altogether, or to relegate accomplishments to a single sentence or bullet point.**

Take a moment and pause before reading any more. Pull out your current resume. Take a quick look at it—no more than ten seconds. Can you immediately spot the accomplishments? Can you differentiate them from your duty descriptions? If you can't find your accomplishments in less than ten seconds in your own resume, consider how hard you'll be making the Human Resources Specialist—and the Hiring Manager—work to find your added value. Strategy 4 is all about telling your accomplishment stories and highlighting them so that they're easy to identify.

First, let's consider what an accomplishment is. People really struggle with this. If you're like most, you might think that unless you received an award or formal recognition, you don't have any accomplishments. But the reality is that accomplishments can take many forms. How often have you done something at work that you haven't received any recognition for? We've all been there. The most important step in thinking about accomplishments is to embrace a broader understanding of what you can, and should, consider as an accomplishment.

An accomplishment can be represented by an award or formal recognition. But it need not be. Have you made some sort of difference to your organization? Have you changed a policy, a procedure, or a process? Have you delivered a recommendation that was implemented? Are there things that you're proud of? Maybe you were a key player in an important project. Maybe you solved a problem. Perhaps you took on an extra duty when no one else was willing. Whatever you've done, be willing to claim credit! Why? Because it may be the difference between getting an interview and not getting one.

We often are asked, "What is the difference between regular everyday job duties and an accomplishment?" It is a fair question. The best response is to separate your regular duties from any special projects you have worked on, problems you have solved, or major customer service work that you have performed. Each of those areas are rich fodder for identifying accomplishments. Kathryn Troutman interviewed a Human Resources Specialist on behalf of a highly qualified Federal jobseeker— an engineer—who was trying to land a job at NASA. Even though he was obviously qualified, his applications were never referred. During the interview, the Human Resources Specialist indicated that the job applicant had not sufficiently demonstrated past performance through accomplishments. It was not enough to simply include the keywords in the resume—the engineer needed to tell stories and show examples of his accomplishments to get referred. That's an important lesson!

People tend to under-report their accomplishments because they're afraid it will come across as "bragging." Here's the thing: the resume is the one place where bragging is not just socially acceptable, *IT IS ESSENTIAL*. Step out of your comfort zone, think about what you're proud of, and share that in your resume. Not only will it make you feel better about your work, it will get the attention of the Hiring Manager.

Second, let's consider how to highlight accomplishments. Each job block in the Federal resume should have a section that is dedicated to your accomplishments for the job. You'll use the keywords-based Outline Format to describe your day-to-day duties, and then you would add in a section that is clearly marked as "ACCOMPLISHMENTS" or "ACHIEVEMENTS" or "KEY HIGHLIGHTS." Whatever wording you choose is less important than to clearly show the reader (i.e., the Human Resources Specialist and/or the Hiring Manager) that you've done something notable and where it can be found in the resume.

Develop some real content for each accomplishment to include in the resume. Don't relegate that important story to a single sentence or bullet point; rather, tell the story. It should be a short paragraph. Provide the reader with some context, formulate what problem you were working on, identify the actions you took, and then conclude with the results and why those results were important. If we go back to thinking about the resume as an argument—an argument to persuade someone to hire you—then the use of storytelling is a particularly effective method because humans are hardwired to appreciate good stories.

Let's look at a real-world example of how this can be a difference-maker:

Original Accomplishment: Received recognition for participating in implementation of cybersecurity awareness campaign.

More Developed Accomplishment: Senior leadership selected me to lead an organization-wide cybersecurity awareness campaign because of my expertise in the area. This had never been done before and came at a crucial time for the organization. I hand-selected a team of five subject matter experts and tasked each with developing different components of our strategy. Next, I coordinated with managers across the organization to define a roll-out plan. Finally, with the strategy and roll-out plan in place, I leveraged technology such as online training modules, webinars, and e-mails to increase cybersecurity awareness. Through my initiative and actions, the organization launched its first-ever cybersecurity awareness campaign, increasing global visibility into a mission-critical topic. I received a written commendation from the Chief Information Officer.

Both versions are true. Both are based on the same set of events. Now, ask yourself which version demonstrates this job applicant's added value? The first merely claims "recognition" for "participation." The second claims credit, tells a story, demonstrates a leadership role, and conveys the significance of the accomplishment.

Writing accomplishments in this more developed format is hard work, which is why this strategy comes with some tools to help you. Let's look at some more examples and the tools that you can use to write better accomplishments for your Federal resume.

Start Writing **Your Accomplishment Stories**

Accomplishment stories don't come from out of nowhere. They come from your experience. So, let's pause for a bit and engage in some self-reflection. Ask yourself: what have I accomplished professionally in the last five years that makes me proud? What have I contributed to my organization's mission? What am I proud of as a professional?

As you reflect on those questions, begin writing out a list of your key professional accomplishments over the past five years. Once you have a list, then you have the items to jog your memory so that you can get into story-telling mode. Remember, a list isn't good enough for the resume. We want you to tell your accomplishment stories. So, the best practice here is to use your list as the beginning of this process. Next, take each item on the list—one by one—and write out a short narrative about what happened. Don't worry too much at this stage about content and grammar—just get the story out. Then, once you have a paragraph, go back and refine using the CCAR (context, challenge, actions, results) formula, which we break down later on in this chapter.

See a sample of a Top Ten List of Accomplishments on pages 120-121.

Write your story with the Resume Place accomplishment tool:
www.resume-place.com/ccar_accomplishment

Using the **CCAR Format**

The Office of Personnel Management has a recommended format for writing KSAs and your accomplishments record in a story-telling format: the Context, Challenge, Action, Result (CCAR) Model for writing better KSAs. This CCAR story-telling format is also great for the Behavior-Based Interview.

CONTEXT

The context should include the role you played in this example. Were you a team member, planner, organizer, facilitator, administrator, or coordinator? Also, include your job title at the time and the timeline of the project. You may want to note the name of the project or situation.

CHALLENGE

What was the specific problem that you faced that needed resolution? Describe the challenge of the situation. The problem could be disorganization in the office, new programs that needed to be implemented or supported, a change in management, a major project stalled, or a large conference or meeting being planned. The challenge can be difficult to write about. You can write the challenge last when you are drafting your KSAs.

ACTION

What did you do that made a difference? Did you change the way the office processed information, responded to customers, managed programs? What did you do?

RESULT

What difference did it make? Did this new action save dollars or time? Did it increase accountability and information? Did the team achieve its goals?

Write your story with the Resume Place accomplishment tool:
www.resume-place.com/ccar_accomplishment

Accomplishment Examples

At the end of your accomplishment writing process, you should have a short paragraph that demonstrates your value-added to the organization and which tells a good story about your accomplishment.

Let's look at some KEY ACCOMPLISHMENTS that you can add to your Federal resume. Since the Federal resume is on average 5 pages, you can add accomplishments in short narratives that will demonstrate your past performance in your work.

EXECUTIVE ASSISTANT; GS-0301-12

Launched a comprehensive reorganization of the Executive Director's library, which had fallen into a state of disarray and disorganization. Proactively envisioned and instituted an entirely new naming and filing system for library binders and coordinated junior staff in implementing my vision. The library is now systematized, standardized, and user-friendly, thereby enhancing executive ability to find and use information critical to the company's mission fulfillment.

Led a file management downsizing effort and streamlined processes under a more organized labelling system. Creatively developed a first-of-kind system to identify files associated with each organization and sub-organization, oversaw the new labeling process, and managed the reorganization effort. As a result, files are more readily accessible, locatable, and trackable. This resulted in reducing time and effort necessary to leverage company information in a competitive marketplace.

PUBLIC AFFAIRS SPECIALIST; GS-1035-13

Drove an outreach effort using project management best practices, resulting in communications touching 18,000 Watabu County, Florida businesses. Guided a 15-member staff across all aspects of the execution and evaluation of disaster assistance media outreach, communication plans. Envisioned and initiated improvements to the communication of agency policies, loan programs, and activities targeting stakeholders and members of the public. Acted as an agency spokesperson and external liaison by making public appearances, preparing presentations, delivering talking points and speeches describing the low-interest, long-term loan programs for physical and economic damage caused by a declared disaster. I successfully leveraged my team leadership, communication, and strategic planning skills to raise crucially important awareness for disaster assistance programs across the Watabu County Community.

Managed the creation and implementation of a Strategic Communication Outreach Plan to target specific communities and demographics in disaster areas. Applied the plan to disseminate SBA disaster assistance loan program informational materials to external customers, the media, Congress, local representatives, academic institutions, small and large businesses, non-profits, and community partners. My leadership to implement the plan resulted in the coordination of media relations, public outreach, and disaster response communications as part of the SBA's response to hurricanes Harvey, Florence, and Sandy across multiple deployments.

NURSE; GS-0610-14

Strategically initiated and led a collaborative effort with the Centers for Medicare and Medicaid (CMS) to develop a Care Coordination Agreement to expand the circumstances under which beneficiaries could receive Federal matching funds at the enhanced Federal matching rate (FMAP) of 100 percent. Leveraged subject matter expertise, professional relationships, and business acumen to collaborate with CMS to update policies allowing our medical facilities to enter into care coordination agreements with external providers to deliver services. My leadership over the process directly resulted in an expansion of access to funds for beneficiaries.

Launched a first-of-kind online training curriculum for the agency to address professional development gaps in an environment with limited funding. Formed a team of subject matter experts to identify critical training needs, engage in process mapping, and develop new training modules. Coordinated with the Office of Information Technology (OIT) to design, test, and implement a training website agency-wide. My efforts standardized training in crucial areas to the agency mission, saved the agency tens of thousands of dollars in travel costs, and increased information accessibility to providers. My approach to standing up the training program has been recognized as a "best practice" and resulted in recognition with the Director's Award.

Emergency Management Specialist; GS-0089-12

Developed emergency response plan for the White Oaks Hospital, including the following key documents: Emergency Operations Center Activation, Hurricane Response Plan, and Active Shooter Response Plan. Incident commander for two disaster events. Wrote and implemented capacity building curriculum for long-term preparedness. Planned and coordinated three training exercises for 400 staff members. Acquired and maintained $150,000 of response equipment to support the hospital's hazardous materials response and decontamination requirements. Equipment included the latest in protective technology: Powered Air Purifying Respiratory Devices, decontamination tents, generators, and personal protective clothing for medical personnel.

PILOT targeting Aviation Safety Inspector; FG-1825-12-13

Developed work-around for Eyjafjallajokull Volcano eruption in Iceland, which shut down European airspace for six days. Analyzed best options to avoid significant safety threat of flying through volcanic ash, without significantly increasing fuel costs. Conducted historical analysis of engine shutdowns and depressurization of B-757/767/777 aircraft to determine and assess risk of flying over cloud. Created procedure for crew to treat cloud as terrain: Instructed pilots to fly over cloud with instructions to fly away from the cloud (one direction or another) if emergency descent was required. Vetted procedure through dispatch and engineering; issued a bulletin to operation manuals of three fleets involved and, lastly, briefed principal operations inspector and pilots' association leadership. The procedure was successfully implemented and flights resumed promptly.

Accomplishment Examples Continued

FINANCIAL MANAGEMENT ANALYST; GS-0501-11 ☺

Innovated new process for running, exporting, and viewing reports within the Budget Office, which improved the efficiency of daily ledger/tracker validation. The new process also reduced manual adjustments, saving 24 work hours/week. The new process was so effective that it was approved by senior leaders as a standard operating procedure for implementation across 4 branches.

Developed a customized Excel spreadsheet incorporating 18 reports and multiple metrics. The spreadsheet introduced advanced cross-referencing tools that improved accuracy, organization, and reporting for all financial data.

Played key role in developing a 15-page Policy and Standard Operating Procedure guide covering all Project Funding Requests, which was approved by HQ as the primary resource for proper methods of receipt and distribution of funds. The new guide will impact $1.2M of disbursements/year.

AIRCRAFT ENGINE MECHANIC; WG-8602-09 ☺

Selected as Relief Shop Supervisor on a quarterly rotation with other qualified shop personnel. Duties include clocking personnel in, meeting attendance, instructing and directing 14 shop personnel on maintenance requirements, and administrative actions as required. I also assist personnel with troubleshooting issues and provide guidance to resolve issues.

Volunteered for one year as an Airframer for the H-53 aircraft line. Gained extensive knowledge and valuable experience in this new work environment. Worked independently and trained three other personnel that were assigned to my work area. My expertise and level of training greatly assisted the Fleet Readiness Center H-53 completion schedule.

CONSTRUCTION CONTROL TECHNICIAN; GS-0809-12 ☺

Directly managed the re-compete for an ending contract across the entire acquisition process including: planning, scope of work development, technical evaluation team leadership, negotiation, and post-award administration. After the new contractor defaulted on numerous orders, I proactively synergized with the Contracting Officer to award a sole source acquisition to avoid imminent work stoppage. Successfully coordinated with senior management and the defaulting contractor to "terminate for convenience," and resolicit the agency requirement, with the contractor agreeing to refund procurement costs. My efforts were recognized with an Outstanding Performance Award and subsequent promotion.

Administered a 10-year Mechanical/Preventative Maintenance Contract, the largest active such contract at the agency. The contract covered all Institution facilities in Washington, DC, and locations in Arizona, California, and New York. I directly monitored and oversaw all aspects of contract performance to ensure preventative maintenance on equipment to sustain compliance, ensure safety, and improve the life of vertical transport equipment. My assignment to this role was based on previous outstanding technical performance.

New Graduate, BSEE MECHANICAL ENGINEER, GS-0083-09

Next Generation Mobile Cloud Computing Technology: Member of team that designed device that could be used for mobile cloud computing; device had stronger processing power than a cell phone, but was more portable than a laptop. The project consisted of modifying and compromising between various available technologies to produce a design that would be functional, reliable, and economical. Design consisted of cell phone that projected a laser keyboard onto any flat surface with glasses to serve as a visual display and gloves to interact with objects on the visual display; the entire system remotely connected to a desktop at home with strong computing power.

Dynamics of a Rotating Baseball: Lead programmer and numerical analysis assistant for five-person team that calculated the aerodynamic forces placed on a rotating baseball as it travels from the pitcher to the batter. Location of fastball pitch was determined, which determined the initial velocities and angles at which the pitch was thrown. Used MATLab code to simulate the movement of a different pitch with a different spin with the same initial angles.

Smoke Wire Flow Visualization Over Car Models: Team leader for project to determine which car design reduced aerodynamic drag the most. Took pictures of streamlines exposed by oil on a heat wire producing smoke trails in the airflow of a wind tunnel. Photos showed which car models experienced flow separation or the extent of the flow separation, the leading cause of aerodynamic drag. Then used photos to determine which car design was best suited for the tested wind speeds.

LICENSED VOCATIONAL NURSE; GS-620-09

Sundowners (veterans with PTSD) were triggered at night and became combative. This was made worse because of construction next door, which often started at 5 a.m. I worked collaboratively with a social worker to identify their needs. Took the patients outside to watch the construction so they could understand what was happening next door. This intervention helped calm the patients and lowered the number of psychiatric incidents due to PTSD.

A resident in the nursing home suffered from many arterial ulcers due to non-compliance with his diabetes care and treatment. I effectively treated the patient's diabetes, resulting in the healing of the patient's arterial ulcers. The patient became mobile and he was able to return home to his family.

CLERK; GS-0303-05

When I arrived at the U.S. Patent and Trademark Office, the department was struggling with disorganization. Hundreds of patent application files were catalogued incorrectly. Shelves were falling down and files were on the floor. This disorganization led to significant delay and confusion in the patent application process. I organized the files into types and color-coded them. Previous employees were unable to reorganize the office because it was physically and mentally demanding and required extreme attention to detail. The reorganization process took two weeks and is still being used. Employees and customers were thrilled with the results, which sped up our ability to respond to both routine and special requests.

Practice Writing the **CCAR** Format

Let's practice putting your accomplishment stories into the CCAR formula. Remember that each component should be straightforward. We like to think of the CCAR formula as something that makes writing easier, rather than harder. It is almost like plug and play. For each element of the formula, you plug in the relevant information (and only the relevant information) and by the end you have a full narrative ready to go for your Federal resume. We typically recommend 1–2 sentences for context and challenge, 2–3 sentences for actions, and 1–2 sentences for results. These are guidelines, not hard and fast rules, and can change depending on the complexity and seriousness of your story!

Context

Challenge

Action

Result

Strategy 5

ADD YOUR CORE COMPETENCIES

Federal agency managers are looking for more than specialized experience, education, and technical skills. What "value-added" competencies can you offer a supervisor?

Core competencies are the characteristics that align with the basic qualities and values of an agency's mission. You will read about the OPM core competencies followed by many Federal agencies ... and the unique customer service and problem-solving competencies required by the IT Specialist and the FBI Core Competencies required now for the FBI Special Agent.

Add Your Core Competencies

What are competencies? OPM defines a competency as a measurable pattern of knowledge, skills, abilities, behaviors, and other characteristics that an individual needs to perform work roles or occupational functions successfully. "Competencies can be seen as basic qualities that employees should exhibit in the work place to maximize their potential for the government."

It goes without saying that not all Federal agencies do the same thing. They each exist for a specific reason, serve different functions, possess different missions, and are driven by distinctive goals. For example, the Social Security Administration (SSA) is a people-focused agency that administers a variety of benefits programs; the Securities and Exchange Commission (SEC) focuses on securities laws and rule-making; while Immigration and Customs Enforcement (ICE) manages homeland security investigations and immigration removal operations. Because each of these Federal agencies does different work, their core values—as reflected in their core competencies—are different.

When you're applying for Federal jobs, it is important to consider the strategic perspective (which jobs you should apply for) as well as the resume-writing perspective (which core competencies you should highlight).

The Strategic Perspective. It isn't uncommon for people to lack a strategy when it comes to applying for Federal jobs. They say, "I just want a Federal job! I just want to get my foot in the door, so the agency doesn't really matter." That's fine, but here's the rub: not all Federal jobs are going to fit you the same way. Let's say that you are applying for positions at all three of the above-mentioned agencies, and you possess a strong orientation toward customer service, enjoy interacting with people, and like making people happy. Do each of these agencies have a customer service component? Sure. But where would you fit best? Let's look at the values they invoke on their own websites:

- ❯ **ICE:** Our mission is to protect America from cross-border crime and illegal immigration. This mission is executed through immigration enforcement, preventing terrorism and combating the illegal movement of people and goods.

- ❯ **SSA:** We are passionate about supporting our customers by delivering financial support, providing superior customer service, and ensuring the safety and security of your information—helping you secure today and tomorrow.

- ❯ **FBI:** MUCH MORE THAN A JOB. The mission of the FBI is to protect the American people and uphold the Constitution of the United States. Special Agents enforce over 300 Federal statutes and conduct criminal and national security investigations.

If you're a "people person," SSA is probably the clear winner in our scenario. It is a people-focused, customer-centric agency; the others, considerably less so. The point here is that you want to consider where you're applying to Federal jobs because some agencies will be a good fit for you and others won't. You need to evaluate this for yourself, because you don't want to end up working in an agency where you'll be miserable. Look at agency websites, mission statements, and statements of values to find the right fit for you.

The Resume-Writing Perspective. Once you know which agencies are good fits, you should think about incorporating their core competencies into your resume. Let's look at the SSA example again.

> **SSA:** We are passionate about **supporting our customers** by delivering **financial support**, providing superior **customer service**, and ensuring the safety and **security of your information**—helping you secure today and tomorrow.

The bolded words represent some core competencies of the SSA: providing customer service and support, financial support, and information security. A job applicant applying to positions within the SSA would do well by demonstrating each of these core competencies throughout the resume. Remember, the Federal resume should be a strategically developed, specifically targeted argument to persuade someone to hire you. If you've considered the mission and values of the agency to which you're applying, that shines through! Don't just focus on describing your experience, education, and technical skills—align them to core competency areas for which the agency is specifically looking.

How Do I Use Core Competencies When Applying for Jobs?

These characteristics go above and beyond skills. You can stand out in a government resume, question/essay narrative, or behavior-based interview by highlighting these competencies. Determine the top five or ten competencies that make you a stand-out employee in your field of work. Add these competencies to your resume in the work experience descriptions for a stronger Federal resume!

Core Competencies Are Your Transferable Skills!

If you are changing your career, these core competencies will demonstrate that you have valuable skills that are transferable to your new career.

Let's look at some more examples...

Office of Personnel Management Core Competencies - these competencies are followed by many agencies.

Various agencies and job title core competencies: IT Specialist, Logistics Management, Program Analyst, Cyber Security, Administrative Officer, Nurse Practitioner

FBI Special Agent Core Competencies - examples of these are required in the Federal resume and in the FBI job interview.

Office of Personnel Management Core Competencies

Find your core competencies and check them off the list. Add a few of these competencies into the "duties" section of your work experience.

Interpersonal Effectiveness

❑ Builds and sustains positive relationships.

❑ Handles conflicts and negotiations effectively.

❑ Builds and sustains trust and respect.

❑ Collaborates and works well with others.

❑ Shows sensitivity and compassion for others.

❑ Encourages shared decision-making.

❑ Recognizes and uses ideas of others.

❑ Communicates clearly, both orally and in writing.

❑ Listens actively to others.

❑ Honors commitments and promises.

Customer Service

❑ Understands that customer service is essential to achieving our mission.

❑ Understands and meets the needs of internal customers.

❑ Manages customer complaints and concerns effectively and promptly.

❑ Designs work processes and systems that are responsive to customers.

❑ Ensures that daily work and the strategic direction are customer-centered.

❑ Uses customer feedback data in planning and providing products and services.

❑ Encourages and empowers subordinates to meet or exceed customer needs and expectations.

❑ Identifies and rewards behaviors that enhance customer satisfaction.

Flexibility/Adaptability

❑ Responds appropriately to new or changing situations.

❑ Handles multiple inputs and tasks simultaneously.

❑ Seeks and welcomes the ideas of others.

❑ Works well with all levels and types of people.

❑ Accommodates new situations and realities.

❑ Remains calm in high-pressure situations.

❑ Makes the most of limited resources.

❑ Demonstrates resilience in the face of setbacks.

❑ Understands change management.

Creative Thinking

- ❑ Appreciates new ideas and approaches.
- ❑ Thinks and acts innovatively.
- ❑ Looks beyond current reality and the "status quo."
- ❑ Demonstrates willingness to take risks.
- ❑ Challenges assumptions.
- ❑ Solves problems creatively.
- ❑ Demonstrates resourcefulness.
- ❑ Fosters creative thinking in others.
- ❑ Allows and encourages employees to take risks.
- ❑ Identifies opportunities for new projects and acts on them.
- ❑ Rewards risk-taking and non-successes and values what was learned.

Systems Thinking

- ❑ Understands the complexities of the agency and how the "product" is delivered.
- ❑ Appreciates the consequences of specific actions on other parts of the system.
- ❑ Thinks in context.
- ❑ Knows how one's role relates to others in the organization.
- ❑ Demonstrates awareness of the purpose, process, procedures, and outcomes of one's work.
- ❑ Encourages and rewards collaboration.

Organizational Stewardship

- ❑ Demonstrates commitment to people.
- ❑ Empowers and trusts others.
- ❑ Develops leadership skills and opportunities throughout organization.
- ❑ Develops team-based improvement processes.
- ❑ Promotes future-oriented system change.
- ❑ Supports and encourages lifelong learning throughout the organization.
- ❑ Manages physical, fiscal, and human resources to increase the value of products and services.
- ❑ Builds links between individuals and groups in the organization.
- ❑ Integrates organization into the community.
- ❑ Accepts accountability for self, others, and the organization's development.
- ❑ Works to accomplish the organizational business plan.

Core Competencies from USAJOBS Announcements

IT Specialist Mandatory Core Comptencies:

❯ Attention to Detail

❯ Customer Services

❯ Oral Communications

❯ Problem Solving

Qualifications

GS-07: You must have one year of specialized experience at a level of difficulty and responsibility equivalent to the GS-5 grade level in the Federal service: This experience must include Information Technology (IT) related experience that demonstrates each of the following four competencies: **1) Attention to Detail, 2) Customer Service, 3) Oral Communication and 4) Problem Solving.** Specialized experience for this position includes: Interviewing subject-matter personnel to get facts regarding work processes and synthesizing the resulting data into charts showing information flow; operating computer consoles where this involved choosing from among various procedures in responding to machine commands or unscheduled halts.

How You Will Be Evaluated

You will be evaluated for this job based on how well you meet the qualifications above.

The assessments for this job will measure the following Competencies:

- Operational Supply Logistics Management
- Planning and Evaluating
- Life Cycle Logistics Support Concept
- Oral Communication
- Education, Training and Awards

Logistics Management Specialist

Program Analyst

You will be rated on the following Competencies for this position:

- Analytical Thinking
- Leadership
- Project Management
- Quality Management

Rating: Your application will be evaluated in the following areas: Research and Analysis, Communication, and Technical Category rating will be used to rank and select eligible candidates. If qualified, you will be assigned to one of three quality level categories: Superior, Good, or Satisfactory depending on your responses to the online questions, regarding your experience, education, and training related to this position. Your rating may be lowered if your responses to the online questions are not supported by the education and/or experience described in your application.

Cyber Security

Administrative Officer

You will be rated on the following Competencies for this position:

- Administration and Management
- Attention to Detail
- Communication
- Decision Making
- Information Management
- Problem Solving Reading

How You Will Be Evaluated

You will be evaluated for this job based on how well you meet the qualifications above.

Your application will be evaluated based on your resume, attached supporting documentation and your responses to the self-assessment questionnaire. Your materials will be evaluated to validate your possession of any required knowledge, skills, abilities (KSA) and/or competencies. The following competencies will be evaluated in the self-assessment questionnaire:

- Medicine & Dentistry
- Decision Making
- Oral Communication
- Teachers Others
- Teamwork

Nurse Practitioner (International Health Coordinator)

It is easy to bypass core competencies in this process if you don't scroll down to How You Will be Evaluated and hit the READ MORE button, but they're really quite important. As you work on your Federal resume, remember that core competencies come into play at the strategic level, such as decisions into what agencies you want to apply to for jobs, and at the writing level, such as how you translate your skills into relevant competencies for those agencies. Like much of the other strategies described in this book, identifying and blending core competencies into your resume can seem like a daunting task. But all it takes is a bit of time, focus, and effort and you'll be well on your way to your next exciting Federal career opportunity!

The FBI has a unique list of Core Competencies that are required for all of the Special Agent Federal Resumes. Look at the competencies and then look at the sample Federal Resume on the next page. This resume is NOT like the other resumes in this book.

FBI Special Agent Core Competencies

FBI Core Competencies

The Federal Bureau of Investigation (FBI) Core Competencies are the categories of knowledge, skills and abilities all FBI employees are expected to cultivate and use in their work.

Collaboration

Establish contacts and interact effectively with external agencies, government officials, the community and internal Bureau contacts; display professionalism while working with others to achieve common goals; and to proactively share information with others when appropriate.

Behaviors/Skills:

» *Liaise* — Establish contacts and interact effectively with federal, state and local agencies; government officials; community; internal Bureau contacts; and other organizations and agencies.

» *Demonstrate Political Savvy* — Navigate effectively within the organization's social, political and technological systems.

» *Show Respect* — Interact with others in a courteous manner; display composure with others; firmly maintain position without becoming defensive; and confront others with tact.

» *Share Information* — Express self concisely and clearly; use appropriate tone in conversation; present information in a well-organized manner; provide sufficient detail to ensure communication is understood; write in a clear, concise manner appropriate for the audience; and proactively identify who needs information and share it when appropriate.

FBI Special Agent **Core Competencies**

Communication

Express thoughts and ideas clearly, concisely, persuasively and effectively both orally and in writing; interpret and understand verbal or written communications; tailor the communication to the experience, exposure or expertise of the recipient; and proactively share information with others when appropriate.

Behaviors/Skills:

» *Persuade* — Influence others to accept an idea or point of view; provide compelling reasons to accept a change or course of action.

» *Listen and Interpret* — Understand and identify key spoken information; be sensitive to verbal and non-verbal cues from others; ask probing questions to collect additional information or clarify a message; respond appropriately to questions; and paraphrase what has been said to ensure understanding.

» *Speak Clearly* — Express yourself concisely and clearly; use appropriate tone in conversation; present information in a well-organized manner; and provide sufficient detail to ensure communication is understood.

» *Write Clearly* — Write in a clear, concise manner appropriate for the audience.

Flexibility and Adaptability

Change is inevitable. To succeed in an unpredictable law enforcement environment, you must be able to adapt to rapidly changing circumstances and quickly respond to urgent needs. Cultivating the quality of adaptability can make you more effective and help mitigate stress.

Behaviors/Skills:

» *Adapt* — Adapt to unanticipated problems or conflicts; respond positively and productively to work challenges.

» *Manage Change* — Respond positively to and successfully manage change at work; support organizational change in a positive and productive manner; and willingly accept new priorities, procedures or goals.

Initiative

Willingness to begin projects/work or to address issues; be proactive and creatively respond to problems/issues/tasks.

Behaviors/Skills:

» *Be Proactive* — Take action in anticipation of future needs or opportunities; initiate activity to accomplish a task or goal; pursue participation in activities; and volunteer ideas, resources or efforts.

» *Develop Self* — Continually strive to develop skills and abilities; learn from others.

» *Follow Through* — Persist at a task despite setbacks; plan for and accomplish follow-up activities necessary to accomplish goals.

Interpersonal Ability

Ability to deal effectively with others; establish and maintain rapport with management, colleagues and subordinates; recognize and show sensitivity to differences in the needs and concerns of others; and mediate concerns between individuals and groups, as well as settle disputes.

Behaviors/Skills:

» *Establish Rapport* — Put others at ease; engage others in conversation; and express empathy and genuine interest in others.

» *Be Sensitive to Differences* — Keep an open mind; understand and appreciate the opinions of others; see things from a different point of view.

» *Resolve and Manage Conflict* — Successfully mediate concerns between individuals and groups while considering organizational objectives; develop agreements and settle disputes equitably; and find common ground and obtain cooperation with minimum disruption.

» *Work with Others* — Collaborate to identify and achieve common goals.

Leadership

★ ★ ★

Motivate and inspire others; develop and mentor others; gain the respect, confidence and loyalty of others; and articulate a vision, give guidance and direct others in accomplishing goals.

Behaviors/Skills:

» *Mentor* — Recognize positive and negative performance in others; provide objective, direct and timely feedback; and provide guidance to others on how to develop skills and abilities.

» *Direct* — Take a leadership role with others; provide clear objectives and goals to others; demonstrate calm and confidence when dealing with others; and clearly articulate responsibilities.

» *Inspire* — Motivate others to work toward a common goal or objective; influence others by articulating a vision.

» *Presence* — Engender respect and loyalty from others by demonstrating credibility, professionalism and integrity.

» *Set Strategic Direction* — Conceptualize, develop and articulate the vision, strategy and goals to set direction; integrate the vision into daily work activities.

Organizing and Planning

Establish priorities, timetables and goals/objectives; structure a plan of action for self and others; and develop both strategic and tactical plans.

Behaviors/Skills:

» *Plan* — Identify a goal and the resources and steps necessary to achieve it by attending to detail; identify potential problems and ways to overcome them; recognize consequences to actions; and establish necessary follow-up steps.

» *Prioritize* — Determine the relative importance of tasks or goals; expend time and effort in proportion to the relative importance of a task; use time and resources efficiently; and avoid being distracted by irrelevant issues.

Problem Solving and Judgment

Critically evaluate conditions, events and alternatives; identify problems, causes and relationships; base decisions or recommendations on data or sound reasoning; and formulate objective opinions.

Behaviors/Skills:

» *Identify Problems and Opportunities* — Recognize when and where problems and opportunities exist; determine the causes of problems; accurately define and understand the nature of a problem; and capitalize on opportunities.

» *Make Decisions* — Solve problems effectively; use appropriate information in determining solutions to problems; and evaluate strengths and weaknesses of potential solutions to problems.

» *Manage Risks* — Identify and mitigate risk; take calculated and innovative risks.

» *Accept Responsibility* — Take ownership of problems and the need to solve them; weigh risks of potential solutions and determine if they are appropriate; make decisions in a timely manner; and defend decisions when challenged.

» *Evaluate and Analyze* — Evaluate data, conditions and events to support conclusions.

These competencies must be shown in the FBI Special Agent Federal resume with examples that demonstrate your experience. See the next FBI resume sample on the next pages.
Read more at *www.resume-place.com/FBI_resume*

FBI Special Agent Federal Resume

Business Owner, Entrepreneur - HIRED!

Robert Zero
1234 Random Street, Phoenix, AZ 85001
(123) 321-0987 | bobzero@emailaddress.com

Date available to begin work for the FBI: Immediately

SUMMARY STATEMENT

Driven entrepreneur and servant leader with a diverse background in accounting, finance, business ownership, and computer programming. Built two successful businesses over the past 10 years. Experienced Finance and Operations Manager of a professional firm for 4 years. Experienced computer programmer. Logical and analytical and yet relatable. Seasoned interviewer having interviewed over 750 people in the past 10 years.

PROFESSIONAL SKILLS

Education	B.S. in Business Administration from Harvard University.
	Computer programming from Codeup (14-week Coding Bootcamp), San Antonio, TX
Employment	My ability to start and grow two successful businesses demonstrates my initiative, extreme work ethic, strong organizing and planning skills, and exceptional problem solving abilities.
Technical Skills	Extremely fast learner of new computer applications and systems. Strong knowledge of Mac/ Apple computers. Experienced with PHP, JavaScript, Angular JS and database management software. Advanced knowledge of all basic applications (i.e., Excel, Word, PowerPoint).
Personal	I strive to be the "hardest worker in the room," yet to be humble and respected by all while maintaining the utmost honesty and integrity. Laser focused. Goal driven. Trustworthy.

PROFESSIONAL WORK EXPERIENCE

Chief Operating Officer (COO) and Co-founder, October 2009 – Present
Always Pure Cleaning, Phoenix, AZ
Job Type: 40 – 60 hours per week, Full-Time
Supervisor: N/A

Always Pure Cleaning strives to be the leader in providing high quality home cleaning services in the downtown Phoenix area. The company currently employs 18 cleaning technicians and 3 full time office staff and services over 250 recurring clients. My responsibilities continually change as the organization grows and develops. Currently, my primary responsibilities are focused on leading and developing our management team and setting the strategic direction for the company with the goal to ensure the firm's continued growth, smooth operation, and profitability. I plan and prioritize company objectives for future growth and oversee all financial reporting and analysis. I teach our leadership team how to mitigate problems, manage risk, and make sound decisions. I also oversee the hiring process and educate staff on how to properly interview and vet candidates.

KEY ACCOMPLISHMENTS

COLLABORATION: After a recent office relocation, I was informed by our neighbor via text message that he did not want our staff accessing a side street through a back alleyway and a gate. He informed me that this was his property and he preferred that we not utilize it as a business entrance or exit. Having access to this alleyway was implied in our lease and served as a crucial operational entrance and exit for our business operations. In light of this conflict, I reached out to the neighbor in order to see if I could understand his concerns and explain how we were planning to use the space. Although we had a legal right to use our neighbor's property in this capacity, I always believe it is prudent to be respectful and not ruin a potential relationship. Both the landlord and I each reached out separately to the neighbor to put him at ease and explain the situation. I went a step further to craft an entrance/exit policy for our staff that fit with our business interests and the concerns of the neighbor. These steps resulted in a peaceful resolution for all involved parties.

FLEXIBILITY/ADAPTABILITY: In mid-2018, we were focusing on aggressive client growth when suddenly our recruiting and hiring pipeline dried up overnight. The employment landscape changed suddenly and we had to immediately adapt priorities if we were to continue to grow – you cannot grow a service business without continued hiring. I immediately started evaluating our recruiting and hiring processes and led our team to focus on a new goal of solving our hiring challenges. I led a redesign of the career section of our website to make it easier to navigate our application process and more succinctly highlight the benefits of employment with our company. I also made the decision to significantly reduce our initial screening requirements to move candidates on to the phone interview stage as a method to increase our applicant pool. Although we still needed to hire carefully in light of the industry we are in, we had to be willing to be flexible to the current economy, recognizing that applicants are like consumers and have many choices in a thriving economy. Being adaptable allowed us to solve our hiring problem quickly and start hiring one new technician per month.

LEADERSHIP: Always Pure cleaning technicians normally work the majority of their schedule alone, cleaning for recurring clients. However, about 10% of the time, our technicians participate in team cleaning assignments, in particular performing an initial deep cleaning for a new prospective recurring client. Since our main focus is solo cleaning, we had focused the majority of our training program on solo cleaning and not as much time on training our team for these team assignments. In 2016, this issue came to a head when I realized that we were receiving many client complaints following these team cleaning assignments, even when we had some our best techs on the job. Analyzing the specifics of the complaints, I found that clients were complaining that the teams worked too slowly, did not seem to have a coordinated plan of action, and missed many obvious areas that needed attention. Solving this problem naturally required me to revamp our training program for team cleaning plus to address a very evident culture issue. I gathered our entire company together for an all hands meeting and set the strategic direction for our company, explaining our mission and vision for team cleanings. As a result of my leadership, our quality on team cleanings improved dramatically, plus our client conversion rate improved.

INITIATIVE: After graduating from Harvard University in 2009, I immediately gained employment and started earning an income. However, I was earning less than expected and due to the recession, my wife was unemployed. Furthermore, I had a large burden of student loans to pay back. It was a financially challenging time for our family. In light of this situation, I decided to be proactive and take control of our financial situation by starting a side business – Always Pure Cleaning. This was a daunting step for me, as I knew absolutely nothing about starting or operating a business. I took the initiative to research the market, design a viable business model, create marketing materials, purchase cleaning equipment, and pursue dozens of other relevant actions.

Most importantly, I had to take the initiative to step out of my comfort zone and develop myself to become a strong business leader. I had to be entrepreneurial and look into every resource and learn from others more successful and further along this process than myself. I consulted with some of the leading experts in the cleaning industry and immersed myself in various learning programs in order to develop into a competent business leader. As a result of my entrepreneurial spirit to start and grow Always Pure Cleaning, my wife and I overcame our financial challenges and have both developed additional personal and professional skills.

INTERPERSONAL ABILITY: At Always Pure Cleaning, 90% of our work is solo cleaning (one technician per home) for recurring clients; however, our staff members periodically also participate in team cleanings. Team cleanings can be a challenge at times for our staff, as they are used to cleaning on their own. A few years ago, we had two individuals working together on a team cleaning who were both fairly strong willed and opinionated. They argued over who should clean which room and also over a specific vacuum cleaning technique. Listening to each one of the team members, I realized that they each had their own long-standing approach to a cleaning job, came from completely different cultural backgrounds, plus had very different working styles. While I listened to their concerns, I also stressed how critical their cooperation was to the success of our team. Listening to their suggestions, I also came up with a few protocols for them to abide by so that they could avoid any potential issues on future team cleanings together. Although these individuals were not the best of friends after this incident, they were able to work together in a more productive fashion during future assignments.

PROBLEM SOLVING/ JUDGMENT: In the early days of Always Pure Cleaning, we faced the challenge of not knowing exactly how a technician was performing without completing a number of random quality inspections. We assumed that clients would inform us if there was a problem. We would hire new employees, train them, inspect their work for a month or so, and then when the pressure was off, we found that the level of quality in their work would decline. Often, we did not realize that their work quality had declined until it was too late – when the client actually canceled the service. In order to fix this problem, I first had to identify that this problem existed. In evaluating our data, I found that clients were canceling service between the 3rd and 6th month after being paired with a technician. This coincided with the period when our training had ended and most of our inspections had stopped. We solved our quality issues by implementing a surveying system that automatically reached out to all clients after the cleaning to solicit their feedback.

Owner, 2016 – Present
Luxury Rentals, Phoenix, AZ
Job Type: 10 - 15 hours per week, Part-Time
Supervisor: N/A

Luxury Rentals provides fully furnished premium apartments in the heart of downtown Phoenix for those looking for short term rentals, vacation rentals, or corporate housing. I started and grew the company from $0 revenue to $650,000 in 3 years while working part time. We now have 10 apartment properties in our portfolio. I currently set the direction for the company by developing our vision and strategy. I also manage all financial performance reports, from budgeting to forecasting, revenue per night, and pricing. In addition to initiating, organizing, and planning growth objectives, I also resolve difficult problems that other staff members cannot handle in a professional and timely fashion.

KEY ACCOMPLISHMENTS

ORGANIZING AND PLANNING: When my wife and I decided to grow our Luxury Rentals portfolio in 2018, we had a unique opportunity to acquire 6 properties all in one building. This is a rather rare opportunity in our industry for a company of our size, so we jumped on it. The unique challenge this posed was that we had to onboard 6 new properties all at one time. Before this acquisition, we had never onboarded more than one unit at a time. This task was equivalent to opening up a small boutique hotel in one month's time with no full-time staff. The opportunity also meant that our business would more than double once the new units were ready. A further consideration was that every day the properties were not onboarded was a day that we were losing money (a lot when multiplied by 6). I immediately laid out a detailed plan with deadlines and identified the responsible party for each task. Tasks included selecting furniture, scheduling and aligning deliveries, arranging for our handyman to build and install various items, decorating, ordering linens, scheduling our cleaning service, coordinating a professional photoshoot, and many other small jobs. My wife and I did most of this work and I tracked our progress using Google Calendar and Excel to make sure everything was aligned for success. I also alleviated some of our financial pressure by negotiating favorable leasing terms, saving $10,000. The result of my planning allowed us to onboard all 6 of the apartments at once within one week of our lease start date.

COMMUNICATION: Starting a business is challenging. One of the challenges I faced when growing Luxury Rentals was having sufficient capital. When you do not have sufficient collateral, are a new business, or are operating a unique business model, it is extremely difficult if not impossible to utilize a traditional bank for funding. Thus, I had to leverage non-traditional financial lenders. I put together our business plans and financial documents in a clear and cohesive form and went out to persuade others to lend us the funding at reasonable interest rates. I had to clearly communicate our business model, market demographics, and business viability in order to persuade others we were a risk worth taking. One of the viable lenders I met with had some reservations, as this was a relatively new business concept and I was asking for a much larger loan than we had borrowed in the past. I needed to listen and understand her concerns and respond in a way that alleviated those concerns. I communicated the viability of our model and presented financial performance information on similar properties, demonstrating that we were a risk worth investing in. As a result of my communications and persuasive abilities, I was able to acquire a $40,000 loan in late 2018 in order to grow our business.

Finance & Operations Manager, June 2009 – March 2013
EFG, Inc, Phoenix, AZ
Salary: $65,000
Job Type: 45 - 55 hours per week, Full-Time
Supervisor: Siva Venuogopalan, Owner

EFG provides in-depth corrosion inspection services for bridges and other infrastructure in order to extend the service life of the structure. During my tenure at EFG, we had approximately 20 staff. I managed all finance and operations of the company, reporting directly to the owner. Acting as the project manager for all projects, I ensured the productivity of all staff and that deliverables were provided on time and under budget. I led all company hiring and interviewed over 100 people in my tenure with the company. This included hiring, supervising, and training a Finance Associate and Executive Assistant.

EDUCATION

B.S. Business Administration: Finance and Economics, June 2009
Harvard University, Cambridge, MA | GPA 3.92

CERTIFICATIONS/ACHIEVEMENTS
Computer Programming Bootcamp, February 2015
Top of Class & first to gain employment
(14-week Coding Bootcamp)
Codeup, San Antonio, TX

FBI Special Agent Competency blog and YouTube by Kathryn Troutman
www.resume-place. com/FBI_resume

★ ★ ★

Strategy 6

WRITE YOUR WORK EXPERIENCE

OPM.GOV

USAJOBS®
"WORKING FOR AMERICA"

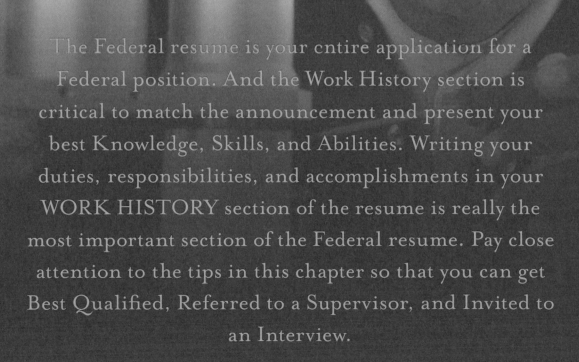

The Federal resume is your entire application for a
Federal position. And the Work History section is
critical to match the announcement and present your
best Knowledge, Skills, and Abilities. Writing your
duties, responsibilities, and accomplishments in your
WORK HISTORY section of the resume is really the
most important section of the Federal resume. Pay close
attention to the tips in this chapter so that you can get
Best Qualified, Referred to a Supervisor, and Invited to
an Interview.

Start Writing Your Work Experience Section

Are you ready to start writing the most important and difficult part of the Federal Resume – your work experience section?

Now that you have your Hats, Keywords, Accomplishments, and Core Competencies, you are ready to write your Work Experience descriptions. Follow these steps to write competitive, complete, and impressive Duties and Accomplishments. Remember that your goal is to get Best Qualified. Your resume needs to MATCH the Requirements / Qualifications section of the announcement (as discussed in Strategy 3, Keywords).

Here is a sample of the Federally-required information for the Work Experience section, taken from USAJOB's website:

https://www.usajobs.gov/ Help/faq/application/ documents/resume/what- to-include/

What should I include in my Federal resume?

Whether you're a current Federal employee or new to the Federal Government, your resume is the primary way for you to communicate your education, skills, and experience.

Before you get started

Read the entire job announcement. Focus on the following sections to understand whether or not you qualify for the position. This critical information is found under:

- ❯ **Duties** and **Qualifications**
- ❯ **How to Apply** (including a preview of the assessment questionnaire)
- ❯ **How You Will Be Evaluated**

Make sure you have the required experience and/or education before you apply. Hiring agencies use the job announcement to describe the job and the required qualifications, including:

- ❯ **Level and amount of experience**
- ❯ **Education**
- ❯ **Training**

Give the following information for your paid and non-paid work experience related to the job you are applying for:

- Job title (include series and grade if Federal job)
- Employer's name and address
- Month and year to month and year; hours per week
- Duties and Accomplishments
- Supervisor's name and phone number

Check out the USAJOBS official instruction on how to write the Work Experience below. As you think about, and possibly get overwhelmed with writing your work history, you're probably wondering how much you have to write, how many years you have to go back, and how many jobs you should include. Read the tips in this chapter.

What should I include in my Federal resume?
Federal jobs often require that you have experience in a particular type of work for a certain period of time. You must show how your skill s and experiences **meet the qualifications and requirements listed in the job announcement** to be considered for the job.

Include dates, hours, level of experience and examples for each work experience

For each work experience you list, make sure you include:

- Start and end dates (including the month and year).
- The number of hours you worked per week.
- The level and amount of experience–for instance, whether you served as a project manager or a team member helps to illustrate your level of experience.
- Examples of relevant experiences and accomplishments that prove you can perform the tasks at the level required for the job as stated in the job announcement. Your experience needs to address every required qualification.

This information is different than a private industry resume and this is REQUIRED for your Federal resume.

Taken from USAJOB's website:

https://www.usajobs.gov/Help/faq/application/documents/resume/what-to-include/

Be Concise

How much should you include in a description of a job? The Federal resume is not a "life history" document.

Taken from USAJOB's website:

https://www.usajobs.gov/Help/faq/application/documents/resume/what-to-include/

Be concise

Hiring agencies often receive dozens or even hundreds of resumes for certain positions. Hiring managers quickly skim through submissions and eliminate candidates who clearly are not qualified. Look at your resume and ask:

❯ Can a hiring manager see my main credentials within 10 to 15 seconds?

❯ Does critical information jump off the page?

❯ Do I effectively sell myself on the top quarter of the first page?

Here are the quick answers to a few typical questions and a review of what's most important to include in your Federal resume.

How far back should you go? Focus on the last 10 years. You will need to cover 10 years of work experience and include all compliance details. Positions you held 15 to 20 years ago will not be of interest to the busy readers. You can add them for the complete picture of your career, but keep the descriptions short.

Should each description be the same length? Summarize or write shorter descriptions of jobs prior to the last 10 years. You can include these jobs if they are relevant to your objectives. Gaps in dates are okay. The HR professionals want to read the recent and relevant positions.

How long should the Federal resume be? The author of this book recommends 5 pages for your Federal Resume. There is NO limit listed on OPM or USAJOBS for all Federal resumes. See these examples of a few agencies with specific page length requirements: USCIS requires 5 pages. NASA requires 32,000 characters. SES resumes can be no longer than 5 pages.

U.S. Citizenship and Immigration Services

Submitting your resume

You must submit a resume as part of the application process. If your resume is longer than 5 pages, the USCIS human resources office will review only the first 5 pages to determine your eligibility and qualifications for the position.

Using Resume Builder

Here are some important tips about using the USAJOBS Resume Builder:

❯ Resume Builder does not show a page count while building a resume.

❯ Resume Builder adds spaces and page gaps to resumes during the automated resume conversion process. This means that our human resources office may receive a version of your resume from Resume Builder with a different page layout than the one you viewed when you were building your resume.

❯ We strongly recommend that if you use Resume Builder, you convert your resume to a PDF, confirm that the first 5 pages contain all the necessary information, and then submit your resume as a PDF.

❯ You are responsible for manually checking your resume and ensuring that you include all content relevant to your eligibility and qualifications in the first 5 pages. Our human resources office will not read beyond the first 5 pages.

Look for the USCIS Core Competencies under "How you will be Evaluated" section in the announcement.

❯ Attention to Detail
❯ Customer Service
❯ Decision Making
❯ Flexibility
❯ Integrity/Honesty
❯ Interpersonal Skills
❯ Learning
❯ Reading
❯ Reasoning
❯ Self-Management
❯ Stress Tolerance

Taken from USCIS website:

https://www.uscis.gov/about-us/careers/how-apply

USCIS Requires 5 pages.

NASA 32,000 Characters in Builder

NASA requires 32,000 characters in the USAJOBS Builder.

How You Will Be Evaluated

This vacancy is being filled through NASA STARS, an automated Staffing and Recruitment System. NASA partners with USAJOBS in providing a seamless application process. Before you begin the application process, please read the vacancy announcement carefully and have all required information available. You may begin the process of submitting your resume by clicking on the "Apply Online" link. In order to be considered, you must submit a resume completed in the USAJOBS site. When completing your USAJOBS resume, please remember that NASA limits resumes to the equivalent of approximately typed pages, or approximately 32,000 characters including spaces. NASA does not accept resumes uploaded to USAJOBS from a second source or documents attached.

Deputy Director for Defense Intelligence (Counterintelligence, Law Enforcement and Security)

DEPARTMENT OF DEFENSE
Office of the Security of Defense

All SES Applications: Not to exceed five pages!

Required Documents

Resume – In addition to your written statements addressing the Executive Core Qualifications, the Mandatory Technical Qualifications, and other qualifications as applicable, submit a resume or any other written format you choose to describe your qualifications, **not to exceed five pages.**

Senior Executive Service (SES) resumes are 5 pages maximum.

What if the most important job I held related to the position was years ago?

If you are returning to a position similar to the one you held 10 years ago, emphasize THAT JOB, even though it was 10 years ago. Many people return to previous careers.

How long should my current job description be?

Most of your time and energy will be spent writing this description (if it is your highest-level position and is most closely related to your objective). You could budget one to five hours for writing this description. The description will be from three paragraphs to 2 pages long. If you have been in your current position for five years, most of the difficult, important writing will be over when you finish this description.

Can I include community service and volunteer or unpaid experiences?

Remember to include both paid and unpaid work experiences related to the job for which you are applying, for positions within the last 10 years. You can include: community and civic leadership positions, association or non-profit positions, teaching, consulting, and small-business experiences. If you want to get credit for the hours per week and time with these volunteer activities, add month and year and hour per week and create an actual "job block" for these positions.

Should Education or Work Experience be listed first?

If the position has a Positive Education requirement, the Education section should be listed first—such as this Instructional Systems Specialist position. Also add your relevant courses in the Federal resume so that the manager will see your course titles (without depending on the transcript).

Instructional Systems Specialist

DEPARTMENT OF VETERANS AFFAIRS
Veterans Affairs, Veterans Health Administration

Education

Basic Requirements

Degree: that included or was supplemented by at least 24 semester hours appropriate to the work of the position to be filled. The course work must have included study in at least four of the following five areas:

1. Learning theory, psychology of learning, educational psychology: Study of learning theories as they relate to the systemic design development, and validation of instructional material.
2. Instructional design practices: study of the principles and techniques used in designing training programs, developing design strategy and models, and applying design methods to the improvement of instructional effectiveness.
3. Educational evaluation: Study of the techniques for evaluating the effectiveness of instructional/education programs, including developing written and performance tests and survey instruments, and determining reliability and validity of evaluation instruments.
4. Instructional Product development: Study of the techniques appropriate for developing training materials, including identifying learner characteristics.
5. Computers in education and training: Study of the application of computers in education and training, including selecting appropriate computer software.

Know Your Audience: **Who Is Going to Read Your Resume?**

HR Professionals

There are at least two audiences for your resume. First the HR professional will review your resume to determine whether you are qualified for the position. The HR professionals will determine whether your stated qualifications fit the formal requirements of the position and, if so, will classify you as "qualified."

The HR professionals will determine whether your stated qualifications match the formal qualifications for the position, and if so, will classify you as "qualified." Depending on the number of qualified applicants, they usually perform a deeper evaluation to select the "best qualified" candidates. Only the best-qualified candidates are forwarded to the selecting official (your potential supervisor).

Do not assume that the staffing specialist is an expert in your career field, although many are quite knowledgeable. Help the specialist understand and interpret your qualifications by writing your work experience descriptions in language they can understand. If you make the specialist's job easier, you will get more benefit of the doubt. Confuse or obscure your qualifications and you will earn a lower score than your experience merits.

The Selecting Official

The second reader will be the selecting official, who has discretion in choosing the candidate she or he likes best from the Best Qualified.

When the hiring official sees your Federal resume, it is in a folder along with resumes from other highly qualified candidates (your competition). The hiring official does not normally have to interview all highly qualified candidates.

Who gets interviewed? Qualifications are important, of course, but so is the SPARKLE that might be visible in your resume. The SPARKLE could be your accomplishments, volunteer experience, locations where you worked. Is your resume interesting? What stands out? Is there a "likeability factor" in your resume?

1. HR Professionals
2. The Selecting Official

> **Use the OPM Standards to write your Federal resume—before you find the perfect USAJOBS announcement!**

Do Your Research

Classification Standards. Please review the Introduction to the Handbook of Occupational Groups and Families. A list of the classification standards for each occupational series is online at www.opm.gov. This OPM resource lists basic descriptions of each major government position, which can help you write your Duties and Responsibilities. Another reason to check the official standards is for keywords and skills. If you use the same language as the official standard for your series, it's easier for the staffing specialists to determine that you possess the needed experience.

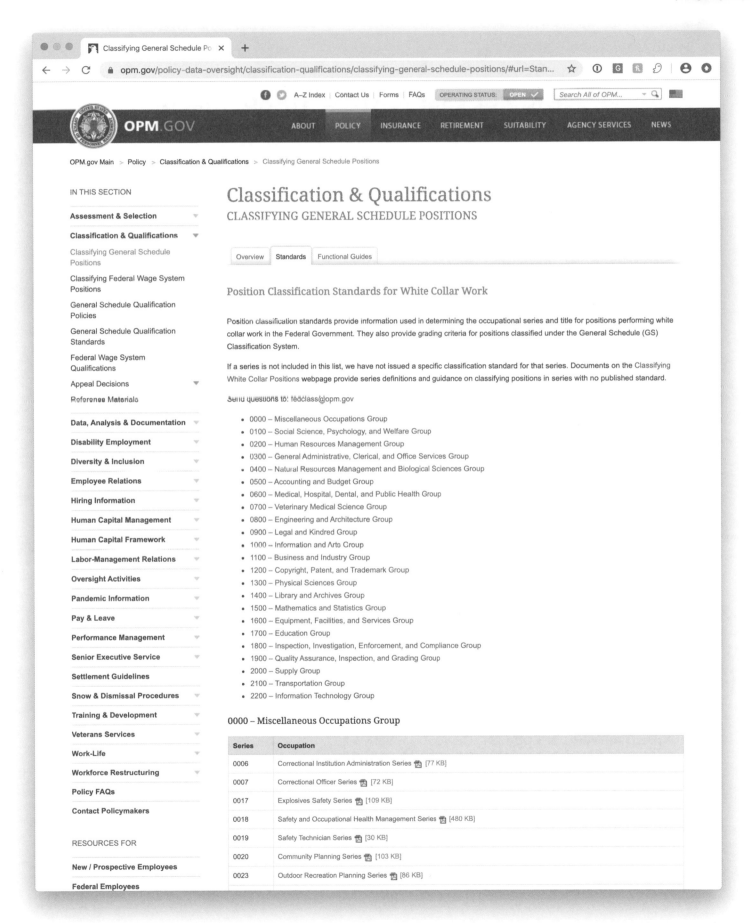

Public Affairs Series, GS-1035   TS-53 July 1981

POSITION CLASSIFICATION STANDARD FOR PUBLIC AFFAIRS SERIES, GS-1035

Table of Contents

SERIES DEFINITION 2

SERIES COVERAGE 2

EXCLUSIONS 3

OCCUPATIONAL INFORMATION 4

TITLES 8

GRADING OF POSITIONS 8

GRADE CONVERSION TABLE 9

QUALIFICATIONS REQUIRED 9

FACTOR LEVEL DESCRIPTIONS 11
    FACTOR 1, KNOWLEDGE REQUIRED BY THE POSITION 11
    FACTOR 2, SUPERVISORY CONTROLS 14
    FACTOR 3, GUIDELINES 16
    FACTOR 4, COMPLEXITY 18
    FACTOR 5, SCOPE AND EFFECT 21
    FACTOR 6, PERSONAL CONTACTS 22
    FACTOR 7, PURPOSE OF CONTACTS 24
    FACTOR 8, PHYSICAL DEMANDS 25
    FACTOR 9, WORK ENVIRONMENT 25

OPM BENCHMARK DESCRIPTIONS 26
    PUBLIC AFFAIRS SPECIALIST, GS-1035-09, BMK # 1 26
    PUBLIC AFFAIRS SPECIALIST, GS-1035-09, BMK # 2 29
    PUBLIC AFFAIRS SPECIALIST, GS-1035-09, BMK # 3 31
    PUBLIC AFFAIRS SPECIALIST, GS-1035-11, BMK # 1 34
    PUBLIC AFFAIRS SPECIALIST, GS-1035-11, BMK # 2 37
    PUBLIC AFFAIRS SPECIALIST, GS-1035-11, BMK # 3 40
    PUBLIC AFFAIRS SPECIALIST, GS-1035-12, BMK # 1 43
    PUBLIC AFFAIRS SPECIALIST, GS-1035-12, BMK # 2 46
    PUBLIC AFFAIRS SPECIALIST, GS-1035-12, BMK # 3 49
    PUBLIC AFFAIRS SPECIALIST, GS-1035-13, BMK # 1 52
    PUBLIC AFFAIRS SPECIALIST, GS-1035-13, BMK # 2 55
    PUBLIC AFFAIRS SPECIALIST, GS-1035-14, BMK # 1 57

EXPLANATORY MEMORANDUM 60

Human Resources Professionals use the FES to evaluate work and to determine its proper level of monetary compensation—in other words, its proper title, series, and grade level. The nine FES factors are useful to you because they form a handy and logical checklist to ensure that your job descriptions are effective, persuasive, and written with the mindset of the reviewer in mind. When you have written a draft of your Federal resume job descriptions, you can review them against the FES factors to ensure that certain key elements are covered. Although you might not need to cover all nine of the FES factors, it is a good idea to include small elements of several of these factors in each of your job descriptions.

The key to using the FES factors as a guide to writing your job description portions of your resume is that human resources professionals in Federal agencies are sensitive to these factors and method of "sizing up" the importance of your job experience. Although you should not use the FES factors to aid you in exaggerating the importance of your experience, you should definitely use them as a means of helping HR officials give you the full credit for the "grade level" of the work you accomplished in each of your jobs.

Grade Conversion Table

Total points on all evaluation factors are converted to GS grades as follows:

GS Grade	Point Range
5	855-1100
6	1105-1350
7	1355-1600
8	1605-1850
9	1855-2100
10	2105-2350
11	2355-2750
12	2755-3150
13	3155-3600
14	3605-4050
15	4055-up

Get a higher score on your Federal resume by writing your Work History duties following the Factor Evaluation System (FES).

The FES Criteria

The FES criteria for each position are the following:

FACTOR 1, Knowledge required for the position (the specific knowledge you applied to your work)

FACTOR 2, Supervisory controls (the level of supervision you received while doing your work; for instance, "Performed the duties of Administrative Assistant with a high degree of independence and sought the advice of my supervisor only on rare occasions.")

FACTOR 3, Guidelines (the written guidelines you followed in doing your work, particularly if they are complicated and required a great deal of independent interpretation on your part)

FACTOR 4, Complexity (the level of complexity that best describes the work that you accomplished)

FACTOR 5, Scope and effect (the scope and impact of your work on the agency, particularly if your work influenced the expenditure of dollars or the use of resources across your organization or agency)

FACTOR 6, Personal contacts (the kind of contacts and the purpose of the contacts you made on a regular basis; for instance, "regularly had contact with members of Congressional office staff")

FACTOR 7, Purpose of contacts (the reason for the contact; i.e., "for purposes of clarifying or exchanging information, scheduling and arranging meetings, and making travel arrangements")

FACTOR 8, Physical demands (the physical requirements of the position; for instance, "PHYSICAL REPORT: Required to climb, bend, stoop, and work in strained and cramped positions. Subject to prolonged standing, walking, and kneeling and must be physically fit to perform daily duties.")

FACTOR 9, Work environment (where work is performed; for example, "WORKING CONDITIONS: Works inside and outside in inclement weather. Work areas may be drafty, noisy, and have toxic fumes present. Exposed to danger of cuts, burns, shock, strains, and broken bones.")

Analyzing Your Work Experience Section to Make Sure It Covers All FES Components

Compare each of your position descriptions against the following criteria.

Knowledge required for the position. What level of knowledge is required? Knowledge in general ("Respond to and assist dire-need and hardship inquiries by underserved Medicare/Medicaid beneficiaries referred by the office of the Administrator and CBC front office. Act as an advocate for beneficiaries by accessing Medicare and other health care benefits, obtaining pro-bono work, and rectifying insurance issues") or specific ("Translate broad agency policy, legislation, regulations, and directives into new policies or methodologies. Serve as subject matter expert in program and operational areas."). This is a powerful factor. It explains, for example, why a Health Insurance Specialist (or other Federal employee) should receive a promotion because of the subject-matter expertise.

FES and Work **Experience Descriptions**

Supervisory controls. If you perform your work independently, lead teams, use judgment, make decisions, use initiative, or plan and execute, it will be clear that you work independently to perform your jobs.

Guidelines. What guidelines are there for you to use? Are there general agency guidelines, detailed technical manuals, or vendor instructions? Are the guidelines current, or are they inadequate and frequently inapplicable? Do you need to apply independent judgment and make difficult decisions?

Complexity. What factors make this work complex, or is it really a simple job? Remember simple and complex are in the eyes of the beholder. If you have 15 years' experience in highly technical work, hold a PhD, and are generally considered a national expert, you might think the problems and situations in your work are simple. An outsider, comparing your work to that of other people, would conclude that your job was highly complex. Do not sell yourself short. You will deal with some of your complexity issues in the knowledge and guidelines criteria. Specific complexity issues include having to make decisions with insufficient data, dealing with competing interests and demands, changing of basic systems, and responding to congressional or public controversy or pressure. Complexity can relate to office politics, but you have to be careful in choosing your words when you write about complexity arising out of office politics.

Scope and effect. Do you support a local office, regional offices, global customers, government, industry, or academia? Give a good description of the scope and effect of your work.

Personal contacts/purpose of contacts. This is the "customer service" factor. Write about your internal and external customers. Who do you talk with on the phone and receive email from? Congress? The Office of the Secretary of Defense? The Office of the Department Secretary? Regional Directors? The American public? PhD Professors. Other agencies? Why do they call or write to you?

Physical demands and work environment. Do you travel? Do you work in the field and in the office? Do you lift lots of boxes? The HR professionals need to know about your work environment so they can understand and envision you at your work.

Congratulations! You have now completed a first draft. It's probably too long and not written powerfully, but it's the first step. Take the rest of the day off and start again after your draft has a chance to cool down. Believe it or not, you can make it better.

See a sample Federal resume with Introduction (scope and effect), Guidelines (guidelines and regulations), Personal Contacts (customers), Purpose of Contacts (what services you are providing), Complexity (accomplishments), Knowledge required (knowledge). Danielle USSS Supervisor, pages 128 to 129; Eric Lower, pages 142 to 145.

The Rewriting Stage

James Michener once said, *"There are no great writers—only great rewriters."* Use a small paragraph format for rewriting the material you have gathered so far. Begin your job description with a general overview paragraph (one or two sentences to describe the work and follow it with small paragraphs, each helping to make the case of your qualifications. Remember to address the components of the FES in your copy. You don't have to address each FES factor—only those that are key to the public goals.

A Before-and-After Example

Here's a before-and-after example of a Short description vs. one that follows the FES and includes keywords, skills, and accomplishments.

BEFORE – MISSING FES CONTENT!

2016 to present; CONTRACT SPECIALIST, ACQUISITION PROFESSIONAL, GS 1101-12. Certified Level III; Robert Morris Acquisition Center, Aberdeen Proving Ground (APG), Aberdeen, MD 20001. Current salary: $74,975; 40 hours per week. Supervisor Edward Waters: 410-222-2222

Manage and administer all contractual actions from pre-award to post-award, including initial planning, contract award, and administration. Contracts include firm-fixed price, fixed-price incentive, fixed-price economic price adjustments, cost plus fixed fee, cost plus award fee, and cost-plus incentive fee. Analyze all procurement requirements to determine contracting method and type and procurement plan. Conduct cost and price analysis, contracting method and type, and procurement plan. Conduct adjustments. Coordinate time extensions, coordinate issue and document contract modifications, and justify emergency procurements as needed. Perform stop-work orders, cure notices, show cause letters, and terminations for default and/ or convenience. Also monitor quality control performance and government property reporting, approve progress payments, and ensure timely closeout of delivery orders and contracts.

The above Contract Specialist "Generalist" description sounds like hundreds of other Contract Specialist descriptions. It doesn't tell what's special, unique, unusual, or outstanding about this person. Read the following impressive rewrite. The FES components are clearly covered in the AFTER Job Block. The accomplishments, numbers, contracts, and problems solved are impressive and will result in interviews and discussions with selecting officials.

> *I have never thought of myself as a good writer. Anyone who wants reassurance of that should read one of my first drafts. But I'm one of the world's great rewriters.*
>
> James A. Michener

AFTER – FES IS COVERED!

Nov. 2016 to present; CONTRACT SPECIALIST, ACQUISITION PROFESSIONAL, GS 1101-12. Certified Level III; Robert Morris Acquisition Center, Aberdeen Proving Ground (APG), Aberdeen, MD 20001. Current salary: $74,975; 40 hours per week. Supervisor Edward Waters: 410-222-2222

Certified Level III Contract Specialist and Acquisition Professional for specialized procurements for the Aberdeen Proving Ground (APG) for 54 tenants and 5 depots throughout the Western region of the US supporting the Soldier Biological Chemical Command (SBCCOM).

FES: Complexity and Scope and Effect

CONTRACT SPECIALIST: Manage and administer all contractual actions from pre-award to post-award, including initial planning, contract award, and administration. Contracts include firm-fixed price, fixed-price incentive, fixed-price economic price adjustments, cost plus fixed fee, cost plus award fee, and cost-plus incentive fee.

FES: Guidelines

PROCUREMENT ANALYSIS: Analyze all procurement requests to determine requirements, contracting method and type, and procurement plan. Conduct cost and price analysis, determine incremental funding, and determine rate and cost adjustments.

PRIMARY INTERFACE with Commanders, Tenant Facility Managers, Government Engineers, Small Business Administration and contractors at the APG and other installations under the Soldier Biological Chemical Command. Recommend procurements to program officials using best value basis.

FES: Contacts and Work Environment

LEAD NEGOTIATOR: Lead contract negotiations on price and technical requirements, as well as action to determine contract terms and conditions. Develop negotiation strategies, lead pre-bid proposal conferences, and negotiate fair contract price and contract negotiations.

FES: Knowledge Required

POINT OF CONTACT for Reverse Auctioning Procurements. Member of the marketing team for the Robert Morris Acquisition Center.

KEY CONTRACTS AND ACCOMPLISHMENTS:

FES: Scope and Effect, Complexity and Work Environment

❯ Key advisor for procurement planning and coordination for maintenance, repair and new construction Base Operation Support Task Order Contracts totaling $75 million, customized to a 10-year master plan for APG, Maryland; Dugway Proving Ground, Utah; Umatilla Proving Ground, Oregon; Desert Chemical Depot, Utah; and Pueblo Chemical Depot, CO.

FES: Work Environment

❯ Administer over 300 individual delivery order contracts in excess of $30 million.

❯ Initiated, and continue to promote, partnering sessions between government agencies and contractors for all specialized procurement contracts. The sessions include preplanning and follow-up meetings with government Contracting Officer Representative and contractors to identify potential problems and evaluate contractor performance, as well as the use of Alternative Disputes Resolution (ADR) to resolve problems. Result: No government claims have been paid on any of the multi-year contracts I have managed.

FES: Guidelines

❯ Because of my facilities-management expertise, I was detailed for 76 months, to the Soldier Biological Chemical Command facility office to accomplish two key assignments: identify excess space and establish an office of utilization policy; and develop and prepare a 1391 for estimated $40 million state-of-the-art Chemical Research Laboratory requiring Congressional funding: Result: Both tasks were accomplished. The 1391 was forwarded to the Army Materiel Command for prioritization and has received DA sponsorship. The space-utilization policy and findings resulted in an estimated overall savings in excess of $1 million. Received performance and special act awards for my accomplishments.

FES: Guidelines

Last Words

Add the Factor Evaluation System factors and get a higher score on your Federal resume. Start on your Federal resume with the OPM Classification Standards!

Strategy 7

EDIT CAREFULLY

No more Passive Voice
Federal Resumes. Only
ACTIVE VOICE!

Editing isn't "fun," but it is important! Before you submit your Federal resume, you should take time to review it closely—line-by-line and word-by-word—to verify you haven't made mistakes, that the key information is there, and that the content is clear and easy to understand.

Edit Carefully

If the Federal resume is the most important document you can write to support your Federal job search, then making sure it is carefully edited is crucial. This simple step is often overlooked, leading to errors that push otherwise qualified candidates out of the running. Remember, what you put into the resume is how you will be perceived by those reading it. A document riddled with errors, sloppy formatting, and poor word choices can doom your application. One of the most common competencies Federal job announcements specifically address is "attention to detail." If you haven't paid attention to the details of what is in your resume and how it is presented, you've failed to demonstrate that competency.

The Plain Writing Act was signed into law on October 13, 2010, requiring Federal agencies to use clear communication that is understandable and useable by the public. Since "plain language" is the law, it makes sense to simplify your resume to reflect the principles of plain language when applying for government positions. The ideas behind plain language—help your reader find what they need, understand what they find, and use what they find to meet their needs—are directly applicable to resumes! You want to help the Human Resources Specialist and Hiring Manager find your qualifications and accomplishments, make it easy for them to understand your experience, and help them make a hiring decision that is in your favor. In other words, you don't want to use bureaucratic words that don't tell the reader anything of value; instead, deploy words that send a clear message. Let's briefly look at a real-world example:

 Poorly Worded Version: Held full responsibility for overseeing and managing a multi-functional team to execute the coordination and integration of financial planning strategy for the organization's multi-million-dollar budget.

Pause. Read that again. Word salad, right? The very worst of bureaucratic-speak. We have no idea what this person does. Let's look at it after some heavy editing with an emphasis on plain language:

 Plain Language Version: Led a 5-member team to strategize financial planning for a $25 million budget.

The plain language version gets to the point and is crystal clear. There's no ambiguity. The words that you use should add value, not distract. So, after you've written your resume, review it and look to see whether it reads like the first example or the plain language example. You want it to be written in plain language.

When we talk about editing, the most common response is for people to think back to their days in high school diagramming sentences, trying to figure out comma placement, and assessing subject-verb agreement. Strategy 7 is less about re-teaching you all those fun "rules"—though they are important—and more about helping you think about a few key puzzle pieces when it comes to resume editing: (1) use plain language and powerful words; (2) use active voice, not passive voice; (3) be consistent with your verb tenses; and (4) don't be afraid to use "I."

Let's dig into some examples of each piece...

Words to Avoid

▼

EXERCISE: Do you have these words in your Work Experience DUTIES SECTION? Circle these words in YOUR RESUME. See Before & After samples page 89.

- ❷ Responsible for / Responsibilities include
- ❷ Duties include
- ❷ Other / Additional Duties include
- ❷ Helped with / in
- ❷ Worked with / in
- ❷ Assisted with
- ❷ Participate in
- ❷ Perform (overused in government resumes)
- ❷ Prepare (overused in government resumes)
- ❷ Serve as
- ❷ Involved in / with

Resume writing is hard work. We know! One of the best practices in writing a Federal resume, or any resume at all, is to edit and revise heavily. Use powerful words and eliminate superfluous content (words that don't add value). When you review your resume, you should look at it with an eye to make it clearer, more concise, and more impactful. If something can be articulated in fewer words, why would you waste space on words that don't add value or impact to your resume? Edit your content down. A good rule of thumb is that your initial draft can by cut by approximately 15%. Let's look at some editing suggestions.

Here are a few before and after examples of better word choices for your resume:

Currently I am working as the Manager of Operations.
> Manage operations.

Major duties include working with other staff.
> Cooperated with staff.

I have experience with planning meetings.
> Plan and coordinate meetings.

I have helped set up office systems.
> Organized new office systems.

I used a variety of equipment.
> Equipment skills include...

Worked with team members
> Member of a team

Being the timekeeper for the office
> Timekeeper for the office

When needed, supervise team members.
> Supervise team members on occasion.

Worked in the capacity of management analyst
> Management Analyst

Assisted with planning, researching, and designing...
> Planned, researched, and designed...

I was responsible for managing the daily operations.
> Managed daily operations.

The information is gathered from...
> Compiled, organized, and managed information gathered from...

My other duties consist of customer services, research, and problem solving.
> Research and resolve problems for customers.

Use Powerful Words

In Strategy #1, we observed that you should think of the Federal resume as an argument—your job is to make the best possible argument as to why you're the best possible candidate for the position. Too often, Federal jobseekers describe their experience and qualifications in weak terms. They use overly simple words and non-descriptive language, and fail to clearly demonstrate their actions. In many ways, this is often a word choice problem. So, once you have a draft of your resume completed, conduct a word-by-word review to replace weak words with powerful words. Powerful words are descriptive, denote action, and are interesting to the reader. Jobseekers often use weak phrases like "worked with" when instead they should instead use stronger phrases such as "built coalitions," "galvanized partners," or "leveraged relationships." Powerful words and phrases add value to your content. This list of more than 100 powerful words for resume writing is based on many years of professional resume writing experience. There are many more options—a thesaurus is a resume writer's best friend, after all!

Creation
assemble
conceive
convene
create
design
forge
form
formulate
invent
implement
initiate
realize
spearhead
plan

Employment
deploy
employ
exercise
use
utilize

Authorship
author
create
draft
edit
generate
publish
write

Leadership
administer
control
direct
govern
head up
lead
manage
oversee
run
supervise

Success
accomplish
achieve
attain
master
score (a victory)
succeed
sustain

Quality
excellent
great
good
high quality
outstanding
quality
special
superb

Competencies
able
adept at
capable
competent
demonstrated
effective
expert
knowledgeable
proven
skilled
tested
trained
versed in

Outcomes
communication
cooperation
cost-effective
efficiency
morale
outcomes
output
productivity

Newness
creative
first-ever
first-of-its-kind
innovative
novel
state-of-the-art

Degree
completely
considerably
effectively
fully
especially
extremely
outstanding
greatly
particularly
powerful
seasoned
highly
significantly
strongly
thoroughly
solidly

Primacy
advisor
coworker
key
major
expert
primary
principal
subject matter
source person
lead
sole source

Persuasion
coach
galvanize
inspire
lobby
rally
persuade
(re)invigorate
(re)vitalize
unify
unite

First or Only
chief
first
foremost
greatest
most
leading
number-one
singular
one
only
prime
single
sole
unparalleled
top
unique
unrivaled

Use **Active Voice**

At the heart of every good sentence is a strong, precise verb. The converse is true as well—at the core of most confusing, awkward, or wordy sentences lies a weak verb. Try to use the active voice whenever possible.

Can you find the Passive Voice Phrases?

Underline the words that should be edited out of this Duties section from a resume:

PASSIVE VOICE

Serve as a staff action officer in the Engineering and Implementation Division. Responsible for overseeing the establishment of new information systems and capabilities. Managing the modernization of existing facilities for the European Theater. Other duties include coordinating and integrating technical aspects of communications and automation working with administrative and management matters. Help in evaluating overall requirements. Made recommendation in policy. Involved with justifying funding equipment requirements, procurement and support services. Utilized my expertise in the overall concepts, theories, analytical processes and techniques of communications/automation, for the requirements of the command. I coordinated and lead assigned projects and reported, directed command project development. Provided advice and assistance on probable impact of proposed standardized systems, new equipment configurations. ADP equipment interface. Work in a lab environment to help support in any Technical assistance as the third tier.

ACTIVE VOICE

STAFF ACTION OFFICER in the Engineering and Implementation Division. Oversee the establishment of new information systems and capabilities. Manage the modernization of existing facilities for the European Theater. Coordinate and integrate technical aspects of communications and automation working with administrative and management matters. Evaluate overall requirements.

RECOMMEND POLICY AND JUSTIFY FUNDING equipment requirements, procurement and support services. Utilize my expertise in the overall concepts, theories, analytical processes and techniques of communications/automation, for the requirements of the command. Coordinate and lead assigned projects and reported, directed command project development.

ADVISOR AND THIRD TIER TECHNICAL ASSISTANCE on probable impact of proposed standardized systems, new equipment configurations in a lab environment to help support ADP interface.

Beware of Acronyms

We know that Federal employees depend on acronyms to communicate, but acronyms are dangerous in a resume. Acronyms can make your resume sound like Greek to a Human Resources Specialist or Hiring Manager who is not familiar with your background or previous work contexts. Remember, the Human Resources Specialist is rating your resume and application based on human resources guidelines. If you don't explain an acronym, they may not know to what you are referring. And if they don't know, you won't get credit! Help the Human Resources Specialist do their job by making it easy for them, and you'll have more success in getting your resume to that coveted referral.

Make sure you spell out your acronyms and give a definition. For example: WAWF (Wide Area Work Flow) could be described in this way in your resume:

> ❯ Train and deliver technical assistance to customers in the use of Wide Area Work Flow (WAWF), the Department of Defense Receipts and Acceptance system.

Be Consistent with Verb Tenses

The rule about tense in resumes is to use present tense for all present responsibilities and skills and past tense for all past responsibilities. For example:

SENIOR COMPUTER TECHNICIAN (September 20XX to present)　　　**PRESENT TENSE**

- Senior Computer Technician serving a fast-paced metropolitan retail outlet for Best Buy, one of the nation's leading retailers and resellers of technology products and services. Lead for the Technical Service Group, a 7-person team providing warranty repair services for the broad range of computer and personal electronics products sold by the company. Repair desktop and laptop computer systems, including digital camera equipment, smartphones, printers, and other computer peripherals.

SENIOR COMPUTER TECHNICIAN (September 20XX to June 20XX)　　　**PAST TENSE**

- Systems administrator for a scientific workgroup computing environment. Planned and delivered customer support services to the organization. Installed, upgraded, delivered, and provided troubleshooting for hardware and software components. Performed file back-ups and restores, system and peripherals troubleshooting, and component repair.

- Provided a high level of customer service for a wide variety of computer and network problems. Monitored, analyzed, and resolved end-user issues and provided informal training and assistance.

- Researched and reported on new technologies, equipment, and software with application to the Naval Surface Warfare Center.

Use "I" Intelligently

In the old days, there was no "I" in a resume. This was probably because it is easy to fall into the trap of starting every sentence with "I," which quickly becomes tedious and egocentric-sounding. The downside to avoiding "I" is that the sentences can end up as verbal contortionism. Today, the resume writer must strike a balance between these extremes. The modern rule of thumb is to use "I" to personalize your resume, but not so often as to become obnoxious.

"I Rules"

- **Don't** use "I" to start every sentence.
- **Don't** use "I" twice in the same sentence, or in two sentences in a row.
- **Do** use "I" when it makes your sentence flow smoothly.
- **Do** use "I" three to five times per page.
- **Do** use "I" with descriptions of accomplishments or "KSAs in the resume."
- **Do** use "I" in a compelling sentence emphasizing complexity, uniqueness, challenge, or outstanding service.
- **Do** use "I" in a summary of skills or competencies.
- **Do** use "I" in project descriptions where you are performing a particular role.
- **Do** use "I" in your Other Qualifications or Summary of Skills section. You can use "I" more frequently in a summary of your personal values, core competencies, and skills.

Here are two examples of good form when using "I":

> My Division Director ordered an audit to be conducted within two business days. The task appeared nearly impossible. After getting input from other team members, I proposed a division of labor that made the challenge more manageable. We completed the audit a half-day ahead of schedule, and the Director awarded me a Certificate of Recognition for my contribution.

> After extensive research I was able to convey to all personnel covering 7 different agencies the proper use/dispatch of government vehicles within Europe. Status of Forces Agreement (SOFA) stipulates if a European country is not part of this agreement, government vehicles cannot be driven there without proper authorization.

As we stated at the beginning of this chapter, what you put into the resume is how you will be perceived by those reading it. A document riddled with errors, sloppy formatting, and poor word choices can doom your application. Most people struggle with writing; even more struggle with revision and editing. If you don't feel comfortable with your own editing ability, we encourage you to have friends, family, peers, or professionals look over your content and offer up suggestions. This is a crucial step because a poorly edited resume won't get you very far at all!

PAY ATTENTION TO DOCUMENT DESIGN AND FORMATTING

Have you ever tried to read a document that was painful to look at? Maybe the layout didn't make sense. Perhaps the font was unusual. Maybe it just looked weird and you couldn't focus on the content. We've all been there. And, yet, most jobseekers pay very little attention to document design. Remember: the resume represents you! So how you present content visually is just as important as the content itself. Document design matters, especially for resumes.

The first thing readers "see" is the design of your document. If your resume doesn't look professional and is difficult to read, your credibility will suffer. Back in 2001, W.H. Baker published an academic article in *Business Communication Quarterly* titled "HATS: A Design Procedure for Routine Business Documents." The title may sound dull, but Baker's HATS formula is exciting, especially if you're trying to think about document design in the context of Federal resume writing. Baker said that to create visually compelling documents that are easy to access and navigate, all you need to do is remember the acronym HATS. No, these aren't the hats from Strategy 2 that you wear at work, but instead are the following core principles:

- ❯ **H**eadings, to promote easy navigation
- ❯ **A**ccess, to promote the finding and understanding of content
- ❯ **T**ypography, to promote readability and information hierarchies
- ❯ **S**pace, to ensure document cohesion

Although the formula is simple, you're probably still wondering exactly what you need to do to implement it, right? Let's get started.

HEADINGS-OUTLINE FORMAT. Earlier, we learned about using headings in the context of the Outline Format resume. They're crucially important because they announce to a reader what information is to follow. As a

> **The Outline Format Federal resume follows W.H. Baker's formula.**

key feature of the Outline Format resume, headings help readers get through documents by prioritizing content and lending to readers' understanding of the flow of information.

ACCESS. Baker believed that documents should be accessible. And we believe that resumes—as a form of professional documentation—should be accessible. What does this mean? When someone reads your resume, they should be able to find and understand important information quickly and easily. Formatting options (use of bullet points, indentation, italicization, bolding, etc.) can be leveraged to highlight key information.

TYPOGRAPHY. The typeface you use sends a message. How would you react, for example, if you read an employment contract in **comic sans** font? Or, how would you feel if your mortgage documents were presented to you in *brush script*? Because typeface sends a message, it is part of your overall consideration of thinking about how to persuade the reader. As a jobseeker, the resume needs to present you as a professional. Good rules to follow: don't use more than two font types in the resume and avoid unusual or unprofessional fonts.

SPACE. If you crunch all your information together, it can be hard to read. Baker argued that space was an important and oft-forgotten principle of document design. So, the last bit of his formula was to use space strategically. Ever wonder why college professors prefer double-spaced documents? They're easier to read. Good rules to follow: always have margins, don't crowd words, and format your content with reasonably-sized, well-balanced blocks of targeted information separated by white space. Sound familiar? It should. That is how we use space in the Outline Format resume.

Ultimately, the goal here is to avoid visual clutter. We've already addressed choosing your content, but avoiding visual clutter is difficult because most of us do not feel comfortable designing things. The simple message here is this: break up your content and categorize it. Keeping it all together in long paragraphs, or an endless run of bullet-points, doesn't serve you well in the context of a resume. When you've pulled together a draft, you should review it and ask yourself these questions:

- Does the design of your resume help clarify your qualifications or hide them?
- Does the design of your resume help you stand out while still representing your professional persona?

If your answer is "no" to either of those questions, go back and re-think your document.

Whatever design choices you make, you MUST be consistent. Inconsistency across your design makes the resume look sloppy, unprofessional, and demonstrates a lack of attention to detail.

There should be a method to your madness. Most resumes do not strategically arrange the content. Strategic arrangement (i.e., making the most important information the most visible) could be the difference between being referred and being rejected. If, for example, a job announcement lists knowledge, skills, and abilities such as effective communication, project management, and contract auditing, those qualifications should rise to the top of every job block and be easy to identify. Do not hide them!

All aspects of your design and formatting choices should account for the realities of the Federal job application process. So, we offer up some actions you should always take and some you should avoid:

- **DO** use the Outline Format, but pay attention to how the content is laid out and how content is emphasized.
- **ALWAYS** approach each resume as a new challenge. Every applicant and job posting is a little bit different. A thoughtful, strategic approach is key. Although there are "best practices," a one-size-fits-all does not apply.
- **DO NOT** use online or word-processing templates.
- **DO** experiment with different ways of using design and applying the Outline Format.
- **ALWAYS** have other people review your work. Can they identify the most important information? Is it easy to read? What is their takeaway after a quick, 20–30 second review?

HOT TIP ABOUT THE USAJOBS BUILDER RESUME!
It's great to build your resume in the USAJOBS builder. But the final output of this resume by the Human Resources Specialist might produce a resume that is small type.

SOLUTION: Print Preview the resume and put the content into WORD format, 11-point type. UPLOAD the resume for easy reading!

 *This example shows what to do!*

CARSON J. GEORGE
1234 Norfolk Lane, Norfolk, VA 63116
666-666-6666 • carsonsample@gmail.com

PROFESSIONAL SUMMARY

SUPPLY CHAIN SPECIALIST with 3 years professional experience supporting US Military equipment, international shipping and logistics. Successful in improving efficiency for an active supply center at Norfolk Naval Shipyard redesigning a customer services center and inventory control. Skilled in cataloging and research with automated supply and accountability systems. Master's in Acquisition and Supply Chain Management.

PROFESSIONAL EXPERIENCE

SUPPLY SPECIALIST, GS-2001-11   **01/2016 – Present**
NAVSUP   40 Hours per Week
100 Hampton Road, Norfolk, VA
Supervisor: Susan Thomas (703) 999-9999
Mission: To provide supplies, services and quality-of-life support to the Navy and Joint Warfighter.

SUPPORT LOGISTICS OPERATIONS: Receive, store, control and issue expendable and non-expendable U.S. Military equipment. Apply knowledge of standardized supply regulations, policies and instructions. Identify, track and assure accountability for variety of supplies, material and equipment for customers.

TECHNICAL EXPERT: Principal representative on property accountability and DPAS (Defense Property Accountability System). Determine supplies or materials needed for planned programs or operations.
- ACCOMPLISHMENT: For Little Creek Maintenance Service Center, I planned logistics, purchasing and renovations for the total renovation of the 2,500sf customer services center. I planned a professional space, including converting to countertops, screens and improved inventory operations. I researched the top purchases from maintenance and supply offices and ordered an additional inventory for 100-line items. Worked with the designers for the shelving and storage plans. RESULTS: Within three months, the new service center was open with faster and more efficient access to needed parts and supplies for maintenance and vehicle operations. I currently visit the center weekly to ensure that the parts are available and review access.

PROPERTY ACCOUNTABILITY: Process requisitions to stock, commodity control, or other appropriate supply requests. Expedite delivery of materials to meet operational needs. Locate and catalog stock for issue and storage. Receive and inspect property equipment and life shelf

Page Two

stock from DOD contractors. Verify material accountability against purchase order (PO) terms and conditions and sign delivery receipts. Ensure the appropriate and safe storage of property.

UTILIZE RANGE OF AUTOMATED SUPPLY AND ACCOUNTABILITY SYSTEMS, including DPAS and PBUSE, to track property accountability and manage requisition, receipt, storage, transfer, purchasing, and inventories. Process documentation for stock item receipts. Prepare standard reports detailing variances between actual and estimated costs.

CUSTOMER SERVICES AND COORDINATE MATERIAL DISTRIBUTION LOGISTICS: Track and maintain accurate property equipment and supply documents in accordance with established procedures and policy. Prepare and forward completed material receipt documentation to the property book officer. Answer inquiries that arise regarding status of equipment ordered. Provide technical guidance to customers.

ENSURE A HIGH LEVEL OF COMMUNICATIONS ON SUPPLY ACCOUNTABILITY: Contact units and prepare issue slips of lateral transfer documentation to ensure property accountability of transferred equipment. Coordinate and resolve data integrity problems. Brief senior leadership on property book activities. Brief management on status, updates, or changes in supplies or material. Relay information to vendors to ensure accurate delivery of material within established schedules.

INTERPRET AND APPLY APPROPRIATE DOD AND DEPARTMENT OF THE ARMY REGULATIONS AND POLICIES pertaining to the management and control of Government-owned property. Create and update Property Book Department SOPs to comply with Government requirements. Clearly conveyed supply policies and procedures to customers to improve customer satisfaction.

EDUCATION

MASTERS IN ACQUISITION AND SUPPLY CHAIN MANAGEMENT, 2016
University of Maryland, Global Campus
— 3.7 GPA; Relevant Coursework: Purchasing and Materials Management; Legal Aspects of Contracting; Contract Pricing and Negotiations; Strategic Purchasing and Logistics; Integration Supply Chain Management; Contemporary Logistics
___Strategic Management Capstone

BACHELOR OF BUSINESS ADMINISTRATION, 2014
American Military University • Charles Town, WV
— Major: Management; Minor: Accounting

CERTIFICATION

Project Management Program, PMP, 2015

This example shows what to do!

GOOD FORMAT, UPLOAD – MILITARY SPOUSE EMPHASIS ON TECHNICAL SKILLS AND MILITARY SPOUSE HISTORY – TARGET GS-5

KATHLEEN G. PAYNE
10000 Cherry Lane
Atlanta, Ga. 30813 US
Day Phone: 222-222-2222
Email: kathleensample@hotmail.com
Military Spouse Eligible for EO 13473

OBJECTIVE: OFFICE AUTOMATION, INFORMATION MANAGEMENT CUSTOMER SERVICES ADMINISTRATION   GS 5

COMPUTER SKILLS:

Microsoft Office Word, Publisher, Excel Spreadsheets, Outlook, Power Point (Expert Level)
Database systems:
Client Tracking System (CTS)
Automated Time Attendance and Production System (ATAAPS)
Installation Support Modules for out processing
Check Appointments Online System
ICE - Interactive Customer Evaluations
Defense Travel System (DTS)
Directorate of Public Works (DPW)
Volunteer Management Information System (VMIS)
Enterprise systems:
U.S. General Service Administration (GSA)
Installation Military One Source
Army Morale, Welfare and Recreation Brand Central (Marking Materials and Branding Guidelines)

Work Experience:
Military Spouse PCS History:
U.S. Army Military Spouse - Various locations, 2001 to present
Extensive experience with military family life, relocations, financial management and services available on military bases worldwide.   30-32 hours per week

Fort Gordon, Georgia	02/2019 - Present
Fort George G. Meade, Maryland	11/2013 - 02/2019
Schweinfurt, Germany	06/2011 - 11/2013
Mannheim, Germany	10/2010 - 06/2011
Fort Bragg, North Carolina	11/2006 - 10/2010
Fort Gordon, Georgia	11/2001 - 11/2006

Work Experience:

Army Community Service
33512 RICE DRIVE & BLDG 35200 279 HERITAGE LANE
Fort Gordon, GA. 30905 United States
05/2019 – Present   Salary: Volunteer   Hours per week: 30-32

ADMINISTRATIVE DUTIES: Provide logistical support to relocation readiness program and staff. Enhance ACS program(s) and service delivery by receiving walk-ins, answering phone lines, recording and distributing messages, clerical duties, updating hand receipts. Update lending closet records in the Client Tracking System (CTS). Notify customers holding overdue items.

Army Community Service
830 CHISHOLM AVENUE
Fort Meade, MD   20755 United States
04/2014 – 02/2019 Hours per week: 40
Office Automation Clerk, GS-0301-04 (This is a federal job); Type 80 wpm.

KEY ACCOMPLISHMENTS:
- Recipient: Excellence in Federal Career Award Winner, Silver and Gold for the following significant contributions to the Ft. Meade Army Community Service, Presidential Lifetime Achievement Award from Fort George G. Meade Army Community Service, Presidential Volunteer Service Family (Gold) Award from Fort George G. Meade (ACS) 2015 Volunteer Service Family (Bronze) Award from Fort George G. Meade (ACS) 2016

CUSTOMER SERVICE: Initial point of contact for Army Community Service (ACS) at Fort Meade. Explain ACS programs and work life related services to approximately 100 community members on the phone and in person daily.

> **Improved Customer Service.** Redesigned the lobby and reception area to make the space more professional and appealing to ACS customers. Quickly recognized that many customers needed detailed information about the installation, so I researched and ordered a large map of the post. My initiative had an immediate and dramatic impact on customer service. It provided clients a great tool that was understandable and easily accessible. Furthermore, by decreasing the need for customers to be shown a small map at the front desk, it increased the amount of time that can be spent on customers with more critical needs.

DATA ANALYSIS AND INFORMATION TRACKING: Extracts data daily to create monthly and quarterly reports on usage and analysis for organization. Maintains, gathers, and complies records of information for management analysis by tracking and logging statistical data of all ACS programs.

KNOWLEDGE OF AND FOLLOW ACS GUIDELINES: Guidelines include ACS AR 608-1, Army Emergency Relief AR 930-4, Preparing and Managing Correspondence AR 25-50, standard operating procedures, agency correspondence procedures, style manuals, MARKS System, relocation automated programs.

Federal Resume Format: **Bad Example #1**

 *These are examples of what NOT to do.*

BAD FORMAT - USAJOBS BUILDER FORMAT – SMALL TYPE

NAVSUP
1000 Hampton Road
Norfolk, VA 23505 United States

01/2019 - Present
Salary: $53,997 USD Bi-weekly
Hours per week: 40
SUPPLY SPECIALIST
Duties, Accomplishments and Related Skills:
Mission: To provide supplies, services and quality-of-life support to the Navy and Joint Warfighter.

SUPPORTED LOGISTICS OPERATIONS: Performed stock receipt, storage, control, and issue of expendable and non-expendable U.S. Military equipment. Applied knowledge of standardized supply regulations, policies, and instructions to identify, track, and assure accountability for supplies, material and equipment. Served as a technical expert and principal representative on property accountability and PBUSE.

PROPERTY ACCOUNTABILITY: Processed requisitions to stock, commodity control, or other appropriate supply organizations. Expedited delivery of materials to meet operational needs. Located and cataloged stock for issue and storage. Received and inspected property equipment and life shelf stock from DOD contractors. Verified material accountability against purchase order (PO) terms and conditions; signed delivery receipts.

UTILIZED RANGE OF AUTOMATED SUPPLY AND ACCOUNTABILITY SYSTEMS, including PBUSE, to track property accountability and manage requisition, receipt, storage, transfer, purchasing, and inventories. Processed documentation for stock item receipts. Prepared standard reports detailing variances between actual and estimated costs.

COORDINATED MATERIAL DISTRIBUTION LOGISTICS WITH CUSTOMERS. Tracked and maintained accurate property equipment and supply documents in accordance with established procedures and policy. Prepared and forwarded completed material receipt documentation to the property book officer. Answered inquiries that arose regarding status.

INVENTORY MANAGEMENT: Inspected, segregated, inventoried, and stored nonexpendable property and expendable supplies. Managed stock levels and reorder points. Conducted physical inventories and adjusted inventory levels in the system based upon needs assessment.

ENSURED A HIGH LEVEL OF COMMUNICATIONS ON SUPPLY ACCOUNTABILITY: Contacted units and prepared issue slips of lateral transfer documentation to ensure property accountability of transferred equipment. Coordinated and resolved data integrity problems. Briefed senior leadership on property book activities. Briefed management on status, updates, or changes in supplies or material. Relayed information to vendors to ensure accurate delivery of material.

+ For Little Creek Maintenance Service Center, I supported the total renovation of the customer services center. I researched the top purchases from maintenance and supply offices and ordered additional inventory for 100-line items. Worked with the designers for the shelving and storage plans. I visited the center weekly to ensure that the parts were available and reviewed access. Within three months, the new service center was open with faster and more efficient access to needed parts and supplies for maintenance and vehicle operations.

+ As a Carcass Tracking manager at ASD Norfolk, in 2012, I recovered $2.5 million in aviation repairable parts. Part of the unit was overseas from Korea. Because of the mission, they had huge inventory and were challenged to keep up. Volume was high and threshold of aircraft parts were high dollar. I identified that these parts could be financial (had taken a loss for the parts). I reported the parts and recouped the finds.

+ Coordinated two evaluations on Introduction to Health Care Data Analytics web-based training course with over 1000 students participating asynchronously over an 8-week term. Received an above industry standard response rate of 27%. Respondents perceived a 35% improvement in their job performance as a result of participating in the program. On average, 77% of respondents agreed the program improved VHA strategic objectives.

+ Created training including real world scenarios and branching decision tree to increase meeting role clarity, inclusivity and diversity, and enable team members to become more effective by meeting overlapping goals and objectives with other VA healthcare providers.

These are examples of what NOT to do.

BAD FORMAT FOR FEDERAL - THIS IS AN UPLOADED PRIVATE SECTOR RESUME

GREG MARTINEZ

5552 November Lane | Silver Spring, MD 20906 | 240-123-4567
GMartinez18@gmail.com

EDUCATION

University of Maryland, Baltimore County	GPA: 3.17/ 4.0
Candidate for B.S. in Computer Science	Expected: December 2018
Minor in Statistics and Economics	

TECHNICAL SKILLS

Operating Systems	Windows, Linux
Programming	C++/C, Python, Java, SQL, JavaScript, Kotlin
Software	VirtualBox, R, QuickBooks, SAS Enterprise, SharePoint
Languages	Fluent in Mandarin

RELATED WORK EXPERIENCE

Department of Energy, Germantown, MD — *November 2017 - Present*
ORISE Fellow
- Create informational sidebar on SharePoint Fellows website.
- Document SharePoint workflow diagram for onboarding prospective ORISE fellows using Visio.
- Update Fellowship Liaison SOP to increase clarity and understanding of ORISE onboarding process for office point of contacts and prospective mentors.

Route 144 Classified, Baltimore, MD — *September 2017 - Present*
IT Consultant
- Clean and manage enterprise databases through QuickBooks and spreadsheets.
- Conduct data analysis using pivot tables and charts to increase sales by understanding consumer metrics.

Student Host International, LLC., Newark, DE — *July 2014 – August 2016*
IT Consultant
- Monitored network activity and increased productivity through Windows parental controls software.
- Created backups and secure sensitive files with Veeam Endpoint Backup.
- Managed software installation and updates through Ninite and batch uninstaller.

PROJECTS

CMSC461 – Database Management Systems — *Fall 2017*
- Created MySQL database from entity-relationship model and a corresponding relational schema.
- Developed a web application that supports SQL queries for selecting, adding, and dropping data.

EXTRACURRICULAR ACTIVITIES

UMBC Cyber Dawgs, Baltimore, MD — *September 2017 - Present*
- Configure CentOS as all-in-one server for DNS, SSH with key pair, MySQL, and Git.
- Configure IPTables to implement state checks, enable HTTP/HTTPS, enable incoming/outgoing SSH, enable mailing protocols and name resolution.

Hack UMBC, Baltimore, MD – Alexa, Rap Me A Recipe — *October 2017*
- Created Alexa skill that uses McCormick and Spotify APIs to create a playlist of rap music soundbites based on descriptions of recipes.

Summary: The Federal Resume Puzzle

Does your Federal resume have all of the puzzle pieces?

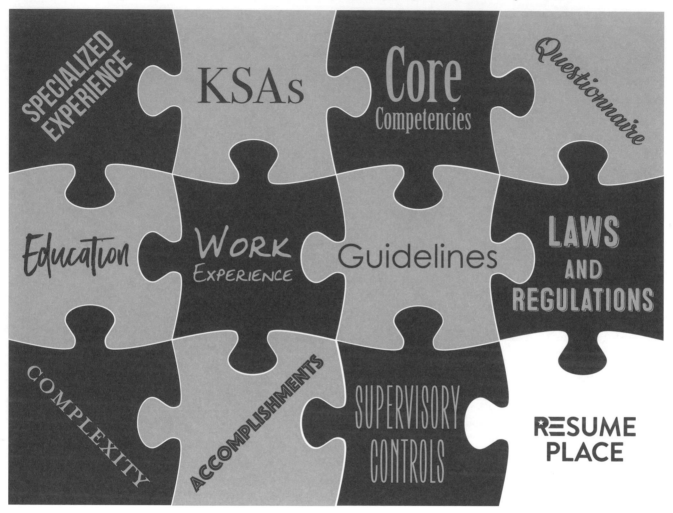

We like to think of the process as similar to putting together a puzzle.

The Federal resume is like a legal document. It must prove, on the page, that you have the qualifications for the job. Resumes get reviewed to prove qualifications and to protect the government against complaints. So, the resume is crucially important and must match the announcement qualifications. Therefore, the pieces of puzzles will help you collect all the right information to match a position and hopefully get you best qualified for the position. From a broad perspective, you should write the resume in the Outline Format, specifically targeting the announcement. Put the resume into USAJOBS. Follow the application directions. That's it! Simple, right?

Well, maybe. Let's dig a bit deeper into the puzzle. Federal job applications are comprised of critical elements—or puzzle pieces—that you have to fit together to create a complete picture of your qualifications.

Here's what each puzzle piece looks like:

 Specialized Experience: Every USAJOBS announcement includes a specialized experience requirement. This is the one puzzle piece you MUST have; without it, you might not even be able to begin the puzzle. No specialized experience? You won't get referred.

 Knowledge, Skills, and Abilities (KSAs): Announcements on USAJOBS list out KSAs for the position. They may seem, at times, like "add on" language, or "fluff," but they are required competencies for the position. Read them carefully. Address them in the resume to round out the puzzle.

 Core Competencies: This is a relatively recent addition to the puzzle, but whether you prove you possess core competencies can be the difference between an incomplete puzzle or a complete image that shows you at your best. Pro Tip: Use accomplishment stories to demonstrate competency areas.

 The Self-Assessment Questionnaire: You're scoring yourself here and basically screening yourself. Think of it as a test. The higher you rate, the more looks you'll get during the evaluation process. Give yourself credit, score yourself as high as possible, and support your self-assessment ratings with resume content. Let Human Resources screen you out; don't do their job for them.

 Education: If the position requires education, make sure you include it. Read the instructions. If a specific number of credits in a particular field is required, you must list out the relevant courses, total number of relevant credits, and prove your claims with a transcript. No proof? Then you're missing a puzzle piece.

 Work Experience: Your work experience should be targeted to the position you're trying to get, not merely summarize your past employment. Don't simply copy-and-paste your position description; rather, fine-tune your experience descriptions based on what the announcement is looking for. Finally, follow the instructions and include all mandatory/required pieces of information.

 Non-Profit & Volunteer Experience: Non-paid work is still work. It counts on a Federal resume. Yes, you read that right! If you have substantial experience with a volunteer position, it can be weighted equally to a paid position. Give it a whole job block; don't leave it as a footnote or small piece of "additional information," especially if it demonstrates specialized experience or KSAs.

 **Guidelines, Laws, and Regulations:** If you're a Federal employee, you're interacting with these puzzle pieces every day. Include them in your resume, and be specific! These can help demonstrate your expertise and your competency areas.

 Supervisory Experience: Do you lead teams? Do you collaborate with others? Are you in a formal supervisory position? Do you manage projects? Whether formal or not, your experience might still qualify as "supervisory." Claim credit for yourself by casting your experiences in the light of leadership and team building. The puzzle will look better for it.

 Accomplishments: Resumes all tend to start looking the same to a Human Resources Specialist who has to review hundreds of them. Make yours interesting. Include stories! Leverage your accomplishment stories to convey your "value added" through past performance and demonstrated excellence. We all like a good story, and telling stories about your accomplishments is the difference between a boring resume and an interesting one. Want to be referred? Want an interview? Include accomplishments in your resume and give them the space they deserve.

Sign In   Help   Sea

eywords

b title, dept., agency, series

, or country

Search

Strategy 9

SUBMIT YOUR RESUME AND QUESTIONNAIRE CORRECTLY ON USAJOBS

AMERICA'S FUTURE

the Federal Government

Profile

Create a US

Explore Opportunities

Create a USAJOBS Profile

Save your favorite jobs and searches

Receive email updates from jobs you're interested in.

Upload your resumes and documents

Save and manage resumes and documents for your application.

Make your resume searchable

Your resume will be visible to recruiters searching our database.

Apply for jobs in the Federal Government

You can only apply online with a complete USAJOBS profile.

Your Outline Format resume must support the answers you provide in the self-assessment questionnaire that you encounter after you "apply" on USAJOBS. The most common reasons qualified applicants fail in their Federal job search are these: they don't give themselves credit on the questionnaire and they don't justify their responses in the resume when they do.

The big thing to remember when submitting an application on USAJOBS is to follow the instructions in the announcement! USAJOBS does a fairly good job of laying out the application process step-by-step and providing clarifications. Even so, many jobseekers still struggle with navigating USAJOBS, so we recommend that you spend some time learning the system and navigating the application process by submitting some test applications.

Aside from the resume, the self-assessment questionnaire is far and away the most important part of the application. The questionnaire isn't in the announcement itself; rather, it is usually located in the Application Manager that the announcement directs you to after you "apply." However, most USAJOBS announcements allow you to "preview" the questionnaire with a link, usually located near the bottom of the announcement. For each question for which you claim expertise or proficiency, your answer must be supported in the resume. You simply cannot ignore this strategy if you want a Federal job. Remember: the resume must be matched to the language of the announcement and your responses to the questionnaire. Those who succeed at applying for Federal jobs are those who emphasize quality over quantity. This isn't a numbers game. Really, it is simply about doing a quality job of reviewing the announcement and reflecting the announcement back in the resume. A key part of that process is the questionnaire.

Know that the Self-Assessment Questionnaire IS A TEST!

Traditional / Commonly used questionnaire format. Give yourself all the credit that you can. The HR specialists need to see a score of 95% on the questionnaire.

3. Participates in the administration of a program to provide internal/external placement to include special placement activities and interpretations of complex guidance.

- A.   I have not had education, training, or experience in performing this task.
- B.   I have had education or training in how to perform this task, but have not yet performed it on the job.
- C.   I have performed this task on the job. My work on this task was monitored closely by a supervisor or senior employee to ensure compliance with proper procedures.
- D.   I have performed this task as a regular part of a job. I have performed it independently and normally without review by a supervisor or senior employee.
- E.   I am considered an expert in performing this task. I have supervised performance of this task or am normally the person who is consulted by other workers to assist or train them in doing this task because of my expertise.

In this case the E answer is the best. There are three ways to be an E for the questionnaire:

❯ I am considered an expert in performing this task.

❯ I have supervised performance of this task.

❯ I am normally the person who is consulted by other workers to assist or train them in doing this task because of my expertise.

Story 1: Bob was a long-time Federal employee. He held his position as an Immigration Services Officer (at the GS-12 level) for several years and was itching for a promotion. A supervisory GS-13 position opened, and Bob got the job, but it turned out that he hated the new job. After a year, despite the increase in pay, he yearned for his old position. Guess what? It re-opened. The exact same job he'd had before his promotion. He excitedly applied and waited for his interview. Here's the kicker: he did not get an interview. Instead, he got a Notification of Results (NOR) that indicated that he was "not referred" because he had not established that he was minimally qualified, for a lower graded position that he had previously held! As crazy as it sounds, this happened because when Bob answered the questionnaire in the Application Manager, he did not take credit for his accomplishments and expertise. He shot himself in the foot because he didn't give himself credit on the questionnaire. This is REALLY common.

Story 2: Michelle was a private sector employee seeking a position as a Program Analyst with the Department of Defense. She was already working in the defense industry as a contractor, possessed substantial amounts of senior-level program management experience, and held a high clearance. Fantastic candidate. When she applied for the Federal position, she gave herself credit on the questionnaire, giving herself high marks and ratings of "expert" across the board. She submitted a single-page functional resume in support of her application. She excitedly waited for her interview. Except she didn't get one. Instead, she got a Notification of Results (NOR) that indicated that she was "not referred" because her questionnaire responses could not be validated. Michelle is the opposite of Bob: she took credit but didn't reflect her questionnaire responses in the resume. Bob had a decent resume, but didn't take credit in the questionnaire.

Story 3: Nicole was a long time Federal employee who wanted to get into a leadership internship within her own agency. She completed a self-assessment form about her awards, performance evaluations, work experience, and accomplishments. She had a list of 12 awards in her Federal resume. Yet she assessed her awards score INCORRECTLY. She was not found to be Best Qualified for the internship.

Select the option that corresponds to the total number of points you should receive for awards. You may receive points for your monetary awards as follows – 1 point for each cash award earned earlier than 5 years from the date of the vacancy (Maximum 5 points) – 1 point for each ECSA award within the prior 5 years – 2 points for each performance award (ROC/Q) within the prior 5 years.

1. Your overall total for monetary awards may not exceed 10 points. Please indicate the number of points you should receive your awards

- ⚪ A.   0
- ⚪ B.   1
- ⚪ C.   2
- ⚫ D.   3
- ⚪ E.   4
- ⚪ F.   5
- ⚪ G.   6
- ⚪ H.   7
- ⚪ I.   8
- ⚪ J.   9
- ⚪ K.   10

Lesson? Don't make these mistakes. Let's take a closer look at some of the key approaches to matching up the resume to the questionnaire so that you don't fall into their shoes…

Self-Assessment Questionnaire **Samples**

Look for the questionnaire preview to review against your Federal resume.

Human Resources Specialist, GS 11, Small Business Administration

> **This is not a good questionnaire answer.**
> **These answers will not get the highest score!**
> **Give yourself all the credit that you can.**

8. Work with multiple types of work schedules such as full-time, seasonal, and intermittent.

- ○ A.   I have no education, training or experience in performing this task.
- ○ B.   I have had education or training in performing the task, but have not yet performed it on the job.
- ◉ C.   I have performed this task on the job. My work on this task was monitored closely by a supervisory or senior employee to ensure compliance with proper procedures.
- ○ D.   I have performed this task as a regular part of a job. I have performed it independently and normally without review by a supervisor or senior employee.
- ○ E.   I am considered an expert in performing this task. I am normally the person who is consulted by other workers to assist them in doing this task because of my expertise or I have supervised performance of this task.

9. Work with both competitive and excepted service appointments.

- ○ A.   I have no education, training or experience in performing this task.
- ○ B.   I have had education or training in performing the task, but have not yet performed it on the job.
- ○ C.   I have performed this task on the job. My work on this task was monitored closely by a supervisory or senior employee to ensure compliance with proper procedures.
- ◉ D.   I have performed this task as a regular part of a job. I have performed it independently and normally without review by a supervisor or senior employee.
- ○ E.   I am considered an expert in performing this task. I am normally the person who is consulted by other workers to assist them in doing this task because of my expertise or I have supervised performance of this task.

10. To support the responses you provided to questions 4-9, please indicate the position(s) in your resume that demonstrates your experience related to Recruitment/Placement and the tasks listed above (provide position title, company and dates only).

> Department of Interior
> Human Resources Office
> Human Resources Specialist, GS 9
> Denver, Colorado
> 9/2015 to present

> **This questionnaire is NOT answered at the highest**
> **level. This will not be a good score. For Question**
> **10, just add your employer where this experience is**
> **demonstrated for each of these fields.**

**THIS QUESTIONNAIRE WILL GET THE HIGHEST SCORE!
GREAT ANSWERS HERE!
GIVE YOURSELF ALL THE CREDIT THAT YOU CAN.**

7. Provides technical advisory services on recruitment and placement actions covered under Title 5, Title 38 and Hybrid 38.

○ A.   I have not had education, training, or experience in performing this task.

○ B.   I have had education or training in how to perform this task, but have not yet performed it on the job.

○ C.   I have performed this task on the job. My work on this task was monitored closely by a supervisor or senior employee to ensure compliance with proper procedures.

○ D.   I have performed this task as a regular part of a job. I have performed it independently and normally without review by a supervisor or senior employee.

◉ E.   I am considered an expert in performing this task. I have supervised performance of this task or am normally the person who is consulted by other workers to assist or train them in doing this task because of my expertise.

8. Ensures compliance with labor contract and applicable regulatory requirements; and evaluates applications for eligibility against regulatory eligibility requirements.

○ A.   I have not had education, training, or experience in performing this task.

○ B.   I have had education or training in how to perform this task, but have not yet performed it on the job.

○ C.   I have performed this task on the job. My work on this task was monitored closely by a supervisor or senior employee to ensure compliance with proper procedures.

○ D.   I have performed this task as a regular part of a job. I have performed it independently and normally without review by a supervisor or senior employee.

◉ E.   I am considered an expert in performing this task. I have supervised performance of this task or am normally the person who is consulted by other workers to assist or train them in doing this task because of my expertise.

9. Reviews and/or develops standards operating procedures (SOPs) and other written documents based on subject matter expertise and regulatory/legal requirements.

○ A.   I have not had education, training, or experience in performing this task.

○ B.   I have had education or training in how to perform this task, but have not yet performed it on the job.

○ C.   I have performed this task on the job. My work on this task was monitored closely by a supervisor or senior employee to ensure compliance with proper procedures.

○ D.   I have performed this task as a regular part of a job. I have performed it independently and normally without review by a supervisor or senior employee.

◉ E.   I am considered an expert in performing this task. I have supervised performance of this task or am normally the person who is consulted by other workers to assist or train them in doing this task because of my expertise.

HOT TIP!
Make sure your resume matches your answers in the questionnaire. In this case, be sure to add: TECHNICAL ADVISORY SERVICES; COMPLIANCE WITH LABOR CONTRACTS; AND REVIEW STANDARD OPERATING PROCEDURES. Those headlines will match this questionnaire.

Tricky Assessment Questions
Program Analyst, GS 341-11
QUIZ: What are the best answers for this questionnaire?

5 | I have planned and performed the following duties as it relates to research and analysis.

Conducted research or studies and provided recommendations for needed revisions in applicable policies and procedures.

Consolidated results of analysis into an overall report for presentation to management.

Participated in the monitoring, tracking and evaluation of operational workload indicators and workload systems

None of the above.

6 | **Please indicate your highest level of experience with Lean Six Sigma process improvement methodologies.**

I have supported and coordinated the implementation of Lean Six Sigma process improvement methodologies across an organization.

I have supported, coordinated, and facilitated the planning and implementation of Lean Six Sigma process improvement methodologies across a business unit.

I have supported the implementation of Lean Six Sigma process improvement methodologies across a division.

I have participated in all aspects of implementing Lean Six Sigma process improvement methodologies across a business unit.

I have supported, coordinated, and facilitated the planning and implementation of Lean Six Sigma process improvement methodologies s across an organization.

I do not have this type of experience.

Although having an excellent resume in the Outline Format is an important step on your Federal career path, not even the best resume in the world will get you a Federal job if you don't navigate USAJOBS correctly and give yourself credit on the self-assessment questionnaire.

Remember, follow the instructions! Familiarize yourself with the process. Also remember that the self-assessment questionnaire is just that: a subjective self-assessment of your own experience. You are being asked to rate yourself. This is often the first step in the process, and if you don't rate yourself correctly, chances are that no one will ever look at your resume.

> **Add these HEADLINES in your resume to match the above questions:**
> **RESEARCH AND ANALYSIS**
> **PROCESS IMPROVEMENT METHODOLOGIES**

★ ★ ★

Part 2

10 STEPS TO GETTING PROMOTED IN GOVERNMENT

USCBP Supervisor
gets a Promotion

Because we receive so many questions about career change and Federal promotion, we are devoting Part 2 and Part 3 of this book to these 4 issues: Getting Promoted; Extreme Career Change in Government; Private Sector to Federal; and Federal to Private Sector.

Step	01	Make a Decision: **It's Time to Get a Promotion**
Step	02	Find and **Update Your Resume**
Step	03	Find and **Review Performance Evaluations**
Step	04	Write Your **Top Ten List of Accomplishments**
Step	05	Research Promotion **Job Announcements**
Step	06	Make a List of **Keywords from the Announcements**
Step	07	Study ECQs to **Understand Leadership Competencies**
Step	08	Write and Target **Your Federal Resume for a Promotion**
Step	09	Prepare for **the Structured Interview**
Step	10	Interview and **Get the Promotion**

Strategic Thinking about Your Leadership Performance and Results

Opportunities for promotion in government are plentiful, but it takes a strategy to develop your skills and prepare your resume to get promoted to the next grade level. As your grade level increases, so does the required level of qualification and scope of responsibility.

Advancement from higher-level grades is much more competitive—you can't wing it! It takes planning and preparation. If your resume does not represent skills for the next higher grade level, you will not get promoted. The good news is that Federal employees (many in higher-grade positions) are increasingly becoming retirement-eligible. That may help you advance to a higher grade more quickly these days than in the past. This chapter is designed to help you do work now so that you can increase your likelihood of moving up in the Federal government.

For Federal promotions, you should develop a game-plan. Rather than non-strategically applying to every new announcement at the next highest grade, step back and assess your own strengths, where the opportunities are to best utilize those skills, and where you will enjoy working. Moving up within the same series is generally easier than moving between series. This is particularly the case as you approach the mid-level grades.

Your "series" experience, especially if it's in the same agency, should be directly relevant to the skills required in the next graded position. Those skills may also translate well to same series positions in other agencies, but the applicant pool will likely include more candidates with agency-specific knowledge and experience. This is also the case, to a somewhat lesser extent, with moving within the same "occupational group" (for example, the 0340 General Administrative group that includes occupational series for e.g., Program Managers, Administrative Officers, Management and Program Analysts, and Logistics Managers). It will be more challenging to meet the "specialized experience" criteria for different series unless you have expertise in the other skills sets.

Keep your eyes peeled for multi-grade career ladder positions. In these positions, employees progressively acquire the background necessary to perform at the "full performance level." You will not be competing against others for a promotion to the next grade, but rather against performance expectations. If you had originally been selected to a GS-12 position with promotion potential of a GS-14, you could have moved up to a GS-14 in as little as two years if you performed well. So, try to identify positions where you have noncompetitive opportunities to move up. As you might expect, these ladder opportunities are harder to find as you get into the mid- and higher-level grades.

At work, always excel. Do your best, achieve in tangible ways, and keep track of your achievements. Produce qualitative work of significant impact that is praised by superiors; exceed the quantitative expectations of your position. If your agency awards superior work, do your best to be acknowledged with letters of commendation, incentive and special achievement awards (both individual and as a member of winning teams), and quality step increases. Be the first to volunteer for the challenging assignments and strive to help your management team succeed. Proactively pursue career-enhancing opportunities.

Review the type of skills that are expected at the next grade level of your series and look for ways to gain those skills. Seek out assignments to be part of special teams or task forces; apply for meaningful details; look for opportunities to "act" at the next level.

Offer to mentor new staff or interns. Be an effective "change agent" and embrace reinvention at your agency.

Pursue in-house or other government agency training that may help you in your current and future positions; you may be pleasantly surprised at the training opportunities that are "there for the asking."

And, remember that relevant "volunteer" work, although unpaid, helps build your competencies. You will be credited for all of your qualifying experience, including volunteer experience, that you clearly include on your Federal resume.

It is important, too, to remember: Don't stay in a job for too long before trying to move up. Once you have a few years of experience under your belt, start looking for opportunities at the next grade level. Even if you don't succeed at first, establishing your interest in upward mobility sends an important message to your management team. If you find your current agency's environment stimulating and there are opportunities to grow, explore those first. If not, you should familiarize yourself with the missions and goals of other agencies (perhaps those where your skills could best be utilized) and apply for opportunities in those agencies.

Finally, we always encourage you to embrace the mantra: "NETWORK, NETWORK, NETWORK!" Join professional organizations, alumni associations, and relevant LinkedIn® groups. Make sure that you have a professional social networking presence. Attend luncheons where you are likely to learn and mingle. If appropriate, seek "informational" interviews with managers in prospective offices.

The following pages are the official Ten Steps to Getting Promoted in Government. Keep going, be persevering, and make it happen!

Step 01 Make a Decision: It's Time to Get a Promotion

Many employees work in a position for five, ten, or more years without exploring opportunities in other positions, in other offices, or even in other agencies. At some point, such employees wake up and realize that a change is needed. They're burned out and need a change of scenery. Or maybe their skills are stagnating. Sometimes, it is a simple pragmatic realization that a higher graded position will help boost their retirement. Whatever the motivations, making a decision to get a promotion is a good one. As we've already noted, it takes a plan of action and serious determination to land the promotion. But it all starts with this: making a decision.

For this chapter we're going to look at a case study to walk through each of our ten steps, so that you can see how each of them get applied to the process.

Meet Danielle

Danielle was a GS-13 Supervisory Law Enforcement Specialist and had been in the position for four years. Even though she had been in the position for a relatively brief time, she was doing the work of three employees and made a decision that it was time for a change. She was overworked but didn't have enough authority to make major changes in her office and felt that she could have more of an impact with better work-life balance in a higher-level position. Here's what she wrote to us:

> *I am looking to move up in my current agency to be able to effect change for the better. I am currently a supervisor and at my level, there is only so little I can do to move my office to the right direction. I have been writing my own resume and I feel that I need to bring in the professionals for I need to ensure I stick out from the rest of the candidates. I recently applied to a position that is one step below from the job announcement that I submitted and was referred. However, the agency decided to go with "no selection made." I was then given a debrief and was told that I need to work on my resume and interviewing skills.*

Knowing that she needed to "up" her game, Danielle made the decision to work hard on getting the promotion and sought out a mentor to help build her resume, target announcements, prepare for interviews, and stick with her goal of achieving a promotion. No matter what situation you find yourself in, remember: it all starts with a decision.

After making the decision to get promoted and to seek out help, Danielle moved to the next step: finding and updating her resume. At this stage, she wasn't worried about the finer details of formatting; rather, she was focused on making sure she had an updated resume that reflected her most recent work and responsibilities. Below is a summary of her job block from the position she held at the time she initiated the effort to get a promotion. This resume obviously needed help, but she worked to update it to get the critical duties included.

DHS / US Secret Service
9999 Secret Service Road

June 2015 – Present
Salary: 103,588 USD Per Year
Hours per week: 40

Supervisory Law Enforcement Specialist
(This is a Federal job.)

Series: 1801 **Pay Plan:** GS **Grade:** 13

Duties, Accomplishments and Related Skills:

Directly responsible for the operations within three major cities in Northern California (San Francisco, Oakland, and San Jose). I ensure the conformance to rules, policies, and law by implementing the process for managing risk to Federal facilities. I currently supervise 15 personnel who are responsible for the compliance of the Interagency Security Committee (ISC) standards across programs such as the Protective Security Officer (PSO), Facility Security Assessment (FSA), and Technical Countermeasure programs for physical security. Additionally, I maintain and ensure that all personnel under my supervision have the proper guidance and all necessary certifications to perform uniform law enforcement duties for the protection of life, property, and the rights of individual citizens by enforcing statutes, laws, and government facility rules and regulations and protecting the civil rights of all persons on the property of U.S. Government and adjacent public areas.

In May 2016, I was specifically selected by senior management as the Acting District Commander for the northern district of California. During my term, I have worked with higher level authorities and other local and Federal law enforcement agencies to ensure assistance for security and emergency procedures were met. I have coordinated with Regional staff and Area Commanders for the entire operational undertakings within the district. Additionally, I have conducted supervisory responsibility for subordinate employees such as assigning work, performance appraisals, leave requests, personnel actions, and disciplinary actions. In result of my endeavors, senior management has submitted a temporary promotion (awaiting HQ approval).

Facility Security Assessment Oversight: I ensure that FSA reports are completed on time, are technically accurate, contain proper formatting, grammar, spelling, and meet policy goals for development and presentation by reviewing and commenting on FSAs. I provide feedback and subject matter expertise to those under my supervision to ensure that threats and vulnerabilities are identified and recommendations mitigate the risk.

I explain risk to stakeholders and subordinates to ensure the decisions are made on the recommended technical countermeasures to mitigate deficiencies, and discuss potential consequence of failing to comply with standards. Additionally, I evaluate technical countermeasures that my subordinates recommend and any existing countermeasures to determine if they are reasonable recommendations and functioning within acceptable standard limits.

Manage and Conduct Post Inspections: I ensure that personnel under my supervision conduct post inspections to ensure proper qualifications such as licensing, identification, uniform, and knowledge of post-specific orders and provide documented results to the COR. Additionally, I ensure that personnel under my supervision initiate, update, review post orders, and conduct Functionality Testing for all technical countermeasures to ensure accuracy and compliance.

Law Enforcement Policing and Patrol: I provide subject matter expertise to internal and external stakeholders and work with personnel within my area of command to ensure areas have sufficient policing and patrol. I provide guidance and best practices to those under my supervision and ensure that they complete all required certifications and qualifications and also provide stakeholder requested training as assigned. I prioritize the scheduling of personnel within my area of command to ensure adequate law enforcement coverage is provided to stakeholders. Additionally, I conduct regular site visits, foot patrols, and interactions with tenants, as well as observe facilities within my portfolio in order to proactively deter crime.

Sometimes, the whole idea of starting on a major project like this can feel overwhelming. But it is less so if you focus on one step at a time. By taking a close look at her resume, she was able to take a major step forward in thinking about revising it towards the goal of getting promoted.

All too often, Federal employees file away their performance evaluations and never look at them again. But performance evaluations are rich sources of data and content for building out a successful resume for promotion. Danielle's next step was to review her evaluations, identify key comments from the evaluator, mine the evaluations for accomplishments and data, and use these pieces to develop new accomplishment stories for the next iteration of her Federal resume. Let's take a look at one of Danielle's performance evaluations.

EXERCISE: Can you underline accomplishments that could be added to her resume?

RATER COMMENTS: During this rating period, Danielle has performed multiple duties and positions simultaneously. Danielle is a Firearms Instructor, a collateral duty responsible for qualifying the majority of the law enforcement officers and regional staff with their assigned firearms. Danielle is the Area Commander and oversees the day to day operations and scheduling in her area. Additionally, Danielle has voluntarily been the point of contact for the Northern District and assumed many of the duties of the District Commander. Her performance of this voluntary duty lead to her selection for a temporary promotion to a District Commander position.

As a Firearms Instructor, Danielle has done an outstanding job in making sure that everyone within her area of responsibility is qualified with their assigned weapons. This can be very challenging due to unforeseen changes in schedules, but Danielle always seems to be able to accommodate those changes and complete with qualifications before the end of the quarter. It has been even more challenging recently, as the firing range where the majority of the firearms qualifications and training took place was closed. Danielle worked diligently to locate acceptable firing ranges for law enforcement qualifications and training. After very time consuming searches and many location visits, Danielle was able to locate some facilities suitable for law enforcement qualification and training. Danielle worked with regional staff to establish agreements for use of the facility by staff, funding and billing to pay the establishment for the use, and liability agreements phrased appropriately for the U.S. Government.

As an Area Commander, Danielle oversees the day to day operations, planning for scheduled and unscheduled events and the Facility Security Assessment (FSA) mission for her area. Danielle reviews the assessments for content and quality and most of the FSAs need little or no additional corrections by the time the District Commander or other manager completed the second level of review. Danielle attends several of the Facility Security Committee meetings for the major facilities in her area and works closely with designated officials and facility mangers to address concerns that impact the security of the facility.

In the absence of a District Commander, Danielle voluntarily accepted a position as the point of contact for the District, and assumed many of the duties of the District Commander. While performing these duties, Danielle's oversight and organizational skills allowed her to track the status, progress, completion, and presentation of the assigned FSAs in her district. These skills contributed to her District completing the FSA mission before the established due date. Her performance of these duties led to Danielle being selected for a temporary promotion as Acting District Commander. In this position, Danielle has been successfully overseeing her District's operations while meeting deadlines, responding to HQ inquiries, making sure significant events are monitored, training requirements are met, scheduling and covering training attendance, and making sure no areas are left unmanned. Danielle has been overseeing and / or conducting these aspects (and more) of the district's operations and performance while working with a depleted workforce due to extended absences, transfers, relocations, and resignations.

Danielle represented the agency in a positive manner when she was working as an Acting Area Commander in charge of FPS staff participating in the Super Bowl 50 operation. Danielle worked in the Emergency Operations Center which was responsible for safety, security, and emergency response to any threats that could impact the Super Bowl Event. During this operation, Danielle formed liaisons with senior managers from various Federal, state, and local agencies while obtaining information and intelligence to enhance the protection of Federal facilities located in close proximity to the event. Danielle also provided informational updates to the overall incident commander so that accurate information was provided to the FPS Joint Information Management Center.

As a Commander and part of the key management staff, Danielle is responsive to calls and emails at all hours of the day and night. Even while on leave out of the country, Danielle was responsive, when HQ requested the region to contact her and check on her status because she was visiting locations that were close to areas of political turmoil and a coup attempt. Danielle responded and provided the required information in a timely manner so the region could respond to the HQ request.

While performance evaluations aren't often compelling reading, they do demonstrate senior management's view of the employee's contributions to the mission as well as major achievements. As you can see from Danielle's evaluation, there's quite a bit of material that can be culled and developed for the resume. Her work during the rating period represented not just getting the job done, but demonstrated initiative, leadership, communication, and the ability to manage complex situations. Each of her achievements, then, needed to get refocused into accomplishment stories for the resume.

Now, if you went back to Danielle's performance evaluation, could you identify major accomplishments? Take a moment and review the rater's comments and underline or highlight the pieces that you think could be developed into accomplishment stories for a resume. What did you find? This is exactly what we asked Danielle to do and she came up with her top ten by looking across her previous evaluations.

Danielle created some of her Top Ten List of Accomplishments from her Evaluations.

Now, why don't you take a moment and dig out some of your performance evaluations and review them for yourself. Can you come up with a list of your top ten accomplishments? These should not be duties, but narratives of accomplishments presented as brief paragraph essays. Your stories should elevate your application above the competition. Accomplishment narratives use the Challenge, Context, Actions, Results format, which we described earlier in the book. Double-check that for each story you've included the challenge, context, actions and results; many applicants forget to describe the actions or results

After you've created your Top 10 list of stories and outlined each one in the CCAR format, it's time to map the stories to leadership competencies. The best way of doing this is looking to the Executive Core Qualifications used for evaluating SES candidates. Even if you're not aiming for Senior Executive Service, these are still the framework for thinking about leadership in the context of the Federal government. If one of your stories talks about forming partnerships, you could map it to the leadership competency called Building Coalitions. If another story focuses on personnel supervision and conflict resolution, it might illustrate Leading People. Even if you write compelling stories in the CCAR format, should they not map to leadership competencies, they won't support your application in the review process.

TOP TEN LIST OF ACCOMPLISHMENTS
DHS, US SECRET SERVICE, 2015 TO PRESENT

In May 2016, I was selected by senior management as the Acting District Commander for the northern district of California. My selection was tied to the need to effectuate changes in organizational security assessment, program oversight, and agent training. *(Leading Change)*

I led sweeping changes in security assessment, program oversight, and agent firearms training. Due to superior performance, and my ability to achieve results, senior management temporarily promoted me to District Commander; GS-1801-14 position on January 2017. *(Results Driven)*

In the absence of a District Commander, voluntarily accepted a position as the point of contact for the District and assumed many of the duties of the District Commander. *(External Awareness)*

Improved supervision and mentoring procedures for Special Agent training, communications and career development. Improved retention, evaluations and morale during complex case investigations and overtime performance. *(Leading People, Developing Others)*

Directed security operations within three major cities in Northern California (San Francisco, Oakland, and San Jose). I ensured the conformance to rules, policies, and law by implementing the process for managing risk to Federal facilities. *(Business Acumen, Human Resources)*

Served as Acting Area Commander in charge of FPS staff participating in the Super Bowl 50 operation. Managed the Emergency Operations Center directing safety, security, and emergency response to any threats that could impact the Super Bowl Event. *(Building Coalitions, Political Savvy, Partnership)*

As a Firearms Instructor, located facilities suitable for law enforcement qualification and training. Worked with regional staff to establish agreements for use of the facility by FPS staff, funding and billing to pay the establishment for the use, and liability agreements phrased appropriately for the U.S. Government. *(Leading People, Developing Others)*

I managed Dakota Access Pipeline Protest that was directed to the Army Corps of Engineers Office in San Francisco. Monitored protest activity of about 2,000 protesters. *(Results Driven, Decisiveness, Problem-Solving)*

Effectively managed critical protective response to post-election protests of Nov 2016. Collaborated closely with Oakland Police Department in the EOC for monitoring protest activity of 7,000 protesters. *(Building Coalitions, Partnering)*

Improved post inspection processes to improve risk assessments and Functional Testing. Created a streamlined checksheet and created online database for improved information management for interviews, inspection and identification of documentation. Resulted in increased non-compliance findings. *(Business Acumen, Technology Management)*

People tend to under-report their accomplishments because they're afraid it will come across as "bragging." Here's the thing, when you're trying to get promoted, the resume is the one place where bragging is not just socially acceptable, it is essential. Step out of your comfort zone, think about what you're proud of, and share that in your resume—not only will it make you feel better about your work, it will get the attention of the Hiring Manager. If we go back to thinking about the resume as an argument—an argument to persuade someone to hire you—then the use of storytelling is a particularly effective method because humans are hardwired to appreciate good stories.

HOT TIP!
Look at the Executive Core Qualification Core Competencies on pages 126 and 127. They can inspire you to write your Top Ten List of Accomplishments.

USAJOBS.gov is the official website for government jobs, managed by the Office of Personnel Management. Here you will find jobs for most Federal agencies. This website is a great starting place for Federal jobs in your geographic region as the search engine allows you to be very specific. You can even save your searches and have notifications sent right to you when there is an announcement that matches your interests! Using USAJOBS to research announcements for your promotion is an important step. Spending time conducting research into what qualities are being sought after for your target promotion will inform your approach to developing keywords, building your resume for promotion, and even preparing for the interview.

In Danielle's case, she was aiming for a GS-14. So, she studied target GS-14 job announcements to get a clear sense of the keywords, qualifications, KSAs, and language that she could use to develop her resume. Research can be time intensive, but it is an important—even crucial—part of the process.

Let's take a look at a few examples of what Danielle found in her announcement research:

Supervisory Criminal Investigator (Group Supervisor) GS-1811-14

DEPARTMENT OF JUSTICE
Bureau of Alcohol, Tobacco, Firearms, and Explosives

Qualifications

Applicants must have one year of specialized experience equivalent to the next lower grade in the Federal service. Specialized experience is experience which is in, or directly related to, the line of work of this position and which has equipped the applicant with particular knowledge, skills and abilities to successfully perform the duties of the position. To meet the specialized experience requirements, you must demonstrate that you possess appropriate experience in, or have shown the potential to develop, the qualities of successful leadership such as: Judgment and Problem Solving; Plan, Organize and Prioritize; Lead Others; Relate to Others; General Investigative Knowledge; Knowledge of Relevant Laws, Regulations, and Policies; measured during ATF's EPAS.

Supervisory Criminal Investigator, GS-1811-14
Small Business Administration
Office of the Inspector General
Salary
$110,231 to $156,758 per year
This position is entitled to availability pay. Availability pay is fixed at 25 percent of a criminal investigator's rate of basic pay.

SPECIALIZED EXPERIENCE STATEMENT:
You must demonstrate one year of specialized experience at a level of difficulty and responsibility equivalent to the GS-13 in the Federal service that is directly in, or related to, the work of the position to be filled. Specialized experience for this position is defined as: independently initiating investigations from informant tips or leads; developing evidence by interviews, documentary searches, surveillance, etc.; establishing interrelationships of facts or evidence; investigating sensitive, controversial subjects; participating on multi-agency taskforce and performing dangerous and extensive undercover and surveillance work.

How You Will Be Evaluated
You will be evaluated for this job based on how well you meet the qualifications above. Applicants meeting basic eligibility requirements will be further evaluated based on the information provided in the Occupational Questionnaire. To preview this questionnaire, click on the following link: https://apply.usastaffing.gov/ViewQuestionnaire/10484569. You will be rated based on your responses to the occupational questionnaire. The occupational questions relate to the following Competencies required to do the work of this position:

- Criminal Investigation
- Oral Communication
- Writing

You will have to spend time playing around with your search criteria to get the right combination of flexibility and specificity, especially if you are researching announcements for a promotion.

Do a treasure hunt search for the link in the announcement that says "View the Questionnaire" (or similar phrase). Here is your magic list of the knowledge, skills, and abilities for the job announcement. If you cannot answer E or Expert for at least 85% of those questions, then you need not apply. Getting closer to 95% is even better. This is true for any job announcement, but even more so if you are aiming for a promotion. It is important to neither deflate nor inflate your answers, though most people tend to shortchange themselves by deflating their answers. Remember to support your answers in your resume!

Remember: the resume must be matched to the language of the announcement. Anything less will result in a failed application. Identifying keywords and key phrases can seem like a lot of work because, well, it is. It can also be tricky. If you're looking at a long paragraph of content in the Specialized Experience section, you might feel overwhelmed by the attempt to essentialize it down into a list of 5-to-7 words or phrases. Even so, remember those who succeed at applying for Federal jobs are those who emphasize quality over quantity—this isn't a numbers game. Really, it is simply about doing a quality job of reviewing the announcement and reflecting the announcement back in the resume.

Let's take a look at a some of the keywords Danielle identified. In this example, we'll look through each component of a job announcement—duties section, qualifications section, and how you will be evaluated section—to identify keywords. We've identified our keywords here. How does your analysis of each section of the announcement match up?

SUPERVISORY CRIMINAL INVESTIGATOR—ATF

PROBLEM SOLVING

PLAN, ORGANIZE, AND PRIORITIZE

LEAD OTHERS / RELATE TO OTHERS

GENERAL INVESTIGATIVE KNOWLEDGE

KNOWLEDGE OF RELEVANT LAWS, REGULATIONS, AND POLICIES

SUPERVISORY CRIMINAL INVESTIGATOR—OIG, SMALL BUSINESS ADMINISTRATION

SUPERVISE SPECIAL AGENTS

CRIMINAL INVESTIGATION

INITIATE INVESTIGATIONS

DEVELOP EVIDENCE FROM INTERVIEWS, DOCUMENT SEARCH, AND SURVEILLANCE

ESTABLISH INTERRELATIONSHIPS OF FACTS AND EVIDENCE

INVESTIGATE SENSITIVE AND CONTROVERSIAL SUBJECTS

MEMBER OF MULTI-AGENCY TASKFORCE

CRIMINAL INVESTIGATOR—DEPARTMENT OF THE INTERIOR

INCIDENT COMMAND SYSTEM

KNOWLEDGE OF FRAMEWORK FOR FEDERAL RESPONSE TO SECURITY INCIDENTS

MANAGE INTERNAL AND EXTERNAL COORDINATED RESPONSE INITIATIVES

AUDIT AND CONDUCT BUREAU INTERNAL AFFAIR PROGRAMS

DEVELOP NATIONAL POLICIES AND STANDARDS FOR LAW ENFORCEMENT AND SECURITY PROGRAMS

Your answers to the online assessment will be used to evaluate your competencies.

Auditing – knowledge of laws and policies surrounding internal affairs investigations and administrative personnel proceedings to audit internal affairs programs.

Security – knowledge of National Security policies, Executive orders, practices and standards pertaining to personnel, physical, information, document, and industrial security in order to develop, implement and administer security programs.

Emergency Management – knowledge of the Incident Command System and the framework for a coordinated Federal response to security incidents, natural disasters, and national emergencies in order to manage both internal and external coordinated response initiatives on behalf of the Department.

Interpersonal Communication – skill successfully communicating verbally with a wide variety of people who may be adversarial, challenging, or difficult including in sensitive, controversial, or critical situations.

Written Communication – skill drafting national policies, standards, guidelines, and procedures pertaining to the law enforcement and security programs.

Step 07 Study Executive Core Qualifications (ECQs)

If you're aiming for a promotion, we recommend spending time seriously studying the **five Executive Core Qualifications (ECQs),** which define the competencies needed to build a Federal corporate culture that drives for results, serves customers, and builds successful teams and coalitions within and outside the organization.

Leading Change – Leading People – Results Driven – Business Acumen – Building Coalitions

Executive Core Qualifications are used for evaluating Senior Executive Service (SES) candidates. Even if you're not aiming for SES, these are still the best framework for thinking about leadership competencies in the context of the Federal government. If one of your stories talks about forming partnerships, you could map it to the leadership competency called Building Coalitions. If another story focuses on personnel supervision and conflict resolution, it might illustrate Leading People. Even if you write compelling stories in the CCAR format, if they do not map to leadership competencies, they won't support your application in the review process. The bottom line here is that if you want to get promoted, you should develop a clear sense of how your professional journey has helped build a Federal corporate culture that drives for results, serves customers, and builds successful teams and coalitions within and outside the organization. Let's take a closer look…

1 – Leading Change
This core qualification involves the ability to bring about strategic change, both within and outside the organization, to meet organizational goals. Inherent to this ECQ is the ability to establish an organizational vision and to implement it in a continuously changing environment.
Creativity and Innovation: Develops new insights into situations; questions conventional approaches; encourages new ideas and innovations; designs and implements new or cutting edge programs/processes.
External Awareness: Understands and keeps up-to-date on local, national, and international policies and trends that affect the organization and shape stakeholders' views; is aware of the organization's impact on the external environment.
Flexibility: Is open to change and new information; rapidly adapts to new information, changing conditions, or unexpected obstacles.
Resilience: Deals effectively with pressure; remains optimistic and persistent, even under adversity. Recovers quickly from setbacks.
Strategic Thinking: Formulates objectives and priorities, and implements plans consistent with long-term interests of the organization in a global environment. Capitalizes on opportunities and manages risks.
Vision: Takes a long-term view and builds a shared vision with others; acts as a catalyst for organizational change. Influences others to translate vision into action.

2 – Leading People
This core qualification involves the ability to lead people toward meeting the organization's vision, mission, and goals. Inherent to this ECQ is the ability to provide an inclusive workplace that fosters the development of others, facilitates cooperation and teamwork, and supports constructive resolution of conflicts.
Conflict Management: Encourages creative tension and differences of opinions. Anticipates and takes steps to prevent counter-productive confrontations. Manages and resolves conflicts and disagreements in a constructive manner.
Leveraging Diversity: Fosters an inclusive workplace where diversity and individual differences are valued and leveraged to achieve the vision and mission of the organization.
Developing Others: Develops the ability of others to perform and contribute to the organization by

providing ongoing feedback and by providing opportunities to learn through formal and informal methods. Team Building: Inspires and fosters team commitment, spirit, pride, and trust. Facilitates cooperation and motivates team members to accomplish group goals.

3 – Results Driven

This core qualification involves the ability to meet organizational goals and customer expectations. Inherent to this ECQ is the ability to make decisions that produce high-quality results by applying technical knowledge, analyzing problems, and calculating risks.

Accountability: Holds self and others accountable for measurable high-quality, timely, and cost-effective results. Determines objectives, sets priorities, and delegates work. Accepts responsibility for mistakes. Complies with established control systems and rules.

Customer Service: Anticipates and meets the needs of both internal and external customers. Delivers high-quality products and services; is committed to continuous improvement.

Decisiveness: Makes well-informed, effective, and timely decisions, even when data are limited or solutions produce unpleasant consequences; perceives the impact and implications of decisions.

Entrepreneurship: Positions the organization for future success by identifying new opportunities; builds the organization by developing or improving products or services. Takes calculated risks to accomplish organizational objectives.

Problem Solving: Identifies and analyzes problems; weighs relevance and accuracy of information; generates and evaluates alternative solutions; makes recommendations.

Technical Credibility: Understands and appropriately applies principles, procedures, requirements, regulations, and policies related to specialized expertise.

4 – Business Acumen

This core qualification involves the ability to manage human, financial, and information resources strategically.

Financial Management: Understands the organization's financial processes. Prepares, justifies, and administers the program budget. Oversees procurement and contracting to achieve desired results. Monitors expenditures and uses cost-benefit thinking to set priorities.

Human Capital Management: Builds and manages the workforce based on organizational goals, budget considerations, and staffing needs. Ensures that employees are appropriately recruited, selected, appraised, and rewarded; takes action to address performance problems. Manages a multi-sector workforce and a variety of work situations.

Technology Management: Keeps up-to-date on technological developments. Makes effective use of technology to achieve results. Ensures access to and security of technology systems.

5 – Building Coalitions

This core qualification involves the ability to build coalitions internally and with other Federal agencies, State and local governments, nonprofit and private sector organizations, foreign governments, or international organizations to achieve common goals.

Partnering: Develops networks and builds alliances, collaborates across boundaries to build strategic relationships and achieve common goals.

Political Savvy: Identifies the internal and external politics that impact the work of the organization. Perceives organizational and political reality and acts accordingly.

Influencing/Negotiating: Persuades others; builds consensus through give and take; gains cooperation from others to obtain information and accomplish goals.

Step 08 — Write and Target **Your Federal Resume**

Part 2

GS-14 Target - Ready to Submit!

Having completed all the previous steps, it is now time to re-write your Federal resume targeted for a promotion. Remember Danielle and the resume we looked at in Step #2? After making the decision to get promoted, she followed each of the steps to get to the stage of rewriting her Federal resume. **Her new Federal resume targeted specific keywords from target promotion announcements and incorporated accomplishment paragraphs that demonstrated leadership competencies.** Below is a summary of her job block from the position she held at the time she initiated the effort to get a promotion.

Supervisory Law Enforcement Specialist; Area Commander (GS-1801-13), Jun 2015 to Jan 2017
DHS / US Secret Service, Oakland, CA
Salary: $103,588
Job Type: 40 hours per week, Full-Time

LAW ENFORCEMENT & FACILITY PROTECTION OVERSIGHT: Oversee and maintain full responsibility of Federal facility protection operations within three major cities in Northern California. Lead criminal investigations involving Federal laws and facilities. Supervise 21 sworn Law Enforcement Officers who are responsible for the security and law enforcement of Federal facilities in the compliance of the Interagency Security Committee (ISC) standards across programs such as Facility Security Assessment (FSA), and Technical Countermeasure programs for physical security. Deliver guidance and direction for all personnel under my supervision, ensuring proper and necessary certifications for performance of uniform law enforcement duties involving the protection of life, property, and the rights of individual citizens.

SUPERVISORY OVERSIGHT OF SECURITY AND PROTECTION OPERATIONS: Closely collaborate with high-level executives and other local and Federal law enforcement agencies to accomplish programmatic goals for security and emergency procedures. Coordinate with senior staff and other supervisors to ensure consistent operational success within the district. Perform full supervisory roles and responsibilities for subordinate employees including assigning work; administering performance appraisals and personnel actions; developing skills; assigning and recommending training; and mentoring. Accept and make proper action upon employee complaints and grievances.

TECHNICAL INVESTIGATIVE GUIDANCE: As Federal security and facilities subject matter expert, provide guidance to internal and external stakeholders and works collaboratively with personnel within area of responsibility to ensure sufficiency of policing, patrol, security, and antiterrorism measures. Advocate for best practices to subordinate employees concerning all law enforcement functions; ensure completion of all required certifications and qualifications. Prioritize scheduling of personnel within area of responsibility to ensure adequate law enforcement coverage is provided throughout the area. Liaise with law enforcement agencies at the local, state, and national level by conducting regular site visits, foot patrols, and interactions with stakeholders, law enforcement agencies.

CRIMINAL INVESTIGATIVE ANALYSIS & EVALUATION: Regularly conduct investigations from the start of the initial crime scene through collections of evidence, interviewing, prosecution, and disposition of cases. Ensure supervised personnel perform preliminary criminal investigations by preserving crime scenes, conducting comprehensive review of all available evidence, collecting statements, and prepare investigative findings and reports and make recommendations for the Criminal Investigator. Review reports and provides senior analytical assistance including the evaluation of allegations and evidence; ensuring compliance of the investigative process with all applicable laws, rules, and regulations of the criminal justice system.

KEY ACCOMPLISHMENTS

Federal FACILITIES PROTECTION: Effectively managed critical protective response to post-election protests. Collaborated closely with Oakland Police Department for monitoring protest activity of 7,000 protesters. Managed operations and staff for two 17-hour days in a row. Maintained staff in the Federal building throughout the protest events. Kept regional staff informed of protests and impacts on Federal facilities and property. Closely monitored San Francisco and San Jose as well, as the only supervisor working both cities. Responded quickly and effectively to emergent challenges—vandalism and a car accident involving one of my officers. Completed the mission despite a small assigned staff and multiple locations to manage. Also, effectively managed a follow-on protest three days later despite budgetary constraints and an overworked staff.

Also in Nov 2016, I managed oversight activities of the Dakota Access Pipeline Protest directed to the Army Corps of Engineers Office in San Francisco. Monitored protest activity of about 2,000 protesters. Collaborated with San Francisco Police Department and ensured the safety of Federal sister-agencies. Prior to the protest, I met with the Designated Official and his staff and briefed instructions in the event of the facility being overrun. I also met with building security to ensure we all had a plan for the worst-case scenario. During the protest, I facilitated the meeting between the organizer of the protest and the Designated Official, while ensuring all persons were safe during the meeting. I also supervised the USSS staff and strategically placed them where most needed. Working together with the local Police Department, we kept protesters off property and denied entry to the facility.

If you're aiming for a promotion, you absolutely must be prepared for the Federal interview format, the Behavior-Based Interview. You'll need to give examples in answers to seven-to-ten questions that will be situation or experience based. If you have an example of how you led a team, delivered training, or managed a project, be prepared to talk about the experience, and your specific actions and the results. The best answers are examples that demonstrate past performance.

Key Tips

Know the paperwork. Know the vacancy announcement, agency mission, and office function. Read your resume and KSAs out loud and with enthusiasm to make sure that you're acquainted with all your materials. Become convinced that you are very well qualified for the job and that the agency needs you to help achieve their mission.

Do Your Research. Go online to research the agency, department, and position. Read press releases about the organization, and even check the news to see if there are any hot topics or recent news events that can inform you about the types of leaders the agency might be looking for.

Focus on Confidence, Knowledge, and Skills. In order to sell yourself for your promotion, you MUST believe in your abilities. Read books and listen to podcasts that will help boost your confidence and give you the support you need to brag on your leadership and work skills. Don't forget or be afraid to use "I"!

Practice – in front of a mirror, a video recording device, a family member, a friend, or even your dog. Practice with anyone who will agree to spend time helping you finetune your storytelling techniques.

Danielle did all of these things in preparation. In fact, Danielle spent a significant amount of time with a senior leader / mentor in her agency to do interview preparation when she found out that she had been referred for her target promotion. She reviewed her accomplishment stories, did her research, and practiced her interviewing techniques to get prepared.

HOT TIP!
Use your Top Ten List of Accomplishments to prepare for your interview. Practice these accomplishments! Try for 1 to 2 minutes per accomplishment.

Danielle made a decision, followed the steps, maintained her patience, and worked persistently to get her materials—and herself—prepared for her promotion. She interviewed successfully and was hired into a GS-14 position! You can do this, too.

Like Danielle, if you want to position yourself to move into a new job or gain a promotion, you need to do something that makes the difference between staying where you are and moving up. No one is going to come along and just promote you or hire you away into your dream job. You must develop a plan. If you will invest just one hour per week in long-term planning and goal-setting for your career development, the investment in yourself will be like money in the bank when you land that new job or a promotion.

Some final pieces of guidance. Know yourself. What are your personal limits? What are you willing to do to move up? Are you mobile? Are you willing to change your geographic location or move to a different agency? There is nothing wrong with wanting to stay where you are, but your career strategy will have to be much different than that of someone who is willing to move or change agencies.

Don't worry that you might not qualify for your dream job right now, that's why you're making a plan. Think about the characteristics of your dream job rather than a specific job title. For instance, do you want a job that allows you to use your communications skills or other special talents? Do you want a job that allows you to use flex time? Thinking in terms of characteristics of the job rather than its classification will help you see possibilities other than the ones you already know about.

Expand your picture. What kinds of jobs would have some or all of the characteristics you'd like? Write them down, even if you aren't qualified for them right now. Consider the obstacles. What stands in your way? Don't be too quick to conclude you need an extra degree or a different credential—what you actually may need are different skills. Make a plan for overcoming each obstacle. You must face the barriers that stand between where you are now and where you want to go. If you don't have the right skills, how can you get them? If you don't know the right people, how can you meet them?

Finally, develop a timeline. Once you identify your goals, the obstacles, and how you'll overcome them, you need to assign a time line to achieve those goals. Ask yourself, "When do I want to achieve my goal?" Then break your plan down into phases or steps. What do you need to do first? Is there a step you need to take before that? Work backward until you identify the very first action you need to take to reach your goal.

One hour a week doesn't seem like a lot of time, and it isn't. But that's all you need to focus on at this point. In one hour, you could gather all the material you need for your resume. In one hour, you could read your or another agency's website to review new programs and mission statements.

The advantage of spending one hour per week is that it keeps you from feeling overwhelmed by a long-term project. In just a few sessions, you will be amazed at how much progress you've made. Setting up and going through this process will give you a feeling of immense control and personal security. If there's a set-back in your agency, you don't have to panic: you're already on your way to something better. If you don't like a particular offer or work situation, you don't have to let desperation drive your decision; you can continue to develop yourself. Invest time in yourself: it will make the difference.

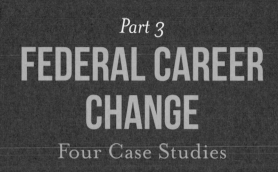

Four important Federal career change stories and case studies will demonstrate how a person can move into government, around in government, and out of government. Have you been in the same position for over five years? Are you ready for a change? If you are a current Federal employee, are you trying to change your job series? If you are a private industry jobseeker, are you trying to change your position or career to enter government service? If you are one of these people, then you need a "career change resume," and this chapter is for you!

Getting **Promoted**

The honest truth is that career change can be tricky. These transitions will require you to overcome additional hurdles and face unique challenges that other jobseekers won't be facing. However, you are not alone. Many people are interested in making a career change, and we have coached hundreds of clients through this transition. Some real life examples of jobseekers who have successfully made a career change include the following:

1 **PRIVATE SECTOR TO FEDERAL**

An overworked veteran and Truck Driver obtains a great career as Material Handler with the US Navy as a civilian.

2 **PRIVATE SECTOR TO FEDERAL**

A deserving Recent Graduate lands a position with the US Army Corps of Engineers.

3 **EXTREME FEDERAL CAREER CHANGER**

An Extreme Federal Career Changer - leaving a stressful Social Work job to become a Park Ranger.

4 **FEDERAL TO PRIVATE SECTOR**

Two Federal Employees need two-page resumes to leave government or start a consulting practice.

How do you get started with a career change?

Make a commitment. A successful career change to the Federal government could increase the opportunities available to you over the remainder of your career. Keep this in mind and commit to putting in the effort that's needed to be hired. Whether you want a more stable career, or want promotion potential that the government is so famous for, or just want a better situation, having your goal (the new position and the benefits it will bring) in focus will help motivate you to be persistent with this Federal resume and campaign.

Get to know the rules. The rules for applying are unique and different between Federal jobs and the private sector. Be aware of this as you try to cross over, no matter which direction you are going. Also be aware that you'll come across additional rules—some undisclosed—as you job hunt. For instance, the procedures can change periodically. The way to be aware of the hidden changes is by "being in the game" and learning through trial and error.

Become acquainted with the playing field. Like athletes who are intimately familiar with their field of play, you'll need to know your targeted agencies or companies inside and out. To research Federal agencies, link to the agency websites from USAJOBS.GOV. Check out each agency's mission, current programs, customers, and new initiatives. Read their press releases. Also, stop by washingtonpost.com to get up to date on related news. In addition, visit whitehouse.gov and scan the President's agenda to see how it may be affecting the agencies you've selected.

Speak the right lingo. No matter where you are applying, using the right keywords is critical to your success. Do your keyword search in the job announcement and match your experience to these words in your resume.

Offer to mentor new staff or interns. Be an effective "change agent" and embrace reinvention at work.

Pursue in-house or other training that may help you in your current and future position. You may be pleasantly surprised at the training opportunities that are "there for the asking."

Remember that relevant "volunteer" work, although unpaid, helps build your competencies. For instance, you will be credited for all of your qualifying experience, including volunteer experience, that you clearly include on your Federal resume.

Don't stay in a job for too long before trying to move up. Once you have a few years of experience under your belt, start looking for opportunities at the next level. Even if you don't succeed at first, establishing your interest in upward mobility sends an important message to your management team. If you find your current environment stimulating and there are opportunities to grow, explore those first. If not, familiarize yourself with the missions and goals of other companies and agencies (perhaps those where your skills could best be utilized) and apply for opportunities in those places.

NETWORK, NETWORK, NETWORK! Embrace this mantra! Join professional organizations, alumni associations, and relevant LinkedIn® groups. Make sure that you have a professional social networking presence. Attend luncheons where you are likely to learn and mingle. If appropriate, seek "informational" interviews with managers in prospective offices.

Sell yourself with accomplishments. Throughout your application, be sure to highlight your best accomplishments in previous jobs. Three to five accomplishments per Federal resume will help the resume to stand out! Each accomplishment should be a short story, 4 or 5 sentences. For Federal the accomplishments can make the difference between getting Qualified or Best Qualified and even Referred to a Supervisor. The Federal accomplishments are longer than the typical private sector version.

Beyond these general guidelines, the following pages review our top ten steps for applying strategic thinking to your goal for a promotion. Let's get started.

Career Change: **Private Industry to Fed**

Moving from the private sector to Federal employment can be daunting, especially if you're unfamiliar with the processes involved in Federal hiring. So, it is a really good idea to follow the recommendations in this book and to spend a significant amount of time familiarizing yourself with Federal hiring. Here are some differences between applying for a Federal job vs. a private sector position:

Amount of Time Invested

Your initial effort to create your first Federal resume (which is on average 3 to 5 pages long) will be at least 10 hours to review the samples in this book, sign up for USAJOBS.gov, start using the Resume Builder, find vacancy announcements, study the announcements for qualifications and keywords, review the OPM standards, and write your Federal resume. When you begin your Federal job search, we recommend that you dedicate at least one and a half hours of prep time to each USAJOBS application.

Furthermore, though the length of time it takes to apply for Federal jobs has been getting shorter, expect that it will still take longer than applying for private industry positions because of the Federal hiring process. Also, considering that it may take some trial and error to get through the entire process correctly, do not be surprised if your Federal job search takes at least six months to complete. The Office of Personnel Management has stated that most hires are supposed to take 80 days from the closing date of the job announcement until you are "sitting in the chair" at work.

Federal Resume Requirements

Use the USAJOBS Resume Builder for your first draft: The Federal resume, unlike the private industry resume, must contain specific information in it, or you will automatically be removed from consideration for the job. We always recommend that first-time Federal jobseekers use the USAJOBS builder to build their first Federal resume. The builder will steer you through WHAT SHOULD BE INCLUDED in the Federal resume. Often newbies to the process will upload their two-page private sector resume into the USAJOBS document section. This can result in ineligibility due to the lack of specific information needed by Federal HR, such as month and years of employment (back at least ten years); supervisor's names and phones; street addresses, cities, states, zip codes, and country. This info must be in a Federal resume, but not necessarily your private sector resume.

Federal Resume Length

Don't use your private sector resume. That resume is too short. The average private sector resume is 2 pages. **The average Federal resume is 3 to 5 pages in length.** ◀

Federal Resume Format

Write a narrative resume in the "Outline Format," which consists of small paragraphs (5 to 10 lines long), narrative statements, including a headline of 3 to 7 ALL CAP KEYWORDS. These keywords match the specialized experience and KSAs in the job announcement. HR specialists can see the match between the resume and the announcement in seconds. The narrative writing style provides more details about a skill set for the HR specialist and the manager.

All of the HAPPY Federal resume samples in this book are in the Outline Format.

What Federal Jobs Are Called

Job titles are worded differently in government. Let's say you're an office manager in the private sector. This position, in the Federal arena, could be labeled an "administrative manager," "quality assurance manager," or "production control manager," etc. How can you translate your job title into Federal language? One option is to read through the vacancy announcements for an agency that interests you; you'll find the announcements through the usajobs.gov site by searching by agency. Analyze the job duties in the announcements, asking yourself which openings you're qualified for.

You can also read the official descriptions of most of the positions in government here: https://www.opm.gov/policy-data-oversight/classification-qualifications/classifying-general-schedule-positions/#url=Standards

Here are some samples of typical private sector positions translated into Federal job titles. Or you can search for OPM Classification Standards.

Federal Job Titles	Private Sector Job Titles
Administrative Officer or Administrative Specialist (GS 0341)	Administrative Assistant
Program Analyst (GS-0343)	Analyst, Market Analyst, Business System Analyst, Pharmaceutical Specialist, General Manager, Operations Manager, even Sous Chef (basically, any position requiring program analysis)
Business and Industry Group (GS-1100)	Sales / Marketing, Realtor, Mortgage Banker, Investment Banker, General Contractor (construction), Business Owner, Property Manager, Retail Sales, and any position that involves developing, negotiating, presenting and managing / administering contracts
Inspection, Investigation, Enforcement, and Compliance Group (GS-1800)	Law Enforcement, Security, Investigator, Quality Assurance, Risk Analyst, Inspector
Supply Group (GS-2000)	Supply Specialist, Inventory Control Specialist, Sales Representative, Wholesale Sales Rep, Manufacturing Rep, Production Control Rep, Merchandise Management

Which Grade or Salary Level Is Appropriate For You?

Many private sector to Federal career changers are challenged by this question.

First, read the GS Schedule and locality pay scales to become familiar with the salaries / GS Schedules in government. Or you can search for OPM GS Salary Schedules.
https://www.opm.gov/policy-data-oversight/pay-leave/salaries-wages/2019/general-schedule/

There are several ways to determine the grade or salary level for which you can qualify the best. Your current salary might match the government salary. Look at the GS Schedule and find your salary in your regional geographic area and see which GS grade you currently match.

For instance, if you currently earn $65,000 and you want to make a min of $65K in government, then you would want to apply for GS-11 or 12 positions (for areas without locality pay added).

If you live in the Washington, DC area, and you want to earn $65K, the locality pay added to the base salary is 27%, so you could apply for GS-9 positions to make $65K. This adjustment could increase your likelihood of getting hired at the lower level as a first-time applicant.

HOT TIP from Federal Human Resources Specialists: Apply for the lowest possible grade that you can afford to take to get into the system. If you can afford to take the GS 9 to begin your career, that could help you get hired faster.

Read the announcements for several grade levels for the position that will match your qualifications the best. Do you have the qualifications for GS 9, 11, 12, 13, 14, 15?

Look for career ladder positions. Some positions have a range of possible grade levels and will have a promotion potential in the vacancy announcement that is higher than the lowest level that the position could be hired at. These positions allow you to qualify at a lower level and later, if your performance is good, you'll be promoted to the highest level indicated without competition.

Start applying. It may take some trial and error. See what your results are, whether you are determined to be Eligible, Ineligible, Best Qualified, or Referred. Research why you were found Ineligible or Referred.

Call the HR person listed on the job announcement. You CAN call or send emails to the HR person on the announcement to ask about WHY you were ineligible or Not Best Qualified.

Adding your salary info in the USAJOBS Builder is optional. If you are trying to get a position that is equal to your current earnings, then be sure to add the salary to your Federal resumes. If you are currently working for less than your desired income level (e.g., at a non-profit or in state government), you could leave the salary information out of the resume.

Next, let's take a look at a couple of examples of private industry resumes rewritten to apply for Federal positions.

Private Sector to Fed: Success Story #1

★ ★ ★

Meet Eric

Eric Lower: Private Sector, Veteran seeking a WG position as Material Handler with a DOD agency
Eric's First Target Position: Material Handler, 6907, WG-8, US Navy

Eric was driving trucks for Goodwill Industries and previously with other carriers and was very unhappy with his work and pay. He was a Veteran and he could use Veterans Preference if his resume would be at least QUALIFIED for a Federal position. His job at Goodwill drove him to want a Federal position where the work would be better quality, consistent, and better pay and benefits. He wanted a steady career with a DOD agency, preferably the Navy as Material Handler, Rigger or Motor Carrier Operator. Success story: He was hired as Material Handler, US Navy; and one year later obtained the Rigger position at the same location, and a promotion. Eric's resume had to match these qualifications and include all of the USAJOBS compliance information.

Success Story: Hired!

TARGET POSITION: MATERIAL HANDLER, 6907, WG-8, US NAVY
TARGET LANGUAGE TO MATCH THE RESUME; HOW YOU WILL BE EVALUATED

This job has a screen-out element which will be used to determine minimum eligibility for this job. Applicants who do not receive a minimum of two points on the screen-out element(s) will be found ineligible: Ability to do the work of a Material Handler without more than normal supervision such as...

- ❯ Performing a full range of Material Handler tasks including work involving ordnance material and operations as related to the receipt, issuing, storage, handling, segregation, renovation, preservation, and pack of such items and accurately maintaining inventories.
- ❯ KNOWLEDGE OF MATERIALS
- ❯ TECHNICAL PRACTICES (THEORETICAL, PRECISE, ARTISTIC)
- ❯ WORK PRACTICES (INCLUDES KEEPING THINGS NEAT, CLEAN AND IN ORDER)

Private Sector to Fed: **Success Story #1**

☹ *This example shows what NOT to do.*

BEFORE RESUME – TOO SHORT, NO USAJOBS COMPLIANCE INFO; NO DUTIES OR MATCHING LANGUAGE TO THE ANNOUNCEMENT

Eric Lower

Work Experience

2017 – UPS Seasonal Delivery Driver

I provide subject matter expertise to internal and external stakeholders and work with personnel within my area of command to ensure areas have sufficient policing and patrol. I provide guidance and best practices to those under my supervision and ensure that they complete all required certifications and qualifications and also provide stakeholder requested training as assigned. I prioritize the scheduling of personnel within my area of command to ensure adequate law enforcement coverage is provided to stakeholders. Additionally, I conduct regular site visits, foot patrols, and interactions with tenants, as well as observe facilities within my portfolio in order to proactively deter crime.

[03/15/14-Current] US Drivers Atlanta GA

- Temp company working for PTG in Lawrenceville GA. Hauling For Masonite to Home Depot Stores in VA, GA, NC, SC, AL, TN. 53ft Trailers Dry Vans, with Full sleeper Freightliner Tractor. Also worked for Salmon Mail carries, Hauled mail during Christmas season 2014 freightliner day cab Northeast coast

[09/01/2012 – Present] Army National Guard

- CDL Driver – Driver, 88M30, Supervisor and Squad Leader
- Flatbed, Containers, Tanker

[04/01/2012 – 08/31/2012] Brown Brothers Inc. Oklahoma City, OK

- CDL Driver - Class A Oil Field Work.
- Tankers, flat beds, dry vans and mobile offices

[01/02/2012 – 03/30/2012] Lone Tree Ridge LLC Killdeer, ND

CDL Driver – Class A Oil Field Work

- Tanker

[09/2010 – 11/30/2011] Georgia National Guard Doha, Qatar

Barrier NCO (MOS 88M)

- Ensured proper placement of concrete barriers at Camp Al Salia. Directed convoys entering camp, including all fuel transport operations. Relieved drivers without clearance and drove tanker vehicles into restricted, high security areas
- Maintained all logs and reports. Ensured all gates were secured per US Army SOP

[06/2010 – 08/2010] Sal Son Logistics Atlanta, GA

Truck Driver CDL Class A

- Transported dry van products to assigned locations in the Eastern United States
- Ensured proper load stability while in transit and maintained timely arrivals
- Maintained all logs and reports pertaining to maintenance.
- Followed Federal and state regulations

BEFORE RESUME – Continued

Summary of qualifications

Management and Administration:

Supervising, scheduling and training personnel, monitoring expenditures and pertinent records. Assessing needs and establishing work priorities. Controlling inventory, purchasing equipment and supplies and assuring compliance with regulations.

Transportation:

Supervising and operating military convoy operations and civilian heavy transport vehicles for a variety of freight cargo to assigned locations with a strong safety record. Utilizing DOD and Army SOP transportation and logistics data management systems to coordinate, planning, priorities and assignments, while assuring load stability and safe transport of hazardous, explosive, flammable, sensitive, fragile or special cargo in local and international environments.

Communications:

Training and experience in installing, operations and troubleshooting communication equipment utilizing digital testing and calibration equipment. Interfacing with design engineers and other technical staff on systems. Setting up and maintaining technical libraries and parts departments

Education

Armstrong State College	Savannah GA
Primary Leadership Development Course	Fort Stewart GA
Georgia National Guard Truck Driver	Fort Jackson SC
Gwinnett Technical College	Lawrenceville GA

Military Awards

- Army Commendation Medal (2), Army Achievement Medal (4), Good Conduct Medal, Southwest Asia Defense Medal, National Defense Ribbon, Overseas Defense Ribbon, Certificate of Achievement, Safe Driving Awards.
- NCO, (E-6 / SSG current rank) - January 1993 to retirement. I have served 26 years in the United State Army National Guard

Private Sector to Fed: **Success Story #1**

☺ *This is an example of what to do!*

AFTER FEDERAL RESUME – HIRED, MATCHES THE QUALIFICATIONS AND IS IN THE USAJOBS BUILDER FORMAT – Uploaded into USAJOBS

ERIC LOWER
1100 East Street, Atlanta, GA 30030 United States
222-222-2222 | ERIC17@GMAIL.COM

WORK EXPERIENCE
Goodwill NG
235 Peachtree St. NE #2300, Atlanta, GA 30303
12/2014 to Present
45 hours per week; $17.50 per hour
CDL Driver Class A

PERFORM TASKS INDEPENDENTLY or with minimal supervision.

DRIVER / WORK PRACTICES: Maintain vehicles and documentation in a clean and organized manner to ensure optimal, timely delivery of loading and unloading donated items by dollies, hand-trucks, manual, and motorized forklifts, to Goodwill stores throughout northern Georgia. Organize and execute pre- and post-trip inspections in accordance with Department of Transportation requirements to ensure safe operation of heavy cargo vehicles such as tractor trailers, box trucks, and forklifts. Identify, report and rectify discrepancies; annotate shipping and inventory records to document identified discrepancies. Follow established procedures to ensure the accuracy and completeness of documentation used to track and receive materials/items.

MATERIALS MANAGEMENT/INVENTORY: Use in-depth knowledge of shipping materials and classes of supply to independently inspect cargo for appropriate packaging, securing and documentation. Use personal computer and smartphone to pinpoint delivery locations. Identify discrepancies such as improperly packaged materials or incorrect documents and take immediate corrective action to avoid further problems.

VEHICLE MAINTENANCE/OPERATION: Perform operator maintenance such as monitoring fluid levels, replacing air filters and interior lights, checking tire pressure and hose connections, and washing vehicles. Utilize technical expertise to drive heavy vehicles safely and effectively in wide range of conditions such as over rough terrain in close quarters, and in heavy traffic on both long and short hauls, while following route directions and time schedules.

Key Accomplishments:
• Provided outstanding customer services with empathy and speed for the fiancée of a renowned athlete who was suddenly imprisoned. I assisted her with donating extensive amounts of household goods under pressure from the government and her family. Provided outstanding services through rain and hurricanes with collecting donated goods from containers from hundreds of locations all over the state of Florida.

US Drivers
5937 Jimmy Carter Blvd, Norcross, GA 30071
03/2014 to 09/2015
40 hours per week
$14 per hour
CDL Driver Class A

DRIVER / WORK PRACTICES: Maintained vehicles and documentation in a clean and organized manner in order to ensure optimal, timely delivery of inventory assets to Home Depot stores in Virginia, Georgia, North Carolina, South Carolina, Alabama and Tennessee. Read, interpreted and followed instructions, including route directions and time schedules, to maximize delivery efficiency.

DEXTERITY AND SAFETY: Conducted pre- and post-trip inspections in accordance with Department of Transportation requirements to ensure safe operation of heavy cargo vehicles. Safely operated a forklift to lift loads in and out of buildings, on and off trucks, rail cars, vessels and other conveyances; safely operated hand trucks, electric jacks and other material handling equipment to gather items for shipment; safely operated motor vehicles including trucks up to 15,000 lbs. to move materials.

VEHICLE MAINTENANCE/OPERATION: Performed operator maintenance such as monitoring fluid levels, replacing air filters and interior lights, checking tire pressure and hose connections, and washing vehicles. Utilized technical expertise to drive heavy vehicles effectively over rough terrain in close quarters, and in heavy traffic on both long and short hauls, while adhering to route directions and time schedules. Vehicles included 53-foot trailers, dry vans, and full sleeper freightliner tractors.

Key Accomplishments:
- Identified issues such as improperly packaged materials or incorrect documents and took immediate corrective action to avoid problems. Drafted discrepancy reports for higher-level managers. Restored complex packaging to specifications by painting, stenciling new material condition tags. Saving expensive and timely returns of hundreds of packages.

Georgia National Guard
1148th Transportation Company, Fort Gordon, GA 30905
07/1988 to 03/2015
45 hours per week $50,000 per year
Transportation & Logistics Supervisor, E-7
Supervisor: Master Sergeant William Smith, 222-222-2222, May Contact

The Installation Transportation Office will provide transportation services for all authorized personnel and activities within the Fort Gordon area of responsibility. The Installation Transportation Office provides that transportation meets force readiness and mobilization requirements as a power-projection platform for 55,000 part-time and activated Reservists.

MATERIALS HANDLING: As supervisor, oversaw the section of 1148th Company's warehouse designated for our shipments. Received, loaded and offloaded weapons, ammunition, combat vehicles and equipment from wide variety of transport vehicles both stateside and in overseas operating environments. Cargo included caliber 4.56mm and 20mm ammunition, grenades and other assets.

HAZARDOUS MATERIALS INVENTORY MANAGEMENT: Determined proper organization and arrangement of materials such as ammunition and highly explosive ordnance in storage facilities as well as proper storage of hazardous and nonhazardous cargo within vehicles in accordance with load plans. Selected necessary assets, including ammunition, explosives, flammable gas, and other hazardous and non-hazardous materials, from specific storage facilities and prepared for shipment per directives for different modes of transport, such as 5-ton trucks and tractor-trailers, while ensuring quantity of item issued agreed with issue documentation.

Key Accomplishment:
- Expert forecasting for multiple deployments from 2002 to 2009 to support the war and 2009 to 2011 for the return of equipment from the theater. Forecasted logistics, manpower, training and operational needs; took all factors into consideration and planned/developed innovative solutions to significantly enhance operations, training, and customer support.

Georgia National Guard
Camp As Sayliyah, Qatar
08/2010 to 08/2011
65 hours per week
Barrier Supervisor
Supervisor: Sergeant First Class William Smith

Key Accomplishments:
- Oversaw accountability and placement of concrete barriers in and along roads of Camp As Sayliyah to maximize safety and security while ensuring logistical operations.
- Scrutinized unit-level Standard Operating Procedures (SOPs) to ensure continual compliance with governing directives. Identified changes to governing directives, made appropriate adjustments to SOPs, and relayed changes to unit leadership and personnel.

EDUCATION
Armstrong State University, Savannah, GA 31419
20 Semester Credits Earned; GPA 3.5/4.0

JOB-RELATED TRAINING
PROFESSIONAL LICENSES AND CERTIFICATIONS:
*Commercial Driver's License, Class A, State of Georgia, #042358833
*Endorsements: X-Tanker and Hazardous Materials, C-Limousine Chauffeur
*Doubles/Triples
*Air Brakes
*Certificate or Training: Powered Industrial Lift Truck Training

TRAINING: Primary Leadership Development Course; Driver Safety Course; Winter Driving Course; Operations Security; Information Security; Hazardous Materials Management Course.

ADDITIONAL INFORMATION

SECURITY CLEARANCE:
Held Secret Security Clearance from 1988 to 2003.

VEHICLE PROFICIENCY:
* Civilian Vehicles: Peterbilt Automatic Transmission; Freightliner Conventional Manual Transmission; International Cab-Over and Conventional Day Cab; Renault Midlum; Volvo Vacuum Tanker Automatic Transmission; Mach Conventional Manual Transmission; Volvo Conventional Manual Transmission.
* Military Vehicles: M35 2-1/2 Ton Manual Transmission; M939 5 Ton Manual Transmission; M915 Tractor; HMMVW.
* Trailers: Flatbed 40-48 ft; Dry Van 20-53 ft; Tanker; Refrigerated Trailer.

AWARDS:
Army Commendation Medal (3); Army Achievement Medal (6); Good Conduct Medal (3); Southwest Asia Service Medal; National Defense Service Medal; Overseas Service Ribbon; Certificate of Achievement; Safe Driving Awards.

RESULTS: HIRED, MAINTENANCE MECHANIC

NEXT APPLICATION – RIGGER, WG 8

Eric asked for help with updating his resume with the new Maintenance position for a Rigger position. We updated the resume with his new Navy position and added Rigger skills:

1. Understand the basic math to determined weights, stresses, and strengths and/ or mechanical advantage of lifts. I had to make sure the weights on axles on the trucks were legal over highways and interstate as well as bridges. Skilled with the stress levels on chains and binders to secure equipment on the back of trucks. Knowledge of the "SWL" of all chains and binders or locate them using the Navy Publications OP 2173 Vol #2, for Mk-85, Mk-86, Mk-87 slings and MK-105 "Orange Legs and Green Legs."
2. Selecting and installing weight handling gear in lifting and moving, and positioning a variety of large and heavy objects. Installing and replacing different Forks on a forklift. Adding adapters to a forklift such as the Mk-45 Fork lift adapter that pulls cargo up with a sling rather than side to side. Understanding the use of a pallet jack or forklift with different size forks to use to off load or on load different items that can be tricky due to the size and shape of the object and tight locations on trucks shelves and warehouses.
3. Perform difficult load routing judgements using factors such as size, shape and location. I work under close supervision of a work or journey-level employee who observes task in progress and upon completion to make sure they are properly performed.

RESULTS: HIRED / PROMOTED INTO RIGGER POSITION

Private Sector to Fed: Success Story #2

Meet Philip

Philip Sang: Recent Graduate Seeking Federal Position or Pathways Internship
Target: Engineering Technician, Aerospace Engineering, Mechanical Engineer,
Interdisciplinary Engineer, Civil Engineer, General Engineer, GS-0802-5/7/9

Philip's mother was a long-time Federal employee with USCG in Hawaii. She was an IT specialist and had a great career. She wanted her son (and other children) to begin Federal careers. Philip found the following job for which he was qualified, and he improved his Federal resume based on education and his courses, papers, projects, and Internships.

Success story: Philip was HIRED with the US Army Corps of Engineers in South Korea!

Philip's target job: Mechanical Engineer, U.S. Army Corps of Engineers

Philip studied the **minimum qualifications** and specialized experience from the announcement and decided that he met these requirements—both Education and One Year Specialized Experience (from his internships):

For GS-9:
Specialized Experience: One year of specialized experience equivalent to GS-9 which includes searching technical reports to obtain information relating to design projects; applying engineering formulas to design calculations; developing plans, drawings, and specifications; and conducting limited equipment inspections.

OR

Education: Master's or equivalent graduate degree or 2 full years of progressively higher level graduate education leading to such a degree in a field which demonstrates the knowledge, skills, and abilities necessary to do the work of the position, such as mechanical engineering.

OR

Combination of Education and Experience: A combination of education and experience may be used to qualify for this position as long as the computed percentage of the requirements is at least 100%. To compute the percentage of the requirements, divide your total months of experience by 12. Then divide the total number of completed graduate semester hours (or equivalent) beyond the first year (total graduate semester hours minus 18) by 18. Add the two percentages.

Private Sector to Fed: Success Story #2

This example shows what NOT to do.

BEFORE RESUME: DID NOT FEATURE EDUCATION OR TARGET POSITION

PHILIP SANG

EXPERIENCE

TUTOR, 09/2012 – present   Honolulu, HI
Mid-Pacific Institute   Hours/week: 10

Provide one-on-one instruction for high-school students in AP Physics, AP Calculus, AP Statistics, IB Physics and trigonometry, in hour-long sessions. Work with students on comprehension of concepts, methods and problem-solving techniques. Review homework and assigned problems, tests, exercises and solutions, ensuring students understand steps and answers. Also, was available for drop-in help after school two days per week.

ENGINEERING TECHNICIAN (Intern), GS-0802-05   05/2018-08/2018
United States Coast Guard, Civil Engineering Unit, Honolulu, HI 96850   Hours/week: 40

APPLIED ENGINEERING PRINCIPLE AND CONCEPT KNOWLEDGE to evaluate designs for $5M C-130 Hercules rinse rack that complied with military regulations and FAA height restrictions. Researched concepts that incorporated a reverse-osmosis water-filtration system to reclaim used water to reduce water usage and that required minimal maintenance over system lifetime. Reviewed plans, manuals, instruction books, technical standards, guides and reports to identify problem areas and assess feasibility. Performed cost analysis on potential rinse rack positions and variety of existing rinse rack systems.

COMMUNICATED ORALLY AND IN WRITING. Worked closely with engineers, senior and support staff and stakeholders. Coordinated meetings with contracting companies regarding site preparation for C-130 rinse rack at the local air station. Contacted State of Hawai'i officials to obtain as-built drawings for a floating dock project that was slated to moor a pair of 100-foot Coast Guard cutters; coordinated site visits to assess ocean swell conditions at the State of Hawai'i floating dock and assessed the dock's performance.

USED TECHNICAL SKILLS to update and maintain engineering drawing database by filing as-built, engineering and surveying drawings with proper descriptions of each drawing.

ENGINEERING TECHNICIAN, GS-0802-05 05/2017-09/2017
United States Coast Guard, Base Support Unit, San Pedro, CA 90731   Hours/week: 40

DEMONSTRATED ENGINEERING KNOWLEDGE AND SKILL in consulting with Civil Engineering Unit Oakland (CEU Oakland) and updating drawing database; introduced the office to the system widely used throughout the Coast Guard, replacing the previous method, which used a collection of on hand copies of drawings obtained from CEU Oakland. Developed drawings for base projects, including a living quarters renovation and office space expansion.

EDUCATION

Master of Science, Aerospace Engineering, 12/2011
University of Southern California (USC), Los Angeles, CA 90089; GPA: 3.3, 24 Total Semester Credits
Emphasis: Propulsion, Fluid Dynamics, and Mechanical Design

Bachelor of Science, Aerospace Engineering, cum laude; Mechanical Engineering (dual degree), 05/2010
Illinois Institute of Technology (IIT), Chicago, IL 60616; GPA: 3.56, 128 Total Semester Credits

LICENSURE AND CERTIFICATION

Engineering License Certification: Engineer-In Training: Mechanical Engineering, 10/2010, State of California
COMPUTER PROFICIENCIES Applications: Microsoft Office, AutoCAD 2010, Pro/Engineer, MathCAD, CAD/CAM with Numerical Control; Programming Languages: C++, MATLAB 2010a

This is an example of what to do!

AFTER RESUME: OUTLINE FORMAT FEDERAL RESUME FEATURING EDUCATION

Philip reworked his resume to put the Education section first in order to clearly demonstrate that he met the qualifications through his education. He added courses, papers, and projects, as well as relevant skills from his internships into the work history.

PHILIP SANG

1333 Key Blvd • Honolulu, HI 96822
Mobile: 888-888-8888 email:

LICENSURE

Engineering License Certification: Engineer-In Training: Mechanical Engineering (10/2010)
State of California

COMPUTER PROFICIENCIES

Applications: Microsoft Office, AutoCAD 2010, Pro/Engineer, MathCAD, CAD/CAM with Numerical Control;
Programming Languages: C++, MATLAB 2010a

EDUCATION

GRADUATE STUDENT, AEROSPACE ENGINEERING   08/2016-12/2018
University of Southern California (USC), Los Angeles, CA 90089
GPA: 3.33, 24 Total Semester Credits

Developed and honed skills in all phases of engineering projects. As part of teams and individually, designed, researched and developed solutions to engineering problems. Made engineering calculations, wrote specifications and selected and identified materials. Conducted testing and troubleshooting to assure design met needs. Observed, tracked and evaluated performance data and prepared reports on findings. Made recommendations for best designs, testing, operations and maintenance.

ACADEMIC DESIGN PROJECTS:

· <u>Next Generation Mobile Cloud Computing Technology:</u> Member of team that designed device that could be used for mobile cloud computing; device had stronger processing power than a cell phone, but was more portable than a laptop. The project consisted of modifying and compromising between various available technologies to produce a design that would be functional, reliable and economical. Design consisted of cell phone that projected a laser keyboard onto any flat surface with glasses to serve as a visual display and gloves to interact with objects on the visual display; the entire system remotely connected to a desktop at home with strong computing power.

· <u>Dynamics of a Rotating Baseball:</u> Lead programmer and numerical analysis assistant for five-person team that calculated the aerodynamic forces placed on a rotating baseball as it travels from the pitcher to the batter. Location of fastball pitch was determined, which determined the initial velocities and angles at which the pitch was thrown. Used MATLab code to simulate the movement of a different pitch with a different spin with the same initial angles.

- COURSEWORK: Dynamics of Incompressible Fluids, Engineering Analytical Methods, Engineering Analysis, Dynamics of Incompressible Fluids, Compressible Gas Dynamics, Advanced Mechanical Design, Project Controls-Planning and Scheduling, Systems Architecting, Combustion Chemistry and Physics, Principles of Combustion, Advanced Dynamics

BACHELOR OF SCIENCE, AEROSPACE ENGINEERING   05/2016
BACHELOR OF SCIENCE, MECHANICAL ENGINEERING
Illinois Institute of Technology (IIT), Chicago, IL 60616
GPA: 3.56 out of 4.00, 128 Total Semester Credits
Supervisor: Candace Thomas (808) 888-8888
Graduated Cum Laude

ACADEMIC DESIGN PROJECTS:

- Smoke Wire Flow Visualization Over Car Models: Team leader for project to determine which car design reduced aerodynamic drag the most. Took pictures of streamlines exposed by oil on a heat wire producing smoke trails in the airflow of a wind tunnel. Photos showed which car models experienced flow separation or the extent of the flow separation, the leading cause of aerodynamic drag. Then used photos to determine which car design was best suited for the tested wind speeds.

- Large-Scale Building Solar Air Conditioning System: As member of six-person team, served as lead for system design and CAD design, and numerical analysis assistant. Researched and designed solar-powered air-conditioning system. The final design used parabolic mirrors that would focus the sun's rays to one point, heating up the molten salt that is then stored in a large silo, capable of holding enough energy to power the system overnight. The salt would heat liquid ammonia into a gas that runs through a heat exchanger with air, which cools the air during summer. During winter, the heat exchanger would run in reverse to warm the facility. The thermodynamic equations were placed into an energy equation solver that solved the unknown parameters through guess and check.

- Light Sport Aircraft Automobile: On four-person team, served as lead for numerical analysis and optimization and design analysis assistant. Designed vehicle that would be capable of driving on any road in the U.S. and be able to fly while carrying at least two passengers. Followed commercial vehicle regulations, which constrained aircraft size and the size of control surfaces, which meant folding the wings. Set maximum allowable flight parameters to match that of a light sport aircraft pilot license.

- Automatic Glove Dispenser: Served as CAD design, structural load analysis and design analysis lead for six-person team. Designed and produced alpha prototype of an automatic glove dispenser. Researched, developed, produced and tested various mockups, including materials selection; settled on a top-loading glove dispenser that would utilize gravity to load gloves into a tray, which would allow users to slide their hands into the gloves without touching the outside of the gloves, keeping the gloves sterile.

- RELEVANT COURSEWORK: Calculus: Multi-variable, Vector and Differential Equations; Statics; Dynamics; Aircraft and Spacecraft Dynamics; Aerodynamics of Aerospace Vehicles; Fluid Mechanics; Compressible Flow; Aerospace Propulsion; Thermodynamics; Applied Thermodynamics (Refrigeration and Heaters); Design of Thermal Systems; Engineering Materials and Design; Analysis of Aerostructures; Systems Analysis and Control; Engineering Measurements; Drafting Physics: Mechanical, Electrical, and Modern; CAD/CAM with Numerical Control, Spacecraft and Aircraft Mechanics; Design of Mechanical Systems; Heat and Mass Transfer; Finite Element Methods in Engineering; Design of Aerospace Vehicles I (Fixed Wing Aircraft Design); Design of Aerospace Vehicles II (Design of Space Launch Vehicles and Satellites).

WORK HISTORY

ENGINEERING TECHNICIAN (Intern), GS-0802-05   05/2018-08/2018
United States Coast Guard, Civil Engineering Unit, Honolulu, HI 96850
Hours/week: 40
Supervisor: Neal Smith (808) 888-8888 May contact

- APPLIED ENGINEERING PRINCIPLE AND CONCEPT KNOWLEDGE to evaluate designs for $5M C-130 Hercules rinse rack that complied with military regulations and FAA height restrictions. Researched concepts that incorporated a reverse-osmosis water-filtration system to reclaim used water to reduce water usage and that required minimal maintenance over system lifetime. Reviewed plans, manuals, instruction books, technical standards, guides and reports to identify problem areas and assess feasibility. Performed cost analysis on potential rinse rack positions and variety of existing rinse rack systems.

- COMMUNICATED ORALLY AND IN WRITING. Worked closely with engineers, senior and support staff and stakeholders. Coordinated meetings with contracting companies regarding site preparation for C-130 rinse rack at the local air station. Contacted State of Hawai'i officials to obtain as-built drawings for a floating dock project that was slated to moor a pair of 100-foot Coast Guard cutters; coordinated site visits to assess ocean swell conditions at the State of Hawai'i floating dock and assessed the dock's performance.

- USED TECHNICAL SKILLS to update and maintain engineering drawing database by filing as-built, engineering and surveying drawings with proper descriptions of each drawing.

Career Change: **Federal to Federal**

Changing careers / occupational series within the government is challenging, because the resume has to show the qualifications and one-year specialized experience in the new target area of work. Sometimes you can change your job series with education alone; but, most of the time, Federal job announcements require you to demonstrate one-year specialized experience doing the work of the job you're applying to.

Making a career change within the Federal government (as a current Federal employee) requires additional care to prepare a top resume because you're competing against other applicants who have already been on that career track and may be more qualified than you. Even a change within the same occupational series and same agency can be considered a career change if the job duties are different enough. This chapter will help you translate your current competencies, knowledge, skills, and abilities into a new occupational series, or a very different job title in your current series. This chapter is designed to offer tips and tools for preparing for your career change and making sure that your resume is up to the task.

A degree of overlap between your previous experience and the requirements of the job you seek will be necessary. In crafting your most effective resume—your ticket to an interview—you must bring this overlap to the forefront while minimizing or outright eliminating content that does not overlap. This is a difficult task for many series-switchers. Finding and articulating relevant overlap is not as easy as it may seem. Years of experience in a given Federal occupational series can impart significant knowledge and skills, but it also can create process, procedural, and linguistic blinders. You have likely grown accustomed to doing certain things a certain way and relating to them using certain words and phrases. But you must translate these words and phrases into the language of the new position so that the reviewers can understand how you fit their hiring needs. Overlap between the job you have and the job you want must be found and leveraged to the maximum extent. This will likely involve rethinking, rephrasing, and generalizing specificity and jargon.

You're heading toward something new and it requires a new resume "wardrobe." But there is a finite space in your resume "closet": the other difficult part of writing the most effective and best-read resume for a series switch is letting go of irrelevance. Most people are rightfully proud of their experience and its reflection in their resume. Experience takes years to develop, and documenting it all within a resume can be arduous. And with lengthiness accepted and even encouraged in Federal resumes, it can be tremendously difficult to trim and feel unnecessary to leave out experience. You certainly need to impart experience and tenure. But irrelevance is irrelevance. The truly unnecessary should be trimmed as it hurts readability. It can be difficult to part with that hard-won experience on paper. It's like the hesitation of donating your favorite old sweater when you have set your sights on moving to the tropics. The old sweater is the unnecessary, dated stuff in your resume that doesn't apply to your future (tropical) job. Tailor your wardrobe, combining exciting and new pieces, with an eye to where you are going—not from where you came.

Fed to Fed - Extreme Career Change Success Story #3

Meet Margaret

Margaret Jones: Current Federal Employee Seeking Career/Agency/Occupational Change
Target
Embedded Clinical Social Worker Seeking Park Ranger, Fish and Wildlife Service or US Army Corps of Engineers

Margaret wanted to make an extreme career change. Her current position was stressful as an embedded Clinical Social Worker with the US Navy. She could afford a downgrade with her GS level and wanted to use her teaching experience to work outdoors in a beautiful environment. She was determined to make this change. In the photo above Margaret was coaching Navaho Indians about Federal job search because their Power Station was closing. She was volunteering with the National Park Service as an instructor in Arizona.

Success story: She was hired at a National Park in Arizona to continue work as an Interpreter and Instructor for the local school systems in partnership with the National Park Service.

Hi Kathryn,

We spoke on the phone a few weeks ago. I am a current government employee looking to do a career change to a park ranger (GS-0025 series). I don't have specialized experience per se for the GS-0025 series, but I do have the generalized experience (investigative work). I also can meet the educational requirement of superior academic achievement for GS-0025 postings since I have a BA in Education with a 3.05 GPA. I am open to full time permanent park ranger positions with the National Park Service, U.S. Army Core of Engineers, and the US Fish and Wildlife Service. I am currently searching for positions. I am seeking a Federal resume to help me with this career change.

Thank you. Margaret

Margaret's target job: Park Ranger, U.S. Fish and Wildlife Service

She determined that she met the **minimum qualifications and specialized experience** required in the job announcement.

You may qualify at the GS-09 level, if you fulfill one of the following qualification requirements:

1. Have at least 1 year of specialized experience that equipped me with the particular knowledge, skills, and abilities to successfully perform the duties of this position. This experience must have been equivalent in level of difficulty and responsibility to that of at least the GS-07 grade level in the Federal service. Experience may have been in technical, administrative, or scientific work, fish and wildlife management, recreation management, law enforcement, teacher / educator or other park-related work. Examples of qualifying specialized experience includes: park guide or tour leader; teacher; law enforcement or investigative work; archeological or historical preservation research work; forestry and/or fire management work in a park, recreation, or conservation area; program specialist work involving the development of policy related to protection, conservation, or management of park areas or similar operations.

How You Will Be Evaluated

You will be evaluated for this job based on how well you meet the qualifications above. Your qualifications will be evaluated on the following competencies (knowledge, skills, abilities and other characteristics):

· Knowledge of interpretive principles, theories, and techniques, with emphasis on conservation principles, and natural and cultural history.

· Ability to use traditional and technological outreach tools to engage the general public and partners.

· Ability to manage a public facility.

· Ability to communicate effectively orally and in writing.

Minimum Qualifications (Screen Out Element):

· Ability to lead or supervise the work of an Mobile Equipment Operator Leader without more than normal supervision performing common Mobile Equipment Operator tasks of operating all classes and types of vehicles to include motor cars, towing equipment, towing vehicles, trucks, forklifts, tractor trailers for loading and unloading materials or equipment.

 *This example shows what NOT to do.*

BEFORE RESUME NEEDS TO BE RE-TARGETED
Margaret found her previous resume, but this resume was written for Clinical Social Work. Now she needs to feature her previous experience as a teacher, degree in education and all relevant instructor skills for Park Ranger.

MARGARET JONES
Address Line 1
Address Line 2
Phone and Email

OBJECTIVE

CLINICAL SOCIAL WORKER

PROFILE

LICENSED CLINICAL SOCIAL WORKER (LCSW), INTERNATIONAL CERTIFIED ADDICTIONS PROFESSIONAL (ICAP) and SOCIAL SERVICES PROGRAM MANAGER with 18 years of professional experience providing behavioral health counseling and mental health services to a diverse patient population. Extensive experience in the delivery of clinical counseling and family advocacy services and support. Top record of performance in addictions counseling, clinical analysis, sexual assault prevention and response (SAPR), victims advocacy, and therapy and counseling for substance abuse programs. Strong individual and group therapy, assessment, treatment planning, crisis intervention, and case management qualifications. Master's degrees in Social Work (MSW) and Public Administration (MPA).

Additional Qualifications include:

- Delivery of counseling services and support for individuals with a broad range of physical and mental health issues, including addictions and substance abuse; family, parenting, and marital problems; stress and anger management; PTSD; domestic, sexual and child abuse; and depression and anxiety.

- Advanced skills in assessing individual family needs and establishing treatment plans with behaviorally specific goals and objectives.

- Excellent problem-solving, analytical, and abstract thinking skills. Solid experience in regulatory oversight, quality assurance, standards review, and program analysis and reporting.

- Developing training and education programs for the prevention of sexual assault and substance abuse.

EDUCATION

MS, Clinical Social Worker, American University, 2014 (GPA: 4.00)
Licensed Clinical Social Worker
Certificate, Biological Technician, University of Southern California, Los Angeles, CA, 2013
BA, Education, University of North Florida, Jacksonville, FL 32224, 2005 (GPA: 3.05)

Teacher's Certification, State of California, 2012

PROFESSIONAL EXPERIENCE

CLINICAL SOCIAL WORKER (LSCW), GS-0185-12, Step 6   4/2016 to Present
Army Substance Abuse Program (ASAP)   Hours per week: 40
Department of the Army, HHD, USAG-Casey

PROVIDE DIVERSE COUNSELING SERVICES AND ACCURATE CASE MANAGEMENT for active duty soldiers, family members, retirees, and eligible Federal civilian employees and others at U.S. Army Garrison (USAG), Casey, Korea. Provide comprehensive substance abuse psychosocial assessments and evaluations for those referred to the Army Substance Abuse Program (ASAP). Manage facilities and resource in a public facility.

TRAINING DELIVERY AND INSTRUCTION; INFORMATION MANAGEMENT: Facilitate planning, development, scheduling and delivery of sexual assault prevention and response training for all personnel, leadership, deploying personnel, volunteer victim advocates, and other key functional stakeholders.

ADVOCACY / TRANSPORTER: Assist victims with gaining access to service providers and available victim support resources. Support and accompany victims of sexual assault through medical and investigative procedures, court/administrative proceedings, and related processes.

KEY ACCOMPLISHMENTS:
   -- Successful in raising awareness with command leadership on the high correlation between alcohol-related incidence (ARI) and sexual assault.
   -- Completed over 75% of 1500 initial psychosocial and clinical assessments for the military command Army Substance Abuse Program (ASAP) assigned to Camp Casey.
   -- Consistently achieved a 90% accuracy rate on patient records and clinical notes.
   -- Developed and delivered a comprehensive presentation on the ASAP program to 175 members of Unit Prevention Leadership during UPL class on a quarterly basis.

INSTRUCTIONAL SYSTEMS SPECIALIST
(SCIENCE – ELEMENTARY)   10/2014 – 10/2016
Department of Defense Education Activity   40 Hours per Week
Europe South DSO • Vincenza, Italy

IMPLEMENT COLLEGE & CAREER READY STANDARDS: Implement college and career ready standards (CCRS) for schools throughout the Europe South District. Build capacity through professional learning, coaching, modeling, and advising in the DoDEA science program. Design individual coaching and support plans. Collaborate with the Center for Instructional Leadership to offer graduate courses, job-embedded professional learning, and data-based decision-making strategies to meet CCRS goals.

LEARNING & PROGRAM EVALUATION – NATURAL AND CULTURAL HISTORY: Model and demonstrate the use of formative and summative assessments from DoDEA-procured resources with teachers during instruction and focused collaboration, ensuring alignment with DoDEA CCRS content standards. Support learning and program evaluation using the ADDIE model, to include data from CRS professional learning sessions, to design meaningful professional learning experiences used by Instructional Systems Specialists.

 This is an example of what to do!

MARGARET JONES
Address Line 1
Address Line 2
Phone and Email

OBJECTIVE
PARK RANGER, GS 9

PROFILE
Possess extensive experience serving the soldiers and the American public first in U.S. Army positions in social services. Bring significant leadership experience gained as a U.S. Army combat veteran, educator and mentor, supplemented by a bachelor's degree in Education, a master's degree in Education, and a passion for the American outdoors and wildlife refuges/park systems.
Experienced educator for DOD Schools. Developed curriculum for history, science and technology courses. Provide activities, course instruction and group lessons.

.

EXPERTISE
- **Interpretative Training/Outreach:** Instructor, Curriculum Designer
- **Communications:** Developing clear and concise communications products that convey complex concepts effectively to technical and non-technical audiences.
- **Outreach:** Combining the effective technical and people skills needed to build and maintain productive customer relationships.
- **Collaboration:** Leveraging a common passion and vision to build and inspire effective teams and partnerships.

CERTIFICATIONS AND LICENSES
Active Colorado State Driver's License, 2018

EDUCATION
MS, Clinical Social Worker, American University, 2014 (GPA: 4.00)
Licensed Clinical Social Worker
Certificate, Biological Technician, University of Southern California, Los Angeles, CA 90089, 2013
BA, Education, University of North Florida, Jacksonville, FL 32224, 2005 (GPA: 3.05)
MA, Education, University of North Carolina, Jacksonville, FL 3224, 2006
Teacher's Certification, State of California, 2012

PROFESSIONAL EXPERIENCE

CLINICAL SOCIAL WORKER (LSCW), GS-0185-12, Step 6   4/2016 to Present
Army Substance Abuse Program (ASAP)   Hours per week: 40
Department of the Army, HHD, USAG-Casey

PROVIDE DIVERSE COUNSELING SERVICES AND ACCURATE CASE MANAGEMENT for active duty soldiers, family members, retirees, and eligible Federal civilian employees and others at U.S. Army Garrison (USAG), Casey, Korea. Provide comprehensive substance abuse psychosocial assessments and evaluations for those referred to the Army Substance Abuse Program (ASAP). Manage facilities and resource in a public facility.

TRAINING DELIVERY AND INSTRUCTION; INFORMATION MANAGEMENT: Facilitate planning, development, scheduling and delivery of sexual assault prevention and response training for all personnel, leadership, deploying personnel, volunteer victim advocates, and other key functional stakeholders.

DEMONSTRATE STRONG INTERPERSONAL AND COMMUNICATION SKILLS when conveying complicated, sensitive, and sometimes controversial issues to high-level officials with tact and diplomacy; as well as when communicating with referring providers regarding a patient's status, treatment needs, and prognosis, where appropriate. Establish working relationships with command to provide victim support assistance.

AS A LICENSED CLINICAL SOCIAL WORKER (LCSW), LEVERAGE ADVANCED TRAINING AND OVER 9 YEARS OF PROFESSIONAL EXPERIENCE across the full spectrum of social science and social work principles, including psychology, to serve as a key consultant to the commander on substance abuse, sexual assault/interpersonal violence prevention and response, and behavioral theories and social services delivery systems related to victim advocacy.

ADVOCACY / TRANSPORTER: Assist victims with gaining access to service providers and available victim support resources. Support and accompany victims of sexual assault through medical and investigative procedures, court/administrative proceedings, and related processes. Transported counseling clients from home, hospital, shelters to counseling centers. Managed cases and intake services.

KEY ACCOMPLISHMENTS:
-- Successful in raising awareness with command leadership on the high correlation between alcohol-related incidence (ARI) and sexual assault.
-- Completed over 75% of 1500 initial psychosocial and clinical assessments for the military command Army Substance Abuse Program (ASAP) assigned to Camp Casey.
-- Consistently achieved a 90% accuracy rate on patient records and clinical notes.
-- Developed and delivered a comprehensive presentation on the ASAP program to 175 members of Unit Prevention Leadership during UPL class on a quarterly basis.

INSTRUCTIONAL SYSTEMS SPECIALIST
(SCIENCE – ELEMENTARY)
Department of Defense Education Activity
Europe South DSO • Vincenza, Italy

10/2014 – 10/2016
40 Hours per Week

IMPLEMENT COLLEGE & CAREER READY STANDARDS: Implement college and career ready standards (CCRS) for schools throughout the Europe South District. Build capacity through professional learning, coaching, modeling, and advising in the DoDEA science program. Design individual coaching and support plans. Collaborate with the Center for Instructional Leadership to offer graduate courses, job-embedded professional learning, and data-based decision making strategies to meet CCRS goals.

LEARNING & PROGRAM EVALUATION – NATURAL AND CULTURAL HISTORY: Model and demonstrate the use of formative and summative assessments from DoDEA-procured resources with teachers during instruction and focused collaboration, ensuring alignment with DoDEA CCRS content standards. Support learning and program evaluation using the ADDIE model, to include data from CRS professional learning sessions, to design meaningful professional learning experiences used by Instructional Systems Specialists.

PROGRAM IMPROVEMENT & SENIOR-LEVEL ADVISING: Support the Superintendent's vision for the One DoDEA and the DoDEA Blueprint by communicating and socializing the Learning Walkthrough Tool. Support PK-12 school principals and assistant principals in providing feedback, conducting walkthroughs, creating master schedules, and facilitating close collaboration. Lead and support school improvement plans and accreditation efforts.

CAPACITY BUILDING & PROFESSIONAL DEVELOPMENT TRAINING DELIVERY: Deliver professional development to K-12 Chemical Hygiene Officers (CHO) to ensure the seamless rollout of CCRS science standards. Collaborate with middle and high school science Instructional Systems Specialists regarding anticipated funding needed to support CCRS science curriculum, Sure Start curriculum, and the living materials component of the science curriculum.

KEY HIGHLIGHTS:

— **Successfully implemented CCRS science standards** during 2017-2018; as a result of my efforts, 270+ teachers across the Europe South District are fully implementing CCRS science standards using the adopted curriculum and institutional practices.

— **Productively facilitated 75+ model lessons** in the classroom using the ELEOT, DoDEA Learning Walkthrough Tool, formative assessment, and CCRS science standards with procured resources.

— **Collaborated with the Center for Instructional Leadership** to manage the message of One DoDEA and ensure rigorous instruction with teachers, Instructional Systems Specialists, and principals. As a result of my efforts, 26 teacher-leaders participated in the "Foundations of Coaching" course.

— **Selected by leadership to train colleagues on best practices** in virtual professional learning and coaching. Virtual Platforms included: Skype for Business, Google Moct, and video teleconferencing.

Career Change: Federal to Private Industry

Each year, many Federal workers think about leaving their government positions to start a new career in the private sector—Retirement, Agency Relocation, Agency Restructure, New Opportunities, Relocation. All that's a critical change for the family!!

CAREER CHANGE – GOVERNMENT TO PRIVATE SECTOR!

There are plenty of options to consider, but if you are considering transitioning to private sector make sure you are prepared with a shorter (two-page) private industry resume that is targeted toward your next job.

Your new private industry resume is actually a "Career Change Resume." The private industry company that hires you will likely be very different from the Federal government—one of the largest employers in the U.S. with a massive budget.

Your private sector target might be a large, global corporation, small business, or even a nonprofit organization. Regardless of the position you want to pursue, you will likely face a number of challenges when creating your new Federal-to-private industry resume.

WHAT'S IMPORTANT FOR YOUR CAREER CHANGE
TWO-PAGE PRIVATE SECTOR RESUME

- **Your current areas of responsibility may be highly specialized and complex,** especially if you work for the Department of Defense. Private industry companies will need your skills, but you will have to translate those skills to the simplest level in order for a private sector recruiter or human resources manager to understand what you do. **Tip:** *Do not use any acronyms or terms that your future employers might not understand.*

- **Your knowledge, skills, and abilities (KSAs) are very government focused** and will need to be translated toward the KSAs needed in private industry. **Tip:** *The work of translating could take some research, thinking, practice, and possibly even coaching.*

- **Your Federal agency probably has many employees.** A smaller private sector business or nonprofit will have fewer employees to achieve their mission. **Tip:** *During your interview, focus on transitional skills like supervision, performance, and training rather than the number of employees.*

- **Your Federal job might support customers in your office, region, or worldwide.** That may or may not be the same in your next job, especially if you want to work for a small company. But customer service is customer service, right? **Tip:** *Emphasize the ways in which you are customer-focused!*

- **Your computer skills in the government might be highly specialized** as a result of your experience working with giant databases and complex enterprise computer systems. **Tip:** *You might need to tune up on Microsoft Office or other computer skills that are relevant to your target job.*

- **Decide on the type of position(s) you are going to pursue.** Are you looking for a position that is similar to what you do now or are you looking to transition to an entirely new career field? **Tip:** *Find and review a job advertisement for that type of position. Your government job could be very different from most private sector jobs. If you are unsure of where to start, you might consider hiring a career coach to get you going.*

- **Take a Myers-Briggs Inventory test to review your personality traits.** The information you learn can help you with knowing your soft skills, such as your communication and work styles. You can even take a mini-version of this test online.

- **Analyze the keywords, duties, qualifications, knowledge, skills, and abilities** for your next job. Make a list of the most important keywords.

- *APPLICANT TRACKING SYSTEMS* - Applicant Tracking Systems (ATS) are used by many companies to manage the high volume of applications they receive. The systems scan your resume and rank and score your qualifications. That's one of the reasons why it is so important to ensure you analyze a target job announcement and define the most important keywords. There are many different systems and they can be quirky about what they can read and not read in your resume. Do your homework.

- **Compare your keyword list to your current Federal resume** and start to translate your Federal resume into the new language for private industry. The process can be tough, but if you want to work in the private sector after you leave the government, you must have a two-page resume that a private sector manager can understand and, most important, can use to envision how you can contribute to their organization.

GUIDELINES & WRITING TIPS FOR CREATING YOUR NEW PRIVATE INDUSTRY RESUME

1. **Decide on a resume format.** Choices include reverse chronological, functional, and hybrid. **Tip:** *A hybrid format will give you the flexibility to highlight skills you want to emphasize, or key transferable skills, at the top of the resume followed by your work experience in reverse chronological order (the most recent experience first and the oldest experience last).*

2. **Ensure your resume is easy to read.** Create your new resume document in Word. Use custom margins that are the same on all sides (top, bottom, left, and right). How long should it be? In general, your new resume should be 2 pages; 1 or 2 pages for a new grad. There are exceptions of course. **Tip:** *Enhance the readability of your resume by incorporating white space. A densely written resume will be too hard to read.*

3. **Don't use crazy fonts or many different fonts.** Use an easy to read sans-serif font. Calibri and Arial are two examples. There are many others. Don't use a font size that is too small (smaller than 10 point). Consistency is important. **Tip:** *Use bold TO emphasize selected text.*

4. **At the top of your new resume, list your name, address, email, and phone number.** If you are searching for a position in the area in which you live, noting your address is important. **Tip:** Use a professional-sounding email. For example: yourname@gmail.com. Do not use a work email. Do not list your SSN. It is not necessary to note your citizenship or veteran's preference. **Tip:** *You can add a link to your LinkedIn profile if you have one.*

5. **A LinkedIn Resume is a highly-recommended addition to your private sector job search and networking.** Use your two-page resume to build your LinkedIn resume. Consider your target keywords and skills in terms of your target new position.

6. **Create a profile section to the resume to reinforce the skills and qualifications that are relevant to your target job.** You can also add a bulleted skills list, but keep that section short. **Tip:** *You could feature a few impressive accomplishments at the start of the resume after the profile.*

7. **Do not list hours worked per week, salaries, supervisor names, and other compliance details required on a Federal resume.** For each work experience (back 10-15 years), list your job title, dates of employment (month/year-month/year or year to year); employer name, city, and state. **Tip:** *Earlier work experiences can be summarized at the end of the resume.*

8. **Write a concise overview of your job duties.** Keep it brief. This is not a Federal resume. Your content needs to be easily scannable and clear to the reader. It is important to include only information most relevant to the job you are targeting. **Tip:** *Take the time to review some private sector resumes samples to become familiar with different styles.*

9. **Accomplishments are the STAR of your private industry resume.** Feature strong, quantifiable accomplishments. **Tip:** *Front load your accomplishment with metrics and add bold text to ensure the most important part of the accomplishment jumps off the page.* For example: Reduced inventory $4M by implementing lean manufacturing techniques and other process improvements.

10. **Education.** If you are a new grad, your education can be included at the start of the resume after your profile. If you are an experienced professional, you should list education near the end of your resume. List degrees and school names. **Tip:** *You can omit graduation dates if you are not a new graduate.*

11. **Professional Training, Certifications & Awards.** If you have space to list training, be selective and list only training classes that are most relevant to your target job. Same goes for certifications. Honors and awards are typically featured in Federal resumes, but less frequently on a private sector resume.

This is an example of what to do!

TWO-PAGE PRIVATE SECTOR RESUME TARGETED TOWARD QUALIFICATIONS AND KSAS – SEEKING PROJECT MANAGEMENT

ANN BENSON

443-444-4444 | annbenson@verizon.net | https://www.linkedin.com/in/ann-benson

TECHNOLOGY INDUSTRY PROFESSIONAL

Systems Integration & Software Development Project Manager ▶ DoD Avionics Systems Engineering
Certified Extensible Markup Language (XML) Developer

10+ years' experience with industry-leading global aerospace and defense technology companies managing development of advanced solutions for avionics and engineering applications. Combines advanced technical skills in software configuration management (CM), requirements management, authoring/developmental languages, and open architecture standards with strong lifecycle project management and team leadership qualifications. Talent for communicating complex technical ideas to non-technical audiences.

Expertise Includes: Systems Engineering | Electronic Warfare (EW), Radar, Weapon & Mission System Specifications SDLC Management | Systems Architecting | Software Configuration Management (SCM) | Physical/Logical Data Modeling | Quality Assurance | Data Visualization, Management, Analysis, Governance & Architecture | Resource Description Framework (RDF)/Triples | Flight Systems Software T&I | Technical Writing | Process Redesign & Optimization

PROFESSIONAL EXPERIENCE

SSP INC., College Park, MD (Defense Contractor) 6-Month contract   April 201X-Present
Project Manager

Role: Lead cross-functional team for a U.S. Air Force aircraft performance project. Producing flight clearance manual performance supplement with newly defined processes to enhance readiness and mission execution.

Tools & Technologies: Support test and evaluation cycles; generate performance data. Conduct independent testing to assure technical documentation data tables align with outputs from USAF's certified performance data software.

Project Highlights & Results: Worked closely with customer to develop lifecycle requirements. Developed program controls and technical documentation management procedures. Led team in developing style guides and templates, aircraft manual text, procedures, tables/graphs and illustrations.

AISCENT LLC, Baltimore, MD (Aerospace Company)   May 201X-April 201X
Data Management Analyst / Data Architect

Role: Led development of technical requirements and specifications to create custom XML data exchange standards and data/information requirements to support financial regulatory compliance. Technical lead for financial interagency standards development working group. Led requirements development and management.

Tools & Technologies: Open Architecture/XML data exchange standards, UML documentation, content management in Team Foundation Server (TFS), error analysis, quantitative feasibility analysis.

Project Highlights & Results:
- Analyzed existing industry XML data exchange standards for suitability and applicability to financial regulatory reporting for the Commodity Futures Exchange Commission (CFTC).
- Created/extended custom XML data standards, including XSD/schema and recommended existing XML data exchange standards, message formats and required modifications and extensions.
- Authored technical guidance documents with data architectures, data dictionaries, and conditions.
- Created use cases, entity relationship diagrams, UML documentation, and supporting documents. Manually created test case XML instance files for verification and validation testing. Managed team of 10 IT engineers.

GENERAL DYNAMICS LAND SYSTEMS, Westminster, MD (Aerospace Company)   January-May 201X
Logistics Analyst / Web Developer

Role: Managed systems integration and software development projects for DoD aircraft improvement programs. Led cross-functional Agile Scrum team in design and development of 3 enterprise web applications.

Tools & Technologies: ColdFusion, HTML4, CSS3, JavaScript. Hardware/software CM. Security control implementation. SQL queries, unit testing, system, technical & user documentation.

Project Results: Redesigned logistics support website for operational H-60 aircraft. Recommended changes to software architecture. Successfully migrated legacy applications to new architecture.

Page Two

ANN BENSON | 443-444-4444 | annbenson@verizon.net | Page Two

TEXTRON SYSTEMS, Cockeysville, MD (Defense Contractor)   June 200X-July 201X
Principal Technical Writer

Role: Led creation and update of the Technical Information Product (TIP), and other technical/tactical reference publications, instructions, and manuals for avionics systems. Managed project lifecycle and IT resources.

Tools & Technologies: XML authoring software, ArborText, MS Office SME. Desktop publishing workstation CM. Applied Open Application Standards. SharePoint Administrator. Classified/unclassified website content development.

Project Results: Completed mission-critical DoD avionics technical documents. Wrote weapon/systems performance data, constraints, safety-of-flight limits and content for permanent flight clearance systems by NAVAIR Airworthiness, including EW, data buses, radar and other aircraft systems. Assured integrity of metadata, data, and graphics.

DATASOURCE INC., Atlanta, GA (Communications Technology Company)   May 200X-June 200X
Applications Developer / XSLT Specialist / Project Manager

Role: Developed interactive communications with highly-targeted personalized content and videos. Authored software application user guides and technical manuals. Performed HCM/SCM. Supervised 2 developers for diverse projects.

Tools & Technologies: XML processing, XSDs, Visio, SQL, ETL (Extract, Transform, Load) process, eXtensible Stylesheet Language Transformations (XSLTs). Test regiments, data validation, source versioning.

Project Highlights & Results:
- Managed project lifecycles and end-to-end requirements to manage traceability and implementation.
- Structured XML produced by applications, created XSDs to define document structures, and developed XSLTs to transform data for user-friendly Graphical User Interface (GUI) display. Verified data and metadata.
- Developed visual layout and graphical design for data presentations and dynamic XML processing.

TEXTRON SYSTEMS, Cockeysville, MD   Feb 200X-April 200X
Software Certifications Tester & Analyst - Ballistics and Weapons Employment Data Branch

Role: Performed test and evaluation (T&E) for DoD weapons/avionics systems and architecture. Software tester for a proprietary application in a Waterfall environment. Supported systems analysis and lifecycle requirements management. Worked on mission planning systems, simulators, and technical/tactical manuals.

Tools & Technologies: Open architecture standards, XSD, XSLT, IBM Rational Suite (DOORS, ClearQuest, ClearCase, etc.), risk assessment & mitigation, quick-look testing, SLIC, eSLIC, and ATAMS.

Project Highlights & Results:
- Performed in-depth studies to identify linear trends and discrepancies among data sets for weapons on aircraft platforms. Updated relational databases.
- Ensured development efforts were consistent with customer needs and provided traceability and mapping to specific test cases to ensure all requirements were tested.

TECHNICAL SKILLS PROFILE

Selected Software: Eclipse, Visual Studio, Stylus Studio, SQL Server Management Studio, MATLAB, Visio, Adobe CS5, IBM Rational ClearQuest, TFS, NetBeans, SAP (ERP, HANA, BW, BE, Expert Analytics), ColdFusion Builder, Wireshark ► **Software Configuration Management:** Rational ClearCase, Visual SourceSafe (VSS), IBM Configuration Management Version Management (CMVM) ► **Requirements Management:** Rational ReqPro & DOORS ► **Authoring/Developmental Languages:** JavaScript, Java, CSS, HTML5, C++, C#, ColdFusion, DHTML, XML, XML Schema Definition (XSD), XSLT, Visual Basic, SQL, Unified Modeling Language (UML).

EDUCATION

Bachelor of Science, Information Science and Technology, University of Pennsylvania, 201X

This is an example of what to do!

ONE-PAGE COVER LETTER TO EMPHASIZE THE MOST RELEVANT SKILLS FOR THE TARGET POSITION. Utilize the Resume Place Cover Letter Writing Tool: *https://www.resume-place.com/resources/cover-letter-builder/*

ANN BENSON

443-444-4444 | annbenson@verizon.net | https://www.linkedin.com/in/ann-benson

November 29, 2019

Tom Edwards, Human Resources Director
Johns Hopkins Applied Physics Laboratory (APL)
11100 Johns Hopkins Rd., Laurel, MD 99999

RE: Avionics Systems Engineer; Job Number: 2223

Dear Mr. Edwards:

I am forwarding resume for your review for the position of Avionics Systems Engineer with APL's electronics systems laboratory. I am very excited about the position and the opportunity to work for a renowned research and development organization.

Briefly summarized my qualifications include:

- **10+ years of experience with aerospace and defense technology companies managing the development of advanced solutions for DOD avionics and engineering applications.** This includes systems integration and software development project management, DOD Avionics Systems Engineering, avionics architecture, system analysis, and requirement definition.

- **Advanced technology skill set,** including open architecture standards, software configuration management (CM), and authoring/developmental languages.

- **Extensive experience managing systems integration and software development teams for DOD aircraft improvement programs.** Track record of delivering client projects on time and in-budget.

Additional qualifications that may be of interest to you include: B.S. in Information Science and Technology; experience in mission computing, flight computing, Model Based Systems Engineering (MBSE), Electronic Warfare, and radar.

Thank you for your consideration. I am confident I have the qualifications and experience you are seeking. I look forward to the opportunity to speak with you in person about my interest in this position and the ways in which I can further APL's mission to apply "advanced science and technology to find solutions to problems of national and global significance." Please contact me at annbenson@verizon.net or 443-444-4444.

Sincerely,

Ann Benson

☺ *This is an example of what to do!*

TWO-PAGE PRIVATE SECTOR RESUME OR NETWORKING RESUME. TARGETING OPERATIONS, BUSINESS ANALYST, AND PROGRAM MANAGER.

WALTER W. SINGLETON
San Francisco, CA 22222 | 666.666.6666 | walter.singleton@comcast.net

OPERATIONS DIRECTOR / BUSINESS PROCESS ANALYST / PROGRAM MANAGER
20+ years of program leadership experience - U.S. & International

Senior Program Manager with extensive experience in strategic planning, operations analysis, business requirements planning, human resources management, and organizational development with the U.S. Military. Record of success establishing vision, strategy and direction for achieving organizational mission, driving continuous process improvement, and leading staff to top levels of performance. Contract management, procurement, logistics, workforce planning, and continuity of operations (COOP) expertise. Lean Six Sigma (LSS) training. TS/SCI Clearance. Willing to relocate.

Key Qualifications / Areas of Expertise

Strategic Business Management | Change Management | Workforce Planning | Forecasting
Expense & Cost Control | Business Process Analysis | Strategic Communications | Stakeholder/Relations
Budget Planning/Administration | Contract Management | Regulatory Compliance

PROFESSIONAL EXPERIENCE

UNITED STATES AIR FORCE (USAF) – 19XX to Present

Deputy Director / Program Director, Manpower & Organization Division　　　201X-Present
Travis Air Force Base, San Francisco, CA

Manage workforce planning, programming, budgeting, and strategic program management for one of the largest of 12 USAF organizations with 94,000 global military and civilian staff in 230 locations and an $8M appropriated budget. Strategic Human Resources (HR) advisor to senior executives with key role in COOP planning. Supervise 20 analysts.

▶ **Business Process Analyst & Strategist**: Assess business processes and systems and lead implementation of short/long-range plans to improve program effectiveness, efficiency, and performance. Lead complex SWOT, LSS and other technical analyses of operational and HR programs. Develop analytical/status program reports.

▶ **Lifecycle Project Manager / Team Leader**: Design and lead in-depth analyses, projects and initiatives to assess program efficiency and performance, identify best practices, and improve operational policy and procedures.

- **Managed start-up of a new Continuous Process Improvement (CPI) office** to provide strategic business management services to 36 installations for driving CPI and reducing costs. Lead the CPI office and 3 analysts.

- **Identified 160 strategic, long-term process improvements** in a strategic USAF program. Developed reports for USAF/Pentagon and presentation to Congress.

- **Played key role in a high-profile transformation of mission-critical intelligence capabilities.** Oversaw comprehensive program analysis, which justified successful merger of an intelligence/surveillance agency and establishment of a new department. Played key role in seamless transfer of 2 departments;18,000 positions.

WALTER SINGLETON | 443-444-4444 | walter.singleton@comcast.net | Page Two

Human Resources Director   201X to 201X
Davis Monthan AFB, Tucson, AZ

Directed HR programs supporting 4,000 active duty military personnel and 10,000 civilians and dependents. Managed hiring, on-boarding, evaluations, promotions, training & development, and retention. Administered $2M budget. Managed facilities operations, resources, and specialized programs valued at $60M. Liaison to the community, government and business organizations. Directed 360 personnel.

▶ **Led high profile projects and change management initiatives that improved the quality and delivery of facilities, services, and programs serving military personnel, their families and the community.**

- **Orchestrated $10M construction project** to renovate an on-base hotel to provide temporary lodging for transitioning military families. Oversaw development and justification of construction budget and led teams.

- **Saved $206K by eliminating excess inventory** following a comprehensive inventory analysis, including depreciation and recapitalization forecasts, freeing funds for other high need areas.

- **Led more than 10+ successful business process improvement projects,** including revamp of an underperforming dining operation. Improved staff retention at the onsite childcare center.

- **Orchestrated turnaround of a golf course** achieving profitability for the first time in 3 years.

- **Led collaboration with city government**, police/fire, and business leaders that resulted in formal partnerships to share community resources and services.

Human Resources Director   201X to 201X
USAF, U.S. Military Entrance Processing Command (USMEPCOM), North Chicago, IL

Managed operations and led 200 staff at 4 U.S. Military Entrance Processing centers in three states. Managed $5.3M operating budget (personnel and operations/maintenance); $2.7M in equipment inventory; and $12M+ in contracts.

- **Oversaw evaluation of 38,000+ applicants;** qualification and processing of 23,000+ new recruits into 6 branches of the U.S. Armed Forces; and assignment to 10 basic training centers.

- **Evaluated business, management and work processes;** implemented changes that improved long-range performance, efficiency, and productivity, reporting accuracy and quality.

EDUCATION

Master of Arts, Management, University of Maryland, College Park, MD

Bachelor of Arts, Criminology & Criminal Justice, University of Maryland, College Park, MD

ADDITIONAL INFORMATION

Selected Professional Training: Green Belt (Six Sigma/LEAN) Course

Professional Affiliations: Society for Human Resource Management (SHRM)

Technical Skills Profile: Microsoft Tasker Management Tool (TMT), Case Management System (CMS), Microsoft Office Suite, SharePoint, PeopleSoft HR System.

Part 4

SPECIAL INSIGHTS FOR INFORMATION TECHNOLOGY SPECIALISTS

Information Technology
Specialist (GS-2210) Resumes

Writing a resume for the IT world has some interesting challenges. On the one hand, you want to impress the reader with your technical expertise, and what better way to do that than to use lots of technical jargon (appropriately, of course)? On the other hand, your resume will likely also be read by a variety of nontechnical personnel, from the junior human resources specialist logging in the resume or performing an initial screening, all the way to the hiring manager, who may or may not have a technical background. How can you satisfy both of these audiences, plus position yourself as "Best Qualified" for the Federal position you want?

That's the purpose of this chapter: to help you first of all to understand the types of IT jobs available in the Federal world so that you can do a good job of the most important step—selecting those positions that are the best matches for your career aspirations and experience—and then knowing how to present your IT education, training, and job experience in an effective marketing format that produces results.

Government IT Jobs in the 21st Century

The most interesting trend in Federal IT jobs is that more and more, the government is taking its lead from industry. In all areas, government managers are challenged to think like entrepreneurs, to focus on the bottom line, and to build standard, repeatable business processes based on industry-wide best practices. Always remember in developing your Federal resume, your cover letter, and any other component of your application package, that IT systems and software are never the end goal; they are merely the tools to build successful, mission-driven business systems. Every job duty and accomplishment you describe should maintain that focus.

What does this mean in the IT arena? First of all, look to the key business drivers in the IT industry and you will find the Federal government in lockstep.

Federal and Industry Certifications

IT positions in both government and industry increasingly require industry certifications. Those most in demand over the recent past have included Microsoft (MCSA, MCSE, MCSD), CompTIA (A+, Network+, Security+), and Cisco (CISSP, CCNA, CCNP) certifications. With the increased emphasis on Information Assurance and Cybersecurity, there are now also quite a few information security certifications that are in high demand, such as the EC-Council's Certified Ethical Hacker (CEH) certification and the ISACA Certified Information Security Manager (CISM). The move to commercial cloud solutions, including Amazon Web Services (AWS), Google Cloud Platform (GCP), and Microsoft Azure, has also opened up a growing need for IT Specialists with the skillsets and associated certifications needed to facilitate the Federal government's cloud initiatives.

There are also certifications within the Federal government that you should definitely highlight in your resume if you have achieved these. This includes certification under the Defense Acquisition Workforce Improvement Act (DAWIA), certification as a Contracting Officer's Representative (COR) or Contracting Officer's Technical Representative (COTR), and Information Assurance (IA) certifications under Department of Defense (DoD) Directive 8570, which governs the IA training and certification for DoD IA professionals *https://public.cyber.mil/cwmp/dod-approved-8570-baseline-certifications/*

If you have one of these or other certifications, you definitely will want to highlight this in the first half of the first page of your Federal resume. If you do not have any certifications, there is no time like the present to get started. Although formal training is important, you can get started on many of these certifications through self-study and the time and cost invested will be well paid back.

Cyber Security

Certainly one of the top drivers in both industry and government is the urgent requirement to protect systems, networks, and data from escalating cybersecurity threat.

Enterprise Architectures

Both industry and government have realized that reinventing the wheel again and again is neither fiscally nor mission responsible. Many job positions posted by the Federal government are derived from Federal-wide initiatives to design "reusable," "interoperable," "accessible," "scalable," "enterprise" systems and solutions. One of the transformational initiatives in the Federal government is the concept of the Federal Enterprise Architecture Framework (FEAF), which advocates a common approach for the integration of business and technology management, with the goals of streamlining citizen access to Federal government agencies and saving taxpayer dollars.

Cloud Technologies

Another key driver in the 21st century has been the phenomenon of "moving to the cloud," and the Federal government has been no exception. In layman's terms, this move to cloud technologies means that Federal agencies are required to first consider using shared data and computing resources before they go out to purchase or develop their own hardware and software. Cloud computing takes advantage of virtualization, which implements a layer of "virtual" systems on top of the physical system, enabling the capability to dynamically allocate resources based on demand. Driven by industry giants like Google and Amazon, the industry has moved toward several new service models, including Infrastructure as a Service (IaaS), Software as a Service (SaaS), and Platform as a Service (PaaS).

Systems Development Life Cycle (SDLC)

The government has learned the lesson that the real cost for a system is the total life-cycle cost—from product or system inception through development, testing, acceptance, implementation, and then life-cycle support and even decommissioning. If you are a software developer or hardware integrator, or even plan, acquire, and then implement new systems, you have had to consider all of these life-cycle aspects. Again, incorporating the appropriate and accepted terms for this experience into your resume demonstrates your expertise and awareness of these imperatives on the IT industry and Federal IT initiatives.

Continuity of Operations (COOP)

Continuity of Operations (COOP) and Disaster Recovery Planning have been high on the Federal government's to-do list since 9/11. One place to start is by consulting FEMA's Federal Preparedness Circular (FPC) 65 (*www.fas.org/irp/offdocs/pdd/fpc-65.htm*). It is very likely that you will have played some role in disaster preparedness in any IT position in which you have served. Highlighting this experience and relating it to the term "COOP" will ring true to the hiring manager for almost all positions.

Business Process Reengineering (BPR)

Remember the focus on documented, repeatable business processes? The buzzword in the business world for developing these is Business Process Reengineering (BPR). If you have been around awhile in the IT world, you have at some point had to think about how you currently manage a process (the "as-is" scenario) and how you could improve it in the future (the "to-be" process). If you have led or participated on projects to map processes like this, you have essentially been involved in BPR (and should take credit for it and use the correct term).

IT Planning and Acquisition

Whether you have formally served as a Contracting Officer's Technical Representative (COTR) in the Federal government, as a Project Manager for a government project, or even researched, recommended, and documented requirements for IT items or services to be procured, this is one area that you should definitely highlight. Become familiar with terms such as Statement of Work (SOW), Statement of Objectives (SOO), and Request for Proposals (RFP). Even for private-industry experience, try to cast your expertise in these terms.

You should also educate yourself on the **Clinger-Cohen Act of 1996** or the **Information Technology Management Reform Act (ITMRA),** which required the Federal government to reform the acquisition, management, and disposal of its IT resources to better enable agencies to keep up with the high pace of technology change. Clinger-Cohen implemented an IT planning process called **Capital Planning and Investment Control (CPIC)** and placed the responsibility for IT planning in each agency under a Chief Information Officer (CIO), with the Office of Management and Budget (OMB) at the center of the process. CPIC requires each agency to follow a disciplined IT planning process aligned with its Enterprise Architecture. Key documents related to this process include:

- ❯ **OMB Circular A-130**, Management of Federal Information Resources, which establishes policies for the management of Federal information resources.
- ❯ **OMB Exhibit 300**, submitted by each Federal agency to justify each request for a major IT investment.
- ❯ **OMB Exhibit 53**, submitted annually by each Federal agency to report its budget estimates for its IT investment portfolio.

Other Emerging Business Drivers Impacting the Federal IT Workforce

Almost all of the technology growth drivers in industry will eventually find their application space in the Federal government. While you can already find job opportunities in the Federal government that will maximize your education and experience in the latest IT growth areas, from big data analytics and Artificial Intelligence (AI) to mobile computing, even relatively new growth areas such as the "Internet of Things" (IoT) will eventually generate new workforce requirements within the Federal government. If you are currently working with these emerging technologies, there will be many opportunities to expand your career directions into the civil service.

IT Job Series: **How the Federal Government Has Organized IT Positions**

The first step in conducting an effective job search for IT positions in the Federal government is to understand the various job series that apply to IT-related positions (see _www.opm.gov/policy-data-oversight/classification-qualifications/_ and then select General Schedule Qualification Standards from the menu bar on the left). Searching via the Occupational Series/Job Categories on USAJOBS (_www.usajobs.gov_) is essential in identifying vacancies compatible with your education and experience.

Jobs in Series GS-2210 and Beyond

If you type in "Information Technology" in the "Occupational Series or Job Category" field in the USAJOBS Advanced Search feature, you will see all of the available IT job series, 2200 ("2200" is the Job Series; "Information Technology" is the Job Category). The overall Information Technology job series is 2200; however, the vast majority of posted jobs are in the 2210 series, Information Technology Management. The Position Classification Standard defines the 2210 series as follows:

> **GS-2210, Information Technology Management:** "This series covers two-grade interval administrative positions that manage, supervise, lead, administer, develop, deliver, and support information technology (IT) systems and services. This series covers only those positions for which the paramount requirement is knowledge of IT principles, concepts, and methods; e.g., data storage, software applications, networking."

INFORMATION TECHNOLOGY MANAGEMENT, 2210 (continued)

OPM has prescribed eleven parenthetical titles for the Information Technology Management series, 2210, covered by this Job Family Standard (JFS):

Policy and Planning	Network Services
Enterprise Architecture	Data Management
Security	Internet
Systems Analysis	Systems Administration
Applications Software	Customer Support
Operating Systems	

Agencies may use only the above listed specialty titles to supplement the basic titles for the Information Technology Management series, 2210. Parenthetical titles may be affixed to any of the basic titles providing applicability.

To accommodate automated systems limitations, you may use authorized specialty abbreviations (see parenthetical listing below) with the full title or with an abbreviated basic title of ITCYBER (IT Cybersecurity); ITPM (IT Project Manager); ITPROG (IT Program Manager), or ITSPEC (IT Specialist). For example, an IT Project Manager (Operating Systems) could be listed as IT Project Manager (OS) or ITPM (OS).

Titling (continued)

Selecting the right job announcement in the first place is just as critical for IT positions as for any other job search. No matter how good your resume materials are, if you truly do not have the credentials required by the hiring manager, it is close to certain that you will not be in the Best Qualified range. So how can you tell from reading an IT job announcement whether you might be minimally qualified or seriously at the top of the pack?

Analyzing a Sample Announcement

Let's take a sample IT job announcement and really look at it. Here is an actual (but abbreviated) job announcement for an Information Security Specialist at the GS-12 level.

MAJOR DUTIES:

IT SPECIALIST (SYSADMIN), GS-2210-12

DUTIES

- Primary responsibilities include the testing, troubleshooting, maintenance, installation, upgrade, and configuration of hardware and middleware software systems.
- Assist application developer, network, infrastructure, and platform service personnel in the evaluation of new applications in the integration infrastructure that fall within the agency's area of responsibility.
- Provide around the clock support for platform as a service (PaaS) on the agency's Infrastructure as a Service (IaaS), which includes: solutions for web and n-tier application hosting, including multiple operating system-based application servers; solutions for client/server applications; and solutions for distributed file transport services.
- Provide incident/problem management, including the analysis of incidents to identify the cause; determination of the corrective action(s), and the following implementation of those actions; the tracking and reporting of the status of the production support utilizing the agency's incident/problem/knowledge management system.
- Provide installation, upgrade, and configuration support for agency supported technologies.
- Facilitate formal and informal meetings involving IT presentations to decision makers.

Specialized Experience includes performing IT System Administration work that involves serving as a member of a team responsible for planning and coordinating the installation, testing schedules, operation, troubleshooting, and maintenance of hardware and software systems, while interpreting regulations on own initiative, in order to ensure availability and functionality of hardware and operating systems. Examples of such experience for the GS-12 could include: Experience as a systems administrator, such as designing, implementing and supporting enterprise business applications in a multitier architecture (often referred to as n-tier architecture) or multilayered architecture such as a client/server architecture.

The first thing you should do is to copy all of the information in the announcement that describes the job itself into a Word document. Be sure to look at all pertinent sections of the announcement—Job Summary, Duties, Qualifications Required, Specialized Experience, as well as the Occupational Questionnaire. For this exercise, ONLY copy the material that describes the job itself (as opposed to eligibility, travel, security clearance, educational requirements, etc). Now, make each sentence and/or skill a SEPARATE BULLET. And lastly, go through and reorganize all the bullets so that similar tasks or skills are together. Just doing this exercise will force you to think through the key categories of skills they are looking for. Those "categories" are the KEYWORDS that you will want to consider using in your Federal resume; they are so crucial in determining if you are truly qualified for the position.

TRANSFORMED, this might look like the text below. Note that there is no one perfect analysis, and some bullets might actually fit under two categories or KEYWORDs.

SYSTEM ADMINISTRATION

- Primary responsibilities include the testing, troubleshooting, maintenance, installation, upgrade, and configuration of hardware and middleware software systems.
- Provide installation, upgrade, and configuration support for agency supported technologies.
- Includes performing IT System Administration work that involves serving as a member of a team responsible for planning and coordinating the installation, testing schedules, operation, troubleshooting, and maintenance of hardware and software systems.
- Experience as a systems administrator, such as designing, implementing and supporting enterprise business applications in a multitier architecture (often referred to as n-tier architecture) or multilayered architecture such as a client/server architecture.

APPLICATION EVALUATION

- Assist application developer, network, infrastructure, and platform service personnel in the evaluation of new applications in the integration infrastructure that fall within the agency's area of responsibility.

APPLICATION SUPPORT/PROBLEM MANAGEMENT

- Provide around the clock support for platform as a service (PaaS) on the agency's Infrastructure as a Service (IaaS), which includes: solutions for web and n-tier application hosting, including multiple operating system-based application servers; solutions for client/server applications; and solutions for distributed file transport services.
- Provide incident/problem management, including the analysis of incidents to identify the cause; determination of the corrective action(s), and the following implementation of those actions; the tracking and reporting of the status of the production support utilizing the agency's incident/problem/knowledge management system.

SYSTEM PERFORMANCE/COMPLIANCE

- While interpreting regulations on own initiative, I ensured availability and functionality of hardware and operating systems.

COMMUNICATIONS

- Facilitate formal and informal meetings involving IT presentations to decision makers.

Developing **Your IT Resume**

This section assumes that you already know the basics of putting together your Federal resume and that you have done the job analysis to identify the key knowledge, skills, abilities, and experience you need to highlight to be fully qualified for the target positions. Here, then, are some recommendations that will help you to develop a really effective IT resume.

Addressing Specialized Experience and KSAs

Almost all USAJOBS vacancy announcements will mention that candidates must possess at least one year of Specialized Experience at or equivalent to the next lower grade in the Federal service in order to qualify for the position. Specialized Experience is experience that is directly related to the position and has equipped the applicant with the particular knowledge, skills, and abilities (KSAs) to successfully perform the duties of the position, to include experience in applying and interpreting IT theories, principles, concepts, practices, knowledge management, and providing customer service support to IT clients. You should include the details under Specialized Experience and any KSA descriptions in your initial KEYWORD analysis; if you do this, your resume should clearly address each element described.

One of the key considerations often is how to address the KSAs. Candidates used to have to specifically address each KSA in a written narrative; however, that requirement has now been discouraged by the Federal-Wide Hiring Reform Initiative of 2010. You will have to read the vacancy announcement very carefully to determine how to address the KSAs. If the announcement stresses a very specific set of KSAs, it might be wise to include paragraph-length narratives within your resume to address each KSA. These could be included in either the job description or accomplishment sections and should be clearly marked as to which KSA they illustrate.

When You Don't Match the Requirements Exactly

The toughest call is when the announcement mentions a specific government application or system that you could have used only if you were already in that job or agency. In this case, consider several factors, including the exact language used (is this required, or desirable?) as well as the overall announcement itself. If there is one position and the posting time is short, the requirement is probably very firm. If there are multiple positions available, you might have a better chance of gaining an interview even if your experience is missing one of the requirements.

The ideal approach, of course, would be to speak with someone in a similar technical environment to ensure that you fully understand the requirements. Don't hesitate to use any technical contacts you have to look over the job announcement with you if you see any terms or requirements that you are not familiar with. As with any position, you can also call the Point of Contact provided with the announcement to better understand what the agency is looking for.

Addressing IT Core Competencies

USAJOBS vacancy announcements almost always also require IT specialists to address the set of 4 Core Competencies in addition to their technical skills. These competencies include Attention to Detail, Customer Service, Oral Communication, and Problem Solving, and assure the hiring agency that you have the experience and skill sets needed to be effective on the job, to be able to work with a broad range of people, and to be able to solve the problems that inevitably arise in any work environment. These core competencies are important for every IT specialist position. Be sure to cover these in your project or duties descriptions.

Attention to Detail - Is thorough when performing work and conscientious about attending to detail.

Customer Service - Works with clients and customers (that is, any individuals who use or receive the services or products that your work unit produces, including the general public, individuals who work in the agency, other agencies, or organizations outside the government) to assess their needs, provide information or assistance, resolve their problems, or satisfy their expectations; knows about available products and services; is committed to providing quality products and services.

Oral Communication - Expresses information (for example, ideas or facts) to individuals or groups effectively, taking into account the audience and nature of the information (for example, technical, sensitive, controversial); makes clear and convincing oral presentations; listens to others, attends to nonverbal cues, and responds appropriately.

Problem Solving - Identifies problems; determines accuracy and relevance of information; uses sound judgment to generate and evaluate alternatives, and to make recommendations.

So how do you address these Core Competencies? There are actually several alternatives, and you can adjust the approach to your specific experience and resume style.

Use Competencies as KEYWORDs: Customer Service would clearly be a key role for many IT professionals, as well as Oral and Written Communications, so either of these competencies could easily be used as a KEYWORD in your resume.

Include Competencies in the Job Role Descriptions: You can also just mention (and CAPITALIZE) these competencies within the job role descriptions associated with other KEYWORDs. The following examples illustrate this approach:

OPERATIONAL ANALYSIS: Apply an ATTENTION TO DETAIL in evaluating and analyzing the impact of proposed new systems and proposed changes to existing operational systems. Complete an Analysis of Alternatives in developing and recommending alternate technical solutions. Develop qualitative and quantitative measures of effectiveness to be applied to project objectives.

NETWORK ADMINISTRATION: Manage all Local Area Network and Wide Area Network (LAN/WAN) components, including Cisco and Juniper routers, switches, and firewalls. Install, configure, upgrade, and maintain local network hardware/software components. Leverage PROBLEM SOLVING SKILLS to troubleshoot and resolve complex network communication outages and performance issues.

Developing Your IT Resume

Highlight Competencies in the Accomplishments: Another equally effective approach is to highlight each of these skills in your accomplishments. See below for some examples using this model.

Capability Maturity Model (CMM): *(Problem Solving)* Project Lead for a team-based effort to implement CMM for the Enterprise Document Archive system, a Knowledge Management (KM) repository. Led the team through a detailed analysis effort to identify process improvements needed for CMM certification. Process improvements recommended and implemented for the software development procedures during this 6-month effort resulted in a 30% gain in efficiency (2014).

Web Proxy Migration: *(Attention to Detail)* Planned and executed a 4-month project to reconfigure the agency's web proxy implementation to split the web environment into two separate dedicated network segments. Led the enterprise network engineering team through the development of a detailed project plan that included network configuration steps, testing, phased implementation schedule, and rollback procedures. Completed the final phase of the migration in June 2015, with no impact to the operational environment (2015).

Highlighting Your Accomplishments

Developing (and maintaining) a list of your top accomplishments really makes it easy to develop or update your resume when you suddenly see that perfect job on USAJOBS. Coming up with a list of accomplishments in the IT field is really no different from any other field, except that it might even be easier to include lots of pertinent numbers, as you will often be able to include statistics like the number of systems, the number of impacted users, the version number of the software, and even the percentage of improvement in ticket closure rates, network latency, or system availability.

Here is a good method to develop an IT-related accomplishment. Let's say that you are applying for a software design and development position, so you obviously need to include examples of software products that you developed or at least updated.

Your first thought: Yes, I designed and developed a database application to make it easier to track the Requests for Change (RFCs) for our customer's organization.

Now gather some information on this achievement by asking yourself all the pertinent questions.

- **What was the name of the database?** It really didn't have one, but we could call it the RFC Tracking Database.
- **What was its purpose?** To track RFCs for our organization so we could keep track of the history, plus be able to track each RFC to its resolution and closure.
- **How did you get this task?** I actually suggested it after it became harder and harder to figure out whatever happened to each RFC.
- **What database and/or software was used?** Microsoft Access
- **What version?** Version 16
- **How long did it take you?** About 3 months.
- **Did you do it all yourself?** Yes, but I did develop and vet the requirements through our Change Control Board.
- **Did you get an award for this effort?** No, but our customer wrote a nice compliment to my supervisor.
- **When did you complete this?** June 2017

Now, you have all the details needed to develop a concise, but information-packed accomplishment:

 RFC Tracking Database: Developed and designed an RFC Tracking Database using Microsoft Access Version 16 to track Requests for Change (RFCs) for the customer organization, from initiation and presentation to the Change Control Board (CCB) through resolution and closure. Vetted requirements with the CCB and implemented the resulting product within a 3-month period. Received a written acknowledgement from the customer noting the significant improvement in RFC accountability (2017).

Below are some IT-related examples of potential accomplishments you could develop, depending on your specific experience and the type of job you are applying for. Remember, developing and then maintaining a list of your personal accomplishments as your career evolves will make it a cinch to update your resume, develop a KSA narrative, or even prepare for an interview!

- Installing or upgrading to a new version of an operating system or layered application.
- Researching, testing, and recommending the application of a new technology.
- Completing a major network reconfiguration.
- Developing a Standard Operating Procedure (SOP).
- Designing and/or delivering a user training class.
- Representing your organization on an IT-related working group or board.
- Being selected to participate in a special study or to attend a technical conference.
- Managing or resolving a major system outage or performance issue.
- Recommending and implementing any business process changes that reduced the time to respond to system or network outages, or improved the user experience.
- Developing and delivering a technical presentation—doing all the research and preparation; tuning the presentation to the specific group you were addressing.
- Developing an IT-related Statement of Work (SOW) and/or assisting with the acquisition of IT systems or services.
- Analyzing an IT policy or regulation and its implications for your organization.
- Leading the Certification & Accreditation of an IT system.
- Resolving information security findings.
- Designing and implementing Active Directory policies.
- Managing a Technology Refresh effort—ordering, building, configuring, and training users on a new desktop platform.
- Designing and implementing a new technology or system configuration like High Availability servers, Network Attached Storage, 2 Factor Authentication, passwordless logins, virtual servers.
- Designing and moving to a new computing facility.
- Developing and testing a Continuity of Operations (COOP) plan.

Recent Graduate **Resume Sample**

:) *This is an example of what to do!*

3-PAGE RECENT GRADUATE IT SPECIALIST - HIRED!

GREG MARTINEZ

5552 November Lane, Silver Spring, MD 20906
Mobile: (240) 123-4567
Email: GMartinez18@gmail.com
United States Citizen | Veteran's Status: N/A

PROFILE

University of Maryland Baltimore County (UMBC) College Senior seeking career focused position maximizing an academic degree in Computer Science and the real-life experience gained through multiple internships and part-time employment. Selected for a highly competitive ORISE Fellowship with the U.S. Department of Energy (2017-2018). Experienced with agile design methodologies, including the design/development of database applications. Participant in multiple hackathon and cyber challenge events, gaining experience with multiple cyber security applications and tools. Seeking internship opportunities for the Summer 2018 as well as permanent employment following a December 2018 graduation date.

EDUCATION

University of Maryland Baltimore County (UMBC), Baltimore, MD 21250. Completed 151 semester hours in a BS degree program in Computer Science (Minor: Statistics and Economics) (GPA: 3.17/4.0). Expected graduation: December 2018. *Relevant coursework*:

> *Computer Science*: Computer Science I for Majors, Discrete Structures, Social/Ethical Issues in IT, Computer Organization & Assembly Language, Principles of Programming Languages, Data Structures, Computer Architecture, Principles of Operating Systems, Software Engineering I, Database Management Systems, Artificial Intelligence

> *Economics*: Principles of Microeconomics, Principles of Macroeconomics, Intermediate Microeconomic Analysis, Intermediate Macroeconomic Analysis, Benefit-Cost Evaluation, Economics of Natural Resources, Health Economics

> *Statistics*: Introduction to Statistics, Probability & Statistics for Science and Engineering, Time Series Data Analysis, Introduction to Probability Theory, Applied Statistics

COMPUTER SKILLS

Platforms: Microsoft Windows Desktop (7/8/10), RedHat Linux, CentOS
Development: C++/C, Python, Java, JavaScript, Kotlin, ARM assembly, Git, Node.js
Applications: VirtualBox, R, QuickBooks, SAS Enterprise, SharePoint, Veeam Endpoint Backup, Ninite, Microsoft InfoPath
Document Management: SharePoint
Database/Web: Oracle, SQL, MySQL, Amazon Web Hosting (AWS)
Office Products: Microsoft Office, Visio, Google Docs

ACADEMIC PROJECTS

- **Academic Coding Project** - *Building Linux Shell in C,* 250 Lines of Code (LOC) (CMSC421/ Principles of Operating Systems): Designed a shell for Linux that supports a few basic features of a full-fledge *nix shell. The shell presents the user with a command prompt; accepts a command input of an arbitrary length; parses command-line arguments from the user's input; and passes them to the user defined program. The application was not allowed to use any external libraries other than the system's C library (2018).

Page Two

- **Academic Database Project/Presentation** – MySQL Database/Application (CMSC461/Database Management Systems): Completed a team project and presentation for a database application supporting a hypothetical rental agreement application. Designed a MySQL database from an entity-relationship model and a corresponding relational schema for use with a web application supporting SQL queries for selecting, adding, and dropping data. Briefed the design in an oral classroom presentation (2017).

- **Academic Coding Project/Presentation** – *Sin/Cos/Tan ARM Project*, 150 LOC) (CMSC411/ Computer Architecture): Completed a team project to design and develop an ARM assembly program that calculates $\cos(x)$, $\sin(x)$, and $\tan(x)$ using the CORDIC algorithm to calculate trigonometric functions. Briefed the development challenges and final design during an oral classroom presentation (2017).

INTERNSHIPS/FELLOWSHIPS

ORISE Fellow (11/2017 – Present)
U.S. DEPARTMENT OF ENERGY
19901 Germantown Road, Germantown, MD 20874
Part-Time: 16 hours/week
Base Salary: $18.00/hour
Supervisor: Nancy Dement, (202) 123-4567; *May contact*

TECHNICAL PROCESS DEVELOPMENT: Selected for a 6-month (11/2017 – 05/2018) ORISE Fellowship supporting the U.S. Department of Energy. The Oak Ridge Institute for Science and Education (ORISE) Program offers internships, fellowships, and research experiences for students pursuing science, technology, engineering, and math (STEM) disciplines. As an ORISE Fellow, complete multiple assigned projects to design and implement SharePoint-based technical and administrative workflows supporting DOE mission. Capture workflow information through interview and documentation review; develop workflow diagrams to capture the proposed workflow; and implement the end-to-end workflow in the SharePoint installation. Employ Microsoft Infopath to design and distribute electronic forms used within the workflow. Develop and present documentation on the proposed workflows.

Design Intern (07/2016 – 08/2016)
SPANISH SATELLITE TELEVISION
3440 Willis Blvd., Los Angeles, CA 90010
Full-Time: 40+ hours/week
Base Salary: Unpaid
Supervisor: Jean Hollis, (626) 111-2222; *May contact*

JOURNALISM RESEARCH/ANALYSIS: Completed a 2-month internship with Spanish Satellite Television, a Spanish-language television broadcaster that services 160M+ Spanish speaking viewers. Completed research projects to develop background for articles on U.S.-related topics for the corporate InfoNews Channel. Used web and other database resources to compile and analyze statistics on assigned topics. Developed comprehensive research papers used for the development of broadcast journalistic articles. Assigned projects included a statistical analysis of minority enrollment at the United States Military Academy (USMA) and Virginia Military Institute (VMI) and U.S. participation and viewpoints on the 2016 Rio de Janeiro Olympics. The internship included an introduction to the corporate broadcast journalism processes.

Page Three

JOB EXPERIENCE

IT Consultant (09/2017 – Present)
ROUTE 144 CLASSIFIED
P.O. Box 21275, Baltimore, MD 21228
Part-Time: 5-10 hours/week
Base Salary: $15.00/hour
Supervisor: Darryl Phillips, (410) 111-2222; *May contact*

DATA ANALYSIS Complete data analysis and market research studies pertinent to the publication needs of a local classified advertising publication. Compile pertinent employment, sales, and other customer-centric metrics and develop Excel pivot tables to highlight trends and produce business forecasts with the goal to increase sales.

CUSTOMER SERVICE: Assist with customer support functions for resume and training customers. Use QuickBooks to receive and post training advertising orders. Manage the advertisement ordering process, from order receipt to publication. Validate and reconcile advertising sales invoices.

IT Consultant/Tutor (07/2014 – 08/2016) *(Summer Job)*
STUDENT HOST INTERNATIONAL, LLC.
101 Penny Brook Drive, Newark, DE 19711
Full-Time: 40+ hours/week *(Also Part-Time; 5 hours/week; 08/2016 – 05/2017)*
Base Salary: $14.50/hour
Supervisor: Jack Simms, (302) 123-4567; *May contact*

ACADEMIC TUTORING/MENTORSHIP: Served as a tutor and mentor for international high school students preparing for U.S. academic and internship programs. Assisted with academic instruction in mathematics and oral and written English. During the academic year, provided part-time tutoring via Skype.

IT CONSULTING: Completed the setup and configuration of Windows-based desktop systems for use by the Student Host summer program. Installed, configured, tested, and troubleshot 10 new Windows-based desktop systems. Restored legacy personal computers to usable condition. Ensured the compliance of each desktop system with a standard, secure Windows configuration. Implemented an automated system backup capability using Veeam Endpoint Backup. Managed the automated batch installation of system software, layered products, apps, and utilities using the Ninite package management system.

VOLUNTEER/EXTRACURRICULAR EXPERIENCE

UMBC Cyber Dawgs: Participant in the weekly UMBC Cyber Dogs non-credit program, which provides hands-on experience with a broad range of cyber security applications and tools. The weekly program includes a one-hour lecture followed by a lab-based, hands-on project. Example projects completed during the 2017-2018 academic year included:

- Configuring CentOS as an all-in-one server for DNS and SSH, using a Public-Private key pair, MySQL, and Git.
- Configuring Linux iptables to implement state checks, HTTP/HTTPS, incoming/outgoing SSH, mailing protocols, and name resolution.
- Configuring a Virtual Machine (VM) to serve Domain Name Service (DNS BIND), SSH, MySQL, and Git (Gogs).
- Exploring the iptables firewall configuration utility in Linux, including forwarding with pre/post routing, writing policy chains, and using other useful commands and flags.

This is an example of what to do!

3-PAGE MID-CAREER IT SPECIALIST FEATURING TECHNICAL SKILLS - HIRED!

MID-CAREER IT SPECIALIST

Michael Cedar

1000 Brooklane Street, Fairfax, VA 22031
Email: cedar123@mail.com
Phone: (321) 456-7890
Security Clearance: Secret

PROFILE

Certified Senior Information Security Services Specialist with hands-on expertise with advanced Cyber Security toolsets and processes that ensure the confidentiality, integrity, and availability of Agency information assets. Possess knowledge of Certification & Accreditation (C&A), Intrusion Detection, Vulnerability Assessment, Security Event Response, and Risk Management in the design of information security requirements, plans, and strategies needed to safeguard highly sensitive systems, data, and communications resources. Self-motivated and goal-oriented, with a demonstrated ability to handle complex responsibilities in a demanding work environment.

CERTIFICATIONS

Cisco Certified Entry Networking Technician (CCENT), 2018
Global Information Assurance Certification (GIAC) Certified Incident Handler (GCIH), 2018
Certified Ethical Hacker (CEH), 2018
Linux Server Professional Certification (LPIC-1), 2018
Certified Information Systems Security Professional (CISSP), 2017
GIAC Security Essentials Certification (GSEC), 2012

COMPUTER SKILLS

Platforms: Windows Server (2012, 2016), Linux (Red Hat, CentOS, Ubuntu), Solaris, Windows Desktop (7/8/10), VMWare

Cyber Security: Core Impact, Core InSight, nCircle, Symantec Data Loss Protection (DLP), Websense Web Security Gateway, Host Based Security System (HBSS), Nessus, Symantec Control Compliance Suite (CCS), Nitro Security Information and Event Management (SIEM), NetIQ, McAfee e-Policy Orchestrator (ePO), Qualys, Open Web Application Security Project (OWASP) Zed Attack Proxy (ZAP), Tenable Security Center, Tripwire, Nmap (Network Mapper), Wireshark, Symantec GDisk, Symantec Ghost, WebScarab

Database: Oracle, MySQL, Microsoft SQL

Data Analysis: SAS, LogLogic

Digital Forensics: EnCase, Helix3

Software Management: Rational ClearCase/ClearQuest

Intrusion Detection: Sourcefire, Snort

Networking: Cisco routers & switches, Cisco ASAs

Development/Scripting Tools: Python, BASH, SED/AWK

Office Products/Groupware: Microsoft Office

EDUCATION
- MS, Information Security & Assurance, Ohio State University, Columbus, OH (2016)
- BS, Information Technology, University of Michigan, Ann Arbor, MI (20013)

Page Two

RELATED PROFESSIONAL EXPERIENCE

IT Specialist (INFOSEC) (NT04) (08/2016 – Present)
Science and Technology Directorate (S&T), Department of Homeland Security
Washington, DC
Full-Time: 40+ hours/week
Base Salary: $99,296

The Science and Technology Directorate (S&T) cyber mission contributes to enhancing the security and resilience of the nation's critical information infrastructure and the internet by among the R&D community which includes Department customers, government agencies, the private sector and international partners.

VULNERABILITY ASSESSMENT: Technical resource to the Vulnerability Scanning Team. Develop custom audit files for file content scanning and provide technical assistance with the analysis and interpretation of scanning data collected by a Nessus-based vulnerability scanner. Provide expert assistance with the development, implementation, and maintenance of custom scripts and other automated tools required to scan Linux systems. Research and recommend new vulnerability assessment strategies and tools.

SECURITY TECHNOLOGIES & TOOLS: Implement, configure, update, patch, troubleshoot, and maintain critical Information Security tools that promote the security of enterprise systems and applications. Manage Websense web proxy implementation to ensure a real time response to network-based threats. Provide technical assistance for the implementation and deployment of a range of security tools, including Symantec Endpoint Protection and Host Based Security System (HBSS). Research, evaluate, recommend, and implement IT security solutions.

INFORMATION SECURITY SERVICES: Member of the Information Assurance Compliance Team. Provide Information Security services across the DHS enterprise. Recognized as a Senior Information Security Services Specialist, providing Information Assurance functions ensuring the confidentiality, integrity, and availability of over 1250 servers and desktop systems in a highly diverse computing and networking environment.

SECURITY EVENT RESPONSE: Monitor and analyze web traffic from Websense to identify, respond, and report suspicious traffic and potential security breaches. Participate in the Security Event Response Working Group, which interfaces with commercial vendors to identify and recommend enhanced intrusion detection solutions.

SELECTED ACCOMPLISHMENTS

- **Websense Proxy Migration:** Planned and executed a project to reconfigure the Websense web proxy implementation to split the web environment into two separate dedicated network segments. Worked with other senior network engineers to develop a detailed plan including rollback steps. Successfully completed the migration in nonworking hours over one weekend, with no impact to operations.

- **IDS Consolidation Working Group:** Participant in the Intrusion Detection System (IDS) section of the IT Consolidation Working Group. Provide information security advice and recommendations during the process to achieve a more consolidated, centralized solution for intrusion detection across all joint-agency fusion centers.

Page Three

Information Security Consultant (09/20013 – 08/2016)
Computer Technology Group
100 Los Angeles Blvd. Santa Barbara, CA 20007
Full-Time: 40+ hours/week
Base Salary: $93,558.40

Oversaw security administration for systems and databases for the General Services Administration (GSA) Federal Acquisition Service (FAS), which provides solutions to Federal clients in the areas of technology, transportation, travel, motor vehicle management, products and services, and procurement. Supported systems and applications for over 40 application development groups across the FAS.

INFORMATION SECURITY SERVICES: Managed security systems with Windows, Linux (CentOS and Redhat), and Solaris servers, as well as multiple database management systems.

SECURITY EVENT RESPONSE: Monitored, analyzed, and responded to local and widespread events generated by the Intrusion Detection System. Investigated and identified potential breaches in network, hardware, and software system configurations.

CUSTOMER CONTACT: Worked with Security Operations Center (SOC) personnel to differentiate false positives from true intrusion attempts and reported all true positives to FAS management and to US-CERT, following US-CERT incident reporting guidelines.

CUSTOMER SERVICE: Provided security engineering expertise to developers and management of the FAS application teams. Responded to network connectivity issues identified by internal business groups. Communicated complex and sensitive technical issues orally and in writing to technical and non-technical professionals to ensure awareness of Information Assurance compliance goals.

SECURITY TECHNOLOGIES AND TOOLS: Maintained and updated information security tools and their underlying host systems. Utilized an advance tool set of commercial and open source products (Nessus, AppDetective, WebInspect, Core Impact, Core InSight, nCircle) to conduct technical security assessments of hosts, websites, and databases.

VULNERABILITY ASSESSMENT: Executed recurring, automated security scans of FAS production systems; coordinated system scanning schedules with the customer, and guided other information security personnel through the scanning process. Performed data analysis of technical security assessments to determine the security posture of IT assets. Validated vulnerabilities using Proof-of-Concept code and open source tools.

SELECTED ACCOMPLISHMENTS

- **Core InSight Deployment:** Task Lead for the implementation of the Core InSight web scanning appliance. Coordinated the hardware/software installation and configuration; designed and verified security credentials and firewall rules; and implemented automated scanning algorithms for all FAS-maintained websites.

- **Symantec Data Loss Prevention (DLP) Implementation:** Managed the full project life cycle to implement Symantec DLP for the FAS infrastructure. DLP is a data security product that discovers, monitors, and protects confidential data assets. Coordinated and evaluated a Proof of Concept implementation; planned and deployed an operational instance; configured file scans across all FAS servers; and implemented data analysis procedures.

FEDERAL CAREER RESOURCES

★ ★ ★

TOP 30 JOB TITLES IN THE FEDERAL GOVERNMENT

Only jobs with an asterisk (*) require a degree or specific education.

Job Title (Series Number)	Number of U.S. employees
0301-MISCELLANEOUS ADMINISTRATION AND PROGRAM	104,942
0610-NURSE	86,400
2210-INFORMATION TECHNOLOGY MANAGEMENT	84,097
0343-MANAGEMENT AND PROGRAM ANALYSIS	74,361
0303-MISCELLANEOUS CLERK AND ASSISTANT	54,026
1802-COMPLIANCE INSPECTION AND SUPPORT	51,890
1811-CRIMINAL INVESTIGATION	43,160
0905-GENERAL ATTORNEY	38,472
1801-GENERAL INSPECTION, INVESTIGATION, ENFORCEMENT, AND COMPLIANCE SERIES	38,175
1102-CONTRACTING	37,752
0602-MEDICAL OFFICER	35,195
0679-MEDICAL SUPPORT ASSISTANCE	30,121
0962-CONTACT REPRESENTATIVE	30,108
0201-HUMAN RESOURCES MANAGEMENT	29,830
0105-SOCIAL INSURANCE ADMINISTRATION	27,538
0801-GENERAL ENGINEERING	26,780
1101-GENERAL BUSINESS AND INDUSTRY	26,675
0501-FINANCIAL ADMINISTRATION AND PROGRAM	25,773
1895-CUSTOMS AND BORDER PROTECTION	22,961
0401-GENERAL NATURAL RESOURCES MANAGEMENT AND BIOLOGICAL SCIENCES	21,130
2152-AIR TRAFFIC CONTROL	20,546
0346-LOGISTICS MANAGEMENT	20,315
1896-BORDER PATROL ENFORCEMENT SERIES	19,261
0620-PRACTICAL NURSE	19,194
0855-ELECTRONICS ENGINEERING	18,556
0007-CORRECTIONAL OFFICER	17,734
0185-SOCIAL WORK	16,995
0340-PROGRAM MANAGEMENT	15,718
0601-GENERAL HEALTH SCIENCE	15,517
0621-NURSING ASSISTANT	14,712
0083-POLICE	14,690

*Original Research, Resume Place, Inc., Dec. 2019.

https://www.fedscope.opm.gov/employment.asp

BEST PLACES TO WORK 2019

Rank	Agency	2018	2017	Change (2017–18)
LARGE AGENCIES				
1	National Aeronautics and Space Administration	81.2	80.9	0.3
2	Department of Health and Human Services	70.9	70.4	0.5
3	Department of Commerce	70.3	69.2	1.1
4	Department of Transportation	67.7	67.6	0.1
5	Intelligence Community	66.3	66.6	-0.3
6	Department of Veterans Affairs	64.2		
7	Department of the Navy	63.2	63.8	-0.6
7	Office of the Secretary of Defense, Joint Staff, Defense Agencies, and Department of Defense Field Activities	63.2	61.1	2.1
9	Department of the Interior	62.8	63.9	-1.1
10	Department of Justice	62.6	63.7	-1.1
MIDSIZE AGENCIES				
1	Federal Trade Commission	84	81.4	2.6
2	Federal Energy Regulatory Commission	83.9	82.9	1.0
3	Securities and Exchange Commission	82.1	80.9	1.2
4	Government Accountability Office	80.7	82.5	-1.8
5	Federal Deposit Insurance Corporation	80.5	81.9	-1.4
6	Peace Corps	79.8	80.7	-0.9
7	Smithsonian Institution	76.7	76.9	-0.2
8	National Science Foundation	75.5	74.7	0.8
9	Architect of the Capitol	75.3		
10	General Services Administration	74.5	73.7	0.8
SMALL AGENCIES				
1	Federal Mediation and Conciliation Service	87.2	86.9	0.3
2	U.S. International Trade Commission	85.7	80.9	4.8
3	Congressional Budget Office	85.3		
4	Farm Credit Administration	81.1	80.5	0.6
5	Pension Benefit Guaranty Corporation	78.3	73.5	4.8
6	National Transportation Safety Board	77.8	77.5	0.3
7	Office of Management and Budget	75	75.4	-0.4
8	National Endowment for the Humanities	74.9	71.4	3.5
9	Federal Maritime Commission	74.4	67.5	6.9
10	Overseas Private Investment Corporation	73.6	79.8	-6.2

*Partnership for Public Service, 2018, *https://bestplacestowork.org/*

TOP HIRING AGENCIES

Agency	Oct–Dec 2016	Jan–Mar 2017	Apr–Jun 2017	Jul–Sep 2017	FY 2017
Agency - All	47408	40690	56361	44905	189364
CABINET LEVEL AGENCIES	45289	38093	54858	40357	178597
Department of Veterans Affairs	9585	8611	9755	12355	40306
Department of Homeland Security	5994	4485	4370	6342	21191
Department of the Army	5450	3154	5703	5074	19381
Department of Agriculture	2027	2461	12033	1295	17816
Department of the Interior	1599	2104	7125	1238	12066
Department of the Air Force	3763	2261	3087	2672	11783
Department of the Navy	2874	1846	3206	3518	11444
Department of Defense	3233	1766	2190	2925	10114
LARGE INDEPENDENT AGENCIES (1000 OR MORE EMPLOYEES)	1798	2137	1219	4290	9444
Department of the Treasury	3123	4316	688	160	8287
Department of Justice	1822	1729	1746	1461	6758
Department of Health and Human Services	2256	1743	1366	1299	6664
Department of Commerce	1593	1660	2295	946	6494
Department of Transportation	1018	1001	930	748	3697
Social Security Administration	104	51	371	1840	2366
Small Business Administration	308	99	24	1564	1995
MEDIUM INDEPENDENT AGENCIES (100-999 EMPLOYEES)	278	378	233	208	1097
National Aeronautics and Space Administration	130	470	66	171	837
Environmental Protection Agency	253	433	75	38	799
Department of Energy	207	242	212	109	770
Department of State	283	225	68	79	655
General Services Administration	254	189	127	77	647
Department of Labor	226	281	23	40	570
Office of Personnel Management	107	147	68	133	455
Department of Housing and Urban Development	137	123	35	78	373
Federal Deposit Insurance Corporation	22	50	170	109	351
Smithsonian Institution	119	125	42	63	349
Department of Education	99	85	26	18	228
SMALL INDEPENDENT AGENCIES (LESS THAN 100 EMPLOYEES)	43	82	51	50	226
National Science Foundation	71	57	38	46	212
National Archives and Records Administration	62	69	7	65	203
Peace Corps	74	63	27	20	184
Federal Reserve System	23	75	59	15	172
Securities and Exchange Commission	79	49	12	11	151
Agency for International Development	42	58	16	27	143
Federal Trade Commission	19	29	56	30	134
Office of Management and Budget	28	45	26	31	130
Corporation for National and Community Service	30	54	8	17	109
Equal Employment Opportunity Commission	38	51	0	3	92
Federal Housing Finance Agency	9	8	48	10	75
Consumer Product Safety Commission	18	9	44	1	72
National Labor Relations Board	17	31	4	13	65
Broadcasting Board of Governors	14	35	3	11.	63
Federal Communications Commission	17	17	7	20	61
Government Printing Office	13	13	22	11	59
Pension Benefit Guaranty Corporation	22	31	0	3	56
National Foundation on the Arts and the Humanities	16	20	4	15	55

*Original Research, Resume Place, Inc., Dec. 2019.

https://www.fedscope.opm.gov/employment.asp

PUBLICATIONS BY THE RESUME PLACE, INC.

Order online at www.resume-place.com | Bulk Orders: (888) 480 8265
BULK PRICES for Bulk Book purchases for Federal agencies
E-books available for immediate download at www.resume-place.com

Federal Resume Guidebook 7th Edition – All New Jan 2020—Now the #2 Resume Book in America! The ultimate Federal Resume Writing and Federal Career Change Guide for Federal government careers! *$15.95. $10 ea for 50+ books + shipping.*

The Stars Are Lined Up for Military Spouses, 2nd Edition—Key book to assist military spouses with navigating USAJOBS and the complex federal job process. Covers four ways to land the major kinds of federal positions for military spouses. *$14.95. $8 ea for 50+ books + shipping.*

Jobseeker's Guide, 8th Edition—Military to Federal Career Transition Resource. Workbook and guide for the Ten Steps to a Federal Job® training curriculum. Federal job search strategies for first-time jobseekers who are separating military and family members. *$18.95. $8 ea for 50+ books + shipping.*

The **New SES Application, 2nd Edition** breaks down this complex application process into a step-by-step guide based on a popular workshop taught for over 10 years. Updated with SES info to help you navigate hiring reforms currently impacting the Senior Executive Service. *$21.95. Bulk rates available.*

Student's Federal Career Guide, 4th Edition—Outstanding book for jobseekers who are just getting out of college and whose education will help the applicant get qualified for a position. 13 samples of recent graduate resumes with emphasis on college degrees, courses, major papers, internships, and relevant work experiences. *$9.95. Available in ebook.*

Creating Your First Resume is a book used at high school and technical school programs nationwide. The new edition boasts brand new resume samples that represent the push toward STEM technical programs to provide training and certifications for high school students. *$12.95. $5 ea for 50+ books + shipping.*

Federal Resume Database—This online resource contains more than 110 resume samples and federal job search resources from the current Resume Place publications. Sample resumes are available in Word & PDF format for easy reading and editing. *Individual and Agency / Base Licenses available.*

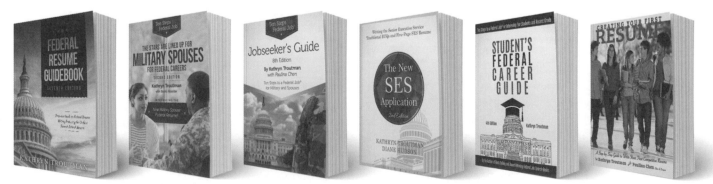

RESUME PLACE

BUILDING CAREERS IN THE US GOVERNMENT

GOVERNMENT AGENCY CAREER WORKSHOPS

Course Titles: Federal Resume Writing, Senior Executive Service Executive Core Qualifications Writing, Behavior-Based Interviews, CCAR-Accomplishment Writing for Interviews, Evaluations and Federal Resumes, Leadership Development.

Formats: Full Day, Half Day, Webinars; Executive Coaching; Writing and Editing; Federal Career courses for Agency Transformation, Recruitment and Retention Objectives.

SES ECQ Writing, Coaching, Interviewing – per agency contract and individual services for agency recruitment of Senior Executive Services executives.

More Info and Request Training Form: *www.resume-place.com*

FEDERAL CAREER CERTIFICATION AND LICENSING

Certified Federal Job Search Trainer / Certified Federal Career Coach - CFJST / CFCC

Three programs: 3-day Live Programs; 7-part, 90 minute Webinars; Hosted Class at your Installation

Learn now to teach government civilians, service members, military spouses, students, veterans, first-time Federal jobseekers about the successful step-by-step approach to Federal job search and Federal resume writing.

Get licensed to teach the following curriculum for 3 years:

1. Ten Steps to a Federal Job®
2. The Stars Are Lined Up for Military Spouses®
3. Creating Your First Resume
4. Ten Steps to a Pathways Internship for Recent Graduates and Students

More Info, Dates, Rates and Registration: *www.resume-place.com*

FEDERAL RESUME WRITING – JOBSEEKER SERVICES – CONSULTING, WRITING, EDITING

RP Certified Federal Resume Writers and Coaches for Jobseekers

Start-up Services: $99 Federal Resume Assessments; $190 Consultation; $199 SES Consultation.

Federal Resume Writing, SES ECQ Writing, Announcement Analysis, Interview, Accomplishment Coaching – Services are quoted within the Assessment and Consultation Start-up Services

https://www.resume-place.com/federalresumequote/

ABOUT THE AUTHOR
KATHRYN TROUTMAN

1. Founder, President, and Manager of The Resume Place®, the first Federal job search consulting and Federal resume writing service in the world, and the producer of *www.resume-place.com*, the first website devoted to Federal resume writing.

2. Pioneer designer of the Federal resume format in 1995 with the publication of the leading resource for Federal human resources and jobseekers worldwide—the *Federal Resume Guidebook*, now in its seventh edition and the #2 resume book on the internet.

3. Developer of the Certified Federal Job Search Trainer®/Certified Federal Career Coach® train-the-trainer program in 2002. Licensing *Ten Steps to a Federal Job®*, a curriculum and turnkey training program taught by more than 5,000 Certified Federal Job Search Trainers® (CFJST) around the world. Recommended by military services for transition and employment readiness counselors around the world.

4. Authored the first-ever book for military spouses on the Federal job search, *The Stars Are Lined Up for Military Spouses*, 2017. Authored and published the second edition with the FIRST-EVER Military Spouse Federal Resume with PCS Military Spouse Career History featured in the resume.

5. Author of numerous Federal career publications (in addition to the *Federal Resume Guidebook mentioned above):*

The *Military to Federal Career Guide* is the first book for military personnel and is now in its second edition, featuring veteran Federal resumes. Troutman recognized the need for returning military personnel from Iraq, Afghanistan, and Kosovo to have a resource available to them in their searches for government jobs.

Ten Steps to a Federal Job was published two months after 9/11 and was written for private industry jobseekers seeking first-time positions in the Federal government, where they could contribute to our nation's security. Now in its third edition.

The *Jobseeker's Guide* started initially as the companion course handout to the Ten Steps book, but captured its own following when it became the handout text used by over 200 military installations throughout the world for transitioning military and family members. Now in its eighth edition.

With the looming human capital crisis and baby boomers retiring in government, the *Student's Federal Career Guide* was originally co-authored with Kathryn's daughter and MPP graduate, Emily Troutman. It was the first book for students pursuing a Federal job. Now in its third edition, it includes the latest information on the changing structure of student programs.